Fifty Years of Higher Education in India

FIFTY YEARS OF HIGHER EDUCATION IN INDIA

THE ROLE OF THE UNIVERSITY GRANTS COMMISSION

Amrik Singh

SAGE PUBLICATIONS
NEW DELHI ❖ THOUSAND OAKS ❖ LONDON

First published in 2004 by

Sage Publications India Pvt Ltd
B1/I-1 Mohan Cooperative Industrial Area
Mathura Road
New Delhi 110044
www.sagepub.in

Sage Publications Inc	**Sage Publications Ltd**
2455 Teller Road	1 Oliver's Yard, 55 City Road
Thousand Oaks, California 91320	London EC1Y 1SP

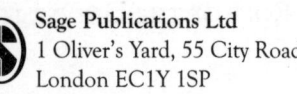

Second Printing 2008

Published by Tejeshwar Singh for Sage Publications India Pvt Ltd, phototypeset in 10 pt Goudy Old Style by Star Compugraphics Private Limited, New Delhi and printed at Chaman Enterprises, New Delhi.

Library of Congress Cataloging-in-Publication Data

Singh, Amrik, 1935–
   Fifty years of higher education in India: the role of the University Grants Commission / Amrik Singh.
      p. cm.
   Includes index.
   1. Education, Higher—India—History—20th century. 2. India. University Grants Commission—History. I. Title.

LA1153.S58	378.54'09'04—dc22	2004	2003025868

ISBN: 10: 0-7619-3216-X (US-Hb)   10: 81-7829-342-0 (India-Hb)
          13: 978-0-7619-3216-1 (US-Hb) 13: 978-81-7829-342-4 (India-Hb)

Sage Production Team: Geetanjali Surendran, Sunaina Dalaya, Sushanta Gayen and Santosh Rawat

In memory of C.D. Deshmukh who, as the first Chairman of the UGC, launched it with an exceptional sense of values and commitments.

Contents

PREFACE

Although I have been a keen observer of the University Grants Commission (UGC) from the day it was established (28 December 1953) and have written extensively about it, two developments combined to prompt me to write this book.

One was the UGC's decision to celebrate 2003 as the Golden Jubilee year of its establishment—big celebrations are being planned for the end of the year. Having written fifty to sixty articles on the UGC, I felt that I had to go beyond that. Hence this book. Besides, I thought to myself, it was odd that no one had so far written a book on the UGC.

Out of the numerous pieces I have written, I selected five for inclusion in this book. One of them was a contribution to a book and had to be updated and partly rewritten. The other four were from research journals and, except for some factual changes, have been reproduced here. For one thing, these articles are detailed as well as analytical. For another, anyone who reads this book from cover to cover will see that what has been said in these articles generally marks a stage in the growth of the UGC. In each case, the date of publication has been indicated so that the argument, as it is emerging, can be understood better.

The other pieces have been specially written during the last few months for this book. While choosing a few of the topics, I decided to focus on some of those issues which have not received as much attention as they deserved.

The second crucial development was the decision of the editor of a leading newspaper in Delhi not to publish me. In writing for newspapers, I thought I would accomplish two things. One was to call attention to a particular point of view or development and the other was to express myself candidly and reach a certain section of the newspaper reading audience. The determined decision to exclude my contributions made me feel strongly that I had to find another channel to express myself. This book which has been brewing in my mind, is the outcome of this combination of circumstances. It is difficult for anyone to realise how much this decision of the said gentleman contributed to the writing of this book. I hereby express my genuine gratitude to him. But for his unintended role, this book might not have been written.

Three other points may also be made. In writing these essays, I have not chosen to be scholarly. Instead I have chosen to be analytical. In quite a few cases towards the end of the analysis, I repeat as well as elaborate my ideas further. My objective in doing so was to make the teachers think about the system by which they were being governed.

Second, this book is not a research piece on the history of the UGC. Instead, it is a piece of critical assessment. I have by and large dispensed with footnotes, endnotes etc. An important reason for doing so was that my idea was to 'prod the community of teachers and analyse things for them so that they in turn begin to take interest in what has been happening to them. This adverse situation will continue to haunt them, if I may venture to say, unless they decide to reflect over their situation more honestly and more critically.

Third, their indifference to how universities are run at the state level and how policy decisions are taken at the central level is perhaps the basic reason for why the educational policy is being implemented as it is and why the UGC has not performed better than it has. This had to be said. Neither the Ministry of Human Resource Development (HRD) nor the UGC feel answerable to anyone. More than other sectors of the middle class, university and college teachers constitute a substantial segment of it. In any case, it is their business to study and analyse and yet this is precisely what they have done all those years even with respect to what happens to them.

As a matter of fact, the book is basically addressed to them. Once the teachers become more critical and more vocal, the Ministry of HRD will have to be more careful about the way it runs the Commission, how its own decisions are made and how experts are nominated on the UGC. Equally important, the Commission needs to be reconstituted radically so that it ceases to be a body which can only bark (often it refuses to do even that) and not bite.

As to its internal working, it needs a total overhaul. But that is not something which can be discussed only incidentally. The need for doing so has been underlined in more than one essay. As to the details, those require a much more detailed exposition and in any case it is for those who are incharge of the administration to work out a system which is both academic and productive.

In the report which I submitted to the Ministry of HRD in regard to the amendment of the UGC Act, one important recommendation made was that the UGC should be run on the lines of the Railway Board. There should be several full-time members dealing with specified subjects. This issue was debated even when the UGC Bill was discussed in Parliament. M.N. Saha, the well known physicist, was strongly in favour of making the UGC an effective and professional body. But the political climate did not seem to be in its favour.

It cannot be said that the climate of opinion has changed in any significant manner. If anything, the passage of time has mercilessly exposed the weaknesses of the UGC. As discussed in the Introduction, the situation is ripe for a drastic change. But those incharge of policy making are unable to understand the nature of the challenge.

There are many more things that can be said here but most of them will be said in the course of the book itself. The reader is therefore invited to read the book rather than hear any more about how or why it came to be written. I do apologise for a certain amount of repetition which, as explained earlier, was unavoidable.

New Delhi
Amrik Singh
August 2003

Introduction

I

Over the last few decades, out of the various professional councils, the UGC has come to be seen as the one that matters the most. But is this the right perception?

The UGC was certainly the first one to be established in pursuit of the constitutional mandate which the union government had been given: to coordinate and determine standards in respect of higher education. In order to fulfil this directive, a year or so after the Constitution was enforced, the union government came up with a proposal to set up a body which eventually turned out to be the ancestor of the present UGC. Since this matter has been discussed at length elsewhere, no more need be said about it here except to call attention to one thing.

While we have a large number of professional councils, the number of staff and students working in the institutions regulated by them on the professional plane, is not particularly large. The bulk numbers are to be found mainly in universities and colleges. In the fifties and the sixties, their rate of growth was 13–14 per cent per year. No other country has had a rate of growth higher than 7–8 per cent per year. Then too, only for a few years with respect to Nigeria during its oil boom. Everywhere else, the rate of growth, even at its highest, has been around 5 per cent or so. It was only in the early seventies that the rate of growth in India stabilised around this figure and the UGC began to breathe somewhat easily. Till then, it was two and a half times higher as stated above. This had unavoidable consequences which do not have to be elaborated here.

Most of the professional councils which were established were set up in the first quarter of a century after 1947. With the unremitting expansion of universities and colleges, the feeling grew that while little could be done to regulate this uncommonly high rate of growth, something should be done to regulate the standards of professional education at least. In a sense, their establishment, one by one, was an attempt to protect higher education from relentless dilution of standards.

Two things happened around this period to thwart this concern for quality which was increasingly projected as an important element in the overall situation. Oddly enough, one was the introduction of the revised pay scales in the mid-seventies. The intention in this case was to attract as well as retain talent in teaching. But this did not happen beyond a point. Since a good deal has been said about this issue too, elsewhere in the book, no more needs to be said about it here.

The second major development was the growing middle class pressure for entry into professional colleges. To start with, more and more engineering and medical colleges were established. The process picked up speed in the mid-eighties and was in full swing by the mid-nineties. So much so that, in the early nineties, the Supreme Court had to intervene. This intervention solved some problems and created some new ones. Once again, details do not have to be gone into here. All that one can say is that, even its latest 2003 judgement, is not free from certain avoidable pitfalls.

At the same time, another parallel development needs to be noted. By the early nineties, expansion in the Information Technology (IT) sector had caught on in a big way. Some of the major private entrepreneurs played a notable role here. Simultaneously, certain enterprising business houses gave an extraordinary degree of impetus to the IT industry. Between the two of them, by the end of the nineties, IT was in full bloom. In addition, its international impact helped it to grow further in India. Indeed two things happened in consequence.

The first one was its impact beyond India that gave a high profile to the Indian IT industry in the international arena. In any case, IT was an area of growth where innovations were being made every few months. These entrepreneurs remained abreast of the changes, indeed there was little that required to be done and was not. The second consequence is now unfolding itself more extensively and with a certain measure of insistence.

The expansion in professional education both in engineering and medicine has not been accompanied by higher standards of performance-in most cases. In point of fact, standards have gone down to some extent. In addition, there was much more expansion than was called for and currently the country is passing through a phase where market forces are forcing the shrinkage of the facilities that have been created.

Acting upon each other and to some extent reinforcing each other, an uncomfortable feeling is growing. It was said that while professional growth was inevitable and expansion too had to take place and was unavoidable beyond a point, the decline of quality that took place was deeply deplorable. Today, people in the professional fields are much more aware of the need for high quality than they were a few years ago.

One additional fact may be mentioned here. The entry of a few hundred foreign promoters—some of whom teamed up with Indian counterparts, at one point posing a serious danger—has passed its peak. Today, because of the concern for quality, there is much less anxiety about their presence in India than there was a few years ago.

To sum up this phase in the history of Indian higher education, two things stand out. One, there has been a certain degree of self-defeating expansion and much less concern for good standards of performance or high quality. Second, more or less as a counterpart of what is being talked about, there is a growing feeling that more attention should be paid to the maintenance and improvement of academic standards. That alone would make Indian-trained manpower competitive in the international arena. This is precisely the job that was assigned to the UGC and the various professional councils which came to be established during the decades after the establishment of the UGC in 1953.

II

Before coming to grips with the issue of the role of the UGC, it needs to be noted that the basic responsibility for the establishment of the various professional councils including the UGC, lay with the union government. It is the union government which, strictly speaking, has neglected its responsibility during the last few decades. Two of its lapses in particular need to be referred to here.

While setting up those professional councils, the union government did not ensure appropriate coordination amongst them. While the Indian Council of Agricultural Research and the Medical Council were established before the UGC was set up and their sphere of operations clearly demarcated, most other councils were established after the UGC had got going. Presumably there were some internal discussions when these various councils were being set up. But if one goes by public evidence, there was hardly any attempt either to allocate responsibilities in such a manner as to avoid overlap in respect of their functioning, or to set up an appropriate mechanism for coordination. These issues have been discussed in Chapters II and III of this book in some detail. The only thing that requires to be added is the following.

The UGC was the one professional council which covered the largest number of teachers and students and at one time also looked after some matters which were later delegated to the various professional councils. The issue of how to avoid duplication and overlap with the other councils had to be given special attention. This was not done.

One example given in those two chapters is that even the word 'teacher' is defined differently in different pieces of legislation. That does not say much for either forethought or planning which would have ensured coordination. This particular issue may be described as minor in character which indeed it is. The real major lapse has been in not having set up the National Council of Higher Education as recommended by the 1986 Policy of Education. Not to have acted upon this suggestion was an act of omission which cannot be defended.

Some bit of defence of what has been happening may be apparent in the political turns and twists that characterised the Indian polity during the last decade and a half. Within a year of the formulation of the Policy on Education in 1986, the then Prime Minister, Rajiv Gandhi, got into political difficulties. After he went out of office, the country had a series of transient prime ministers. It was only in 1999 that the NDA government was formed and it has been reasonably stable since then. What is stated below is therefore more applicable to the NDA government than any earlier government.

Indeed this is the second issue that needs to be taken up here. As the National Council of Higher Education has not come into existence, by implication, the responsibility for coordinating the work of the various professional councils, including the UGC, devolves upon the Ministry of HRD.

It so happened that as several of these professional councils, in the course of settling down to work, tried to tell the universities what to do and what not to do, matters started going to the courts. In every single case, the courts opined that the professional councils had to work within their prescribed field of operations and by and large it was the universities which still controlled the functioning even of the professional institutions. Opinions expressed by the various high courts and the Supreme Court did not oblige the UGC to either intervene as a party or file a separate suit. But this fact does not absolve the Ministry of HRD from its failure to have discharged its basic responsibility. During the last five years, not a single step has been taken to ensure that some kind of mechanism for coordination is evolved. The explanation may be political in character but the nature of the damage caused is by and large professional.

Talking to the chief executives of these various councils, one gets the distinct feeling that each one of them has some grievance or the other. But there is no platform where they can come together and decide about things which are of mutual interest and coordinate their functioning in the desired way. This is precisely what the National Council of Higher Education was planned to do.

Two additional examples may be given. In 1998, i.e., within a few weeks of coming to power, there was a controversy in Parliament regarding what are called the 'fake' universities. According to the UGC Act, no one other than a duly established university can describe itself as a 'university'. In fact there is a penalty prescribed and that penalty is a fine of Rs 1,000. One particular fake university which is older than the UGC has been operating for more than half a century despite the passage of the UGC Act. Within a few years of its establishment, the UGC filed a case against it. But the law is so lax that, even after half a century, that institution still continues to describe itself as a university. Clearly, the UGC Act needs to be tightened up.

When this issue came up in Parliament, the minister for HRD announced the appointment of a committee to go into the amendment of the UGC Act. This writer was named as the chairman of that committee. A report was submitted within the next few months. Several years later, that amended Act is still to be brought before Parliament. Not only that, there has been some further thinking about the matter. Even before this committee reported, the UGC had gone into this issue in considerable detail. Since then, it has continued to address the issue and a more recent draft is again pending with the Ministry of HRD. But there is no firm indication that the UGC Act will be shortly amended.

As a footnote to this discussion, it might be mentioned that the fine has been raised from Rs 1,000, to Rs 1,000,000 and, what is more relevant, mandatory imprisonment for one year. Unless something of this kind is done, no one would really feel discouraged from taking liberties with the law.

The institution of fake universities is one problem. The second related phenomenon is the entry of a large number of foreign institutions into India, sometimes on their own and sometimes in collaboration with their

Indian counterparts. This is such a serious matter that, as far back as 1995, the Ministry of HRD itself had moved a Bill entitled the Private Universities Bill.

There was some criticism of the provisions suggested and the presumption was that appropriate changes would be made and the Bill would be brought back to the House. This was more than five years ago but the Bill has not been reintroduced in Parliament. Even in the draft amendment of the UGC Act, the issue of foreign universities entering India had been dealt with and a remedy suggested. So even if a separate Bill dealing with private universities was not brought up, the problem could have been taken care of as part of the amendment of the UGC Act.

There is no one to question the ministry for these two indefensible lapses. It is difficult to say why when so many other Bills have been introduced and passed by Parliament under the NDA regime, these two Bills could not have been brought up and appropriate decisions taken. Either it indicates a lack of concern or understanding or there is an unwillingness to face the Parliament. Whatever be the explanation, this single omission will go down in history as something which amounts to an abdication of its responsibility by the Ministry of HRD. Legislative support, as and when required, is an important dimension of support to a professional council by the parent ministry. In its absence, the functioning of the councils gets retarded and this is precisely what has been happening.

III

In order to illustrate this particular point, a reference may be made to the overlaps and contradictions in the non-formal sector of education. It was in 1985 that the Indira Gandhi National Open University (IGNOU) was established. Ordinarily speaking, financial aid to open universities established by the states would have been provided by the UGC. In this particular case, following the UK model, IGNOU was given an independent status and the ministry decided to deal with it directly rather than through the UGC. There should have been no problem about this particular arrangement except that, in addition to IGNOU being independent of the UGC, it was also decided that support to state-level open universities would also be through it. This was not spelt out in the IGNOU Act itself. Instead, a Distance Education Council (DEC) was established through a statute passed as part of the IGNOU Act. Now both the open universities and DEC are looked after by IGNOU.

From 1985, when IGNOU was established, to this day, rules and regulations dealing with the assessment and release of grants are matters that are yet to be defined. As an outcome of the protest made by this writer about this particular infirmity in the functioning of IGNOU, some steps to regulate this matter are now being taken. It will be some time however before the matter is finalised.

What has been happening during the last 18 years has been one of the following two things. Either the functioning of the DEC was neglected and IGNOU concentrated upon the functioning of its own campus and little else. Or, equally deplorable, once in while, a meeting or two were held to discuss certain matters connected with the DEC but sometimes even that was not done. The vice chancellor, on his own discretion, took certain decisions and released funds. Some universities were patronised and some were left out and so on. This was in a situation where almost one-fifth of the student population of the country is enrolled in the distance education mode!

This indifference to the overall management of the distance education mode underlines the point that the Ministry of HRD has not cared to attend to the problems of an important sector of education. As a matter of fact, there is more to it. Even before IGNOU was established, quite a number of universities had established correspondence courses in several popular subjects. Even after the establishment of IGNOU, this process did not change. Even today about 50–60 universities in the country run correspondence courses.

Most of them, right from the first day, started with the assumption that correspondence courses or the distance education mode as it came to be called later, was an inferior type of education. Indeed most of those. connected with policy making found that they were not obliged to maintain what are called high standards. What is worse and patently dishonest, a good part of what they charged from the students purportedly to provide all kinds of facilities was mostly not used as such and promises were made which were never meant to be kept.

The most notorious case was of that of B.Ed through correspondence. Two universities in particular made very large sums of money by building upon the eagerness of students to get a B.Ed degree. This issue has been dealt with in the second chapter of the book in detail and no more need be said about it here. Fortunately the National Council for Teacher Education (NCTE) was able to take care of this problem.

But what about correspondence courses at the Master's degree level? In a number of subjects, the public demand was fairly high and quite a few universities did more or less the same thing as they had done in respect of B.Ed students: they exploited the students. In one of the states, income from this source was taken into account while releasing grants to the universities. In other words, a stamp of legitimacy was conferred upon the extravagant fees charged from the students as also the lack of provision for appropriate facilities.

Some years ago, this and several other matters were discussed by the UGC and IGNOU. They decided that while the open universities would continue to receive funding from IGNOU, the other universities would deal with the UGC. As far as the UGC is concerned, it hardly deals with the problem of correspondence course students in any serious or sustained manner. If there is a situation, the UGC intervenes, otherwise the universities continue to function on their own in their lacklustre way. To put it bluntly, a substantial number of students enrolled in these courses are made to subsidise the mainstream universities.

As if this was not objectionable enough, various technical universities got into the act. They started using the medium of correspondence education. Furthermore, several of them established study centres in different parts of the country. One particular technical university established close to a 100 study centres in different states. While doing so, it franchised its name and designation to private entrepreneurs. Only a few of them provided appropriate facilities; the rest got the students to pay the extravagant rates charged and denied them what they had been promised.

Different institutions did what suited them and nobody worried about the students. It was in this undefined and chaotic situation that several hundred foreign universities and colleges entered India. Each one of them started enrolling students and nobody bothered about the constitutional mandate given to the union government to coordinate and determine standards.

By the mid-nineties, the situation had become fairly serious. It was in that background that the Ministry of HRD itself moved a Private Universities Bill referred to already. The Bill could not be passed owing to the various criticisms made but everyone expected this matter to be taken up again. But, to repeat, the matter has not gone to Parliament a second time.

In 2002, rattled by the various developments that were taking place, the UGC issued a circular to universities. It disapproved of the steps being taken by most of them. Within a few weeks, IGNOU too issued a somewhat similar circular. Both were ignored by the offending universities and students continued to be exploited. That the right kind of education was not being imparted and some manipulative people were making fabulous money out of the eagerness of students to get on to the bandwagon, are facts of life. We do not have to elaborate them here.

When all this was happening, the Ministry of HRD remained resolutely unconcerned despite the anxiety expressed by a number of councils, including the UGC, AICTE and so on. The Ministry of HRD was repeatedly requested to do something about the matter. But it remained stubbornly immobile and that is where the situation stands today.

How is it that there was no public protest? The explanation is simple. In our country, it is rare for people to come together over matters educational. Even in newspapers, these things are written about largely when vested interests are affected. Admissions to engineering and medical colleges belong to this category. All these years, vested interests have grown. Scores of dubious characters have got into the act and made millions out of the leaderless and confused situation that had arisen. Whenever any kind of change was attempted, it was resisted by these people. When the initiative came from the Supreme Court in 1991, again there was considerable resistance. Vested interests were seriously affected and they mobilised the press.

As far as the teachers in these institutions or even teacher bodies are concerned, no one chose to protest. None bothered about standards in higher or professional education. The teachers could have been a formidable force against the various moves made from time to time but they never bothered to inform themselves about the issues or even assert their right to be consulted. That they were successfully bribed by the wage policy evolved in the seventies is something so obvious that one need not dwell on it. As long as that wage policy remains intact, they are not bothered about most other things. In any change of policy, they apprehend that the college teachers would stand to lose and they are 80 per cent or so of those who decide how their representatives function. For them, the status quo policy is the best policy. Some of the teacher leaders who understood what was happening chose to keep quiet because safety lay in doing so rather than in speaking out.

IV

There is much more to reinforce what has been stated earlier. Each one of the details underline either the lack of involvement on the part of the UGC or its impotence. When I headed a committee to review the working of Andhra Pradesh Universities in the mid-nineties, we noticed one thing. Open universities from other states had penetrated the state of Andhra Pradesh even though Andhra had been the first state in India to set up an open university. Its Open University was working reasonably well and, even today, it is functioning better than most other state universities of that description. Despite this positive fact, two negative factors were noticed.

One was the fact that universities other than the Open Universiy in Andhra were also handling quite a number of correspondence courses. This was not because they could handle them better than the Open University could but because this meant additional income for them and they had been generally longer in the game. The good old formula of double-crossing the students was at work all the time. Fees were charged in the higher range on the understanding that certain facilities would be provided. But they were not provided those facilities with the result that there was additional income for the concerned university.

Therefore, two issues were raised in the report. The first one concerned how to rationalise the system. Nobody paid any attention to it and things continued as before. It was the second issue however which was more relevant in respect of the problem under discussion. Should universities from other states encroach into Andhra? In terms of territorial jurisdiction, they had no business to do so. Why was the Andhra Government permitting this and creating a situation in which their own Open University suffered in the bargain? As in so many other cases, vested interests had grown and nobody took notice of these objections.

An additional curious incident may also be referred to. The Vishwa Bharati University founded by Tagore has no jurisdiction outside its campus. In order to raise additional revenue, the university decided to give franchise to some private agencies in respect of MBA courses in different parts of the country. Students were enrolled and things started in full swing. When the matter was brought to the notice of both the Ministry of HRD and the UGC, they started moving in the matter. The university took the position that commitments had been made with the private entrepreneurs as also the students and these could not be gone back upon. The Ministry of HRD, which chose to intervene under pressure from the public also took the view that the whole thing was outrageous and some action had to be taken. The UGC was told to withhold some of its grants. Instead of accepting this decision with due humility, the university retaliated in an ingenious manner.

Meanwhile the matter had gone to court. The chairman of the UGC was asked to personally appear in a Calcutta court in order to explain the UGC point of view. The earlier chairman had had to do so and his successor has had to do the same. The university is entirely in the wrong but the UGC has been dragged to court through false representations and misleading statements. Eventually, the issue will be sorted out but meanwhile considerable harassment would have been caused.

The curious thing is that though it is more than a year old, no enquiry has been held so far and no one has been held responsible for having done something which was patently illegal. The plain fact is that, over the years, several universities have become a law unto themselves. Rules have been violated with impunity and the universities have generally got away with their misdeeds. One reason of course is that the legal position of the UGC is weak. Another is that, in line with what is happening in other sectors of life, the universities too are acting lawlessly.

One dimension of this problem needs to be underlined. Most of these deviations from the norm have taken place in respect of actions taken on what is known as the 'distance education mode'. Poaching into alien territory and minting money are the twin attractions. Students do not mind joining these courses because, at the end of the year, they expect to get a university degree.

Despite all the academic dilution that is taking place, university degrees still carry some value in the market. That a central university should be guilty of such academic misdemeanour and the UGC should be unable to enforce even its limited powers has led to only one conclusion—the law needs to be defined better than what obtains today. In any case, those in charge of decision making have to be more assertive than they have given evidence of being so far.

The plain fact is that, for the last several years, quite a few universities have become a law unto themselves. Violation of law is not considered a serious enough matter. The UGC at present is so toothless that it cannot blame anyone else except itself. What it therefore needs is strong statutory support from the Ministry of HRD. So far, at any rate, that has not been forthcoming.

V

More than any other state, it is the state of Chhattisgarh which has taken specific advantage of these gaps in the constitutional powers with which the UGC has been vested. When the 1951 Bill was moved, it was opposed by the universities as a whole. The matter was reconsidered and then a fresh Bill was drawn up and presented to Parliament in 1953. This was referred to a Joint Select Committee and a final Bill was passed in 1956. All this is known and has been discussed elsewhere in the book.

Even though mentioned elsewhere, it needs to be recalled that the 1956 Act does not have two important provisions which figured in the 1953 Bill. One was that no university could be established till the UGC had given its concurrence in the matter. Second, the UGC had the right to derecognise any degree. Both these provisions were deleted by the Joint Select Committee. In this connection it may not be out of place to refer to the parliamentary debate which took place when the Bill was being discussed. M.N. Das, who was the parliamentary secretary of the Ministry of Education and piloted the Bill, observed on 22 November 1955:

> In fact if I may say so, the committee has reduced the UGC into a mere advisory and consultative body, having no power to enforce its recommendations as decisions.

Upon which a member commented that the Bill should be withdrawn.

> M.N. Das replied, The penalty clause about which many members spoke with great vehemence(?) has been drastically revised and today UGC has been authorized to give only this punishment, namely, that if a university does not agree or refuses to carry out its recommendations, then it can only withhold its grants' no other punishment can be imposed on it.

This exchange of comments as recorded in the parliamentary proceedings sums up the situation as far as the UGC Act is concerned. Experience over the last 50 years has shown that the UGC is given attention mainly owing to the fact that its decisions, particularly in respect of pay scales, affect almost 400,000 teachers and around 9 million students today. It is these two facts which, more than anything else, give some weight to what the UGC says. For the rest, the UGC is a toothless body. What makes it even more toothless is the fact that it has neither developed the right system of internal management nor does it always contain the more enlightened and knowledgeable academics on its executive body.

These details will be gone into elsewhere. The fact remains that the UGC, after 50 years of its existence, has been comprehensively defied by the state of Chhattisgarh. That state adopted a Bill in terms of which the establishment of a university did not have to go before the Legislative Assembly as had been the practice hitherto. As per Chhattisgarh's latest regulation, a university can be set up through executive action and its establishment notified in the official gazette! After about one year of this decision which incidentally cannot be legally challenged, something like 50 universities have been established in that state in the manner described above.

These may have their headquarters in the state of Chhattisgarh but their scene of operations is located elsewhere. India is still passing through a phase where a university degree does matter to some extent. Therefore, some of the private entrepreneurs who wish to make money have always wanted the fig leaf of a university degree. They have taken advantage of what Chhattisgarh has done and gone ahead with their shameless fleecing of students with the help of a duly established state government.

A somewhat similar Bill was mooted in Madhya Pradesh (MP). The governor of that state had the good sense to refer it to the UGC for opinion. Chhattisgarh did not choose to do that and the Act was enforced right away and the UGC was merely informed of it. The Chhattisgarh Bill is constitutionally defective in one crucial respect. It does not include, with its text, the First Statutes or Ordinances which have to be a part of any university act.

Regardless of these imperfections, Chhattisgarh has gone ahead and spawned a large number of universities. As if what was happening earlier was not shocking enough, Chhattisgarh has demonstrated beyond any doubt that, unless the UGC Act is amended and given some teeth, the UGC will continue to exist but will not be able to deliver the goods. It is not for the UGC to decide what to do in this situation. Those who understand the constitutional position do not take the matter seriously. And as to funding, there is never enough of it. If the situation has to be saved, the only way it can be done is to remodel both its functions and powers.

In this connection, it needs to be added that what the ministry of education sought to do in 1951 was in accordance with the provisions of the

Indian Constitution. If, in the eventual outcome, the UGC was turned into 'an old aunt who can be coaxed into doing anything', as I wrote in the late sixties on one occasion, in this moment of crisis, the basic responsibility is that of the Ministry of HRD and not the UGC. The UGC can only do what it is permitted to do. It cannot go beyond that and that is why, without a basic reordering of what the UGC has been empowered to do, it will only continue to flex its muscles but this will not necessarily lead to any positive outcome.

VI

Assuming that the UGC Act would be amended and it would also forbid foreign institutions from operating in India except after approval by the UGC, what would be the situation? Obviously regulating the foreign institutions would have a distinctly positive effect. But that is not the only problem. There are various other chronic ones also and those need to be identified though not discussed here.

1. The first problem is that, in addition to an amendment of the UGC Act, the union government should make more funds available to the UGC. What is being provided now is clearly inadequate. Since the whole thing is linked up with the process of planning, no more can be said except to make the point that the UGC, in addition to being empowered and given teeth, should also be enabled to provide better funding. Details of how this has to be done have been discussed in the course of the book. Issues regarding autonomous colleges, affiliated colleges, postgraduate teaching and several related matters have been discussed. Those would have to be codified and the details of the rules and regulations laid down.

2. Though this could have been made the first issue, it needs to be said that the UGC must be vested with greater statutory powers. Whether the centre would have assertion enough to bring back that particular provision whereby it was open to the UGC to derecognise any degree, will depend upon the political situation. Likely enough, the states would still oppose such a provision and it may not get reintroduced. But something close to it could

still be done. What are called Fitness-to-Function-Norms can be defined much more precisely even without taking on the power of derecognising a degree. Once that is done, the situation would undergo a marked change. One of its side effects would be that the UGC would have to have a much more vigilant legal cell than it has at the moment. This is a dimension of the problem to which adequate attention has not yet been paid.

3. The role of accreditation must not only be strengthened, it must also be expanded. Something has been said about this issue in the essay on accreditation. In point of fact, this whole issue has to be gone into much more deeply than has been done so far. At the same time, the process of accreditation has to be extended to cover a larger number of institutions than has been possible so far. What is being argued is nothing but using both the 'carrot' and the 'stick'. Accreditation is the 'carrot' and it is the UGC which will wield the 'stick'. Unless one is seriously mistaken, the impact of accreditation is likely to increase in every sense of the word during the next few years. There is a good deal of creativity only waiting to be identified and promoted. The channel for doing so would be through the process of accreditation.

4. Student assessment of teachers needs to be given a big push. This cannot be done without the active cooperation of the union government. No other set of reforms under discussion will have as much impact as this particular one. Since the state governments are directly involved in it, their goodwill and cooperation is also indispensable. And this cannot be secured without strong and continuing support of the union government.

5. Academic reform will not receive the right kind of attention unless two things are done. One is to establish more autonomous colleges and the other is to introduce a new mode of testing in universities and colleges. Once this is done, the situation would start changing. When a large number of autonomous colleges are set up, they will examine their own students. This in turn will influence and shape a new mode of testing as also the functioning of the universities. Both universities and colleges should begin at the Master's level and then gradually go down to the undergraduate level. This issue has been discussed in considerable detail in a number of essays. What is being done here is to call attention to its importance.

6. To assume that these reforms can be introduced or enforced without the willing cooperation of the academics would be an oversimplification. To start with, they may not be enthusiastic but if both the centre and the states pull their weight together and the UGC opts to follow an enlightened and pragmatic policy, things can change.

7. The glass is not half empty but half full; this is what needs to be understood as also acknowledged. Everything is not negative as quite a few people presume. The fact of the matter is that, as far as professional education is concerned, there is an acutely uncomfortable feeling which recognises that, without improving the standards of performance, nothing will be achieved. This will have both a positive and a negative impact.

   The highly favourable experience of IT during the last few years has prompted more and more people to think along these lines. Problems will certainly arise in those institutions which are handled basically by the UGC. The kind of students who join most affiliated colleges are not equipped well enough to join the fast moving train of development. But, even amongst them, there are quite a few who have potential and, given an opportunity, will do well for themselves.

   That is why a different mode of functioning of the UGC is called for. The crux of the matter is what do we do at the level of affiliated colleges. Once this problem has been taken care of to some extent by setting up large numbers of autonomous colleges, things will start changing. The rest of the job, if one may say so, can be performed by strengthening the UGC and upgrading its functioning.

8. Upgrading its functioning is an objective which will not be achieved overnight. Once the Act is amended and, in addition to the vice chairman, there are other full-time members, the UGC secretariat will start responding differently. This particular innovation and the expanding role of National Assessment and Accreditation Council (NAAC) can bring about spectacular changes within a couple of years. That the UGC staff will have to be retrained, strengthened as also professionalised are issues that do not need much elaboration.

9. The only thing that remains to be added is that changes at the central level, even if carried out as visualised above, will not lead to automatic changes at the state level. Those will have to

be made if the universities as well the colleges in the states are to perform better. In a sense, the existing situation is quite a bottleneck. But it has to be overcome. Strengthening the educational apparatus at the state level is an indispensable step which has to be taken and the centre (which means both the Ministry of HRD and the UGC) must take a hand in it.

10. Two decades ago, the concept of the State Councils of Higher Education was put out. Several states have also set them up. None of them, however, has been given the same status and role as the UGC has been given at the centre. In point of fact, it is when these councils begin to function more or less like the UGC functions at the centre, that things will start moving in the right direction.

PART I

Statutory
Issues

I

FOUNDATION AND ROLE OF THE UNIVERSITY GRANTS COMMISSION*

The UGC in India is different from any grant-giving agency in any country of the world in one significant respect.

It is possibly only in India that the UGC has been vested with two powers simultaneously. One is the power to provide funds and the other is the power to determine and coordinate standards. In other countries, for instance, Canada, Australia, USA, even West Germany, funds are provided by the federal government and there is a good deal of argument about the quantum of grant, the procedures of release and other related issues. In none of these countries however does the federal government have the same right in respect of the determination and coordination of standards as the union government in India has.

According to the Constitution adopted in 1950, the centre was given the requisite powers in respect of higher and professional education. In respect of the other levels of education, the centre has come to acquire increased powers after the 42nd Amendment was adopted in 1976. Whatever be the political realities on the ground, on the constitutional plane, the union government in India has powers which perhaps no other

---

* This article was originally published in the UGC sponsored *Journal of Higher Education*, 7(1), Monsoon 1981.

federal country has. How this came about is a matter that does not have to be discussed here. The focus of discussion in this chapter is on how the UGC came to be established and how it was decided to vest it with the powers that it commands today.

The greater part of this story is a forgotten chapter in the history of higher education. To recall some of those controversies and the circum-stances in which the UGC came to be established can throw a certain amount of light on how the UGC came to be vested with powers which are hardly to be found in any other grant-giving body in a democratic country. Whether those powers have been used or not is another question. A number of committees appointed by Parliament as also a Review Com-mittee appointed by the Ministry of education have gone into those ques-tions. Those who wish to know about this aspect of the problem may refer to these various sources. The point just now is to trace the process of thinking which, step by step, led to the establishment of the UGC as we know it today.

II

The Republic was inaugurated on the 26 January 1951. A few months later the ministry of education prepared a draft Bill entitled 'The Univer-sities (Regulation of Standards) Bill'. The sub-title of the Bill was 'To Regulate Certain Matters Relating to the Coordination and Determination of Standards in Universities'. The statement of Objects and Reasons was as follows:

> The Constitutions of India vests Parliament with exclusive authority in regard to 'coordination and determination of standards in insti-tutions for higher education'. It is obvious that neither coordination of the institutions nor determination of their standards is possible unless the Central Government has some control over the estab-lishment of new universities, the definition of territorial jurisdiction and the determination of standards of teaching and examination in Universities, both old and new.

With this objective in view the proposed Bill put forward certain proposals and the principal ones are enumerated below:

(i) No university established after the commencement of this Act by or under a State Act shall be deemed to be a university unless the central government by notification makes a declaration to that effect.

(ii) It is open to the central government to declare any institution for higher education other than a university to be a university.

(iii) No institution other than a university would have the right to confer degrees.

(iv) In order to carry out the work of coordination and determination of standards, a Central Council of University Education is to be established. At least one-third of the members of the Council would be vice chancellors.

(v) The Central Council can ask for information about any aspect of university work from a university and would have the powers to direct the executive authority of any university to take such action as may be specified.

(vi) In case any university fails to comply with the directions issued within a reasonable time, the Central Council would be authorised to advise the central government to derecognise any degree conferred by such a university for the purpose of employment under the central government or for any other purpose.

This draft Bill was circulated to state government as well as to universities for opinion. Except for one, none of the state governments opposed the Bill. This was stated by Humayun Kabir at a conference of vice chancellors and representatives of universities in India which was held in September 1952, i.e., approximately a year after the Bill was circulated. During this period, however, the universities opposed the Bill strongly and with a certain measure of persistence. As far as the state governments were concerned, they had little to say in criticism of it, possibly for the reason that the Indian Constitution had been adopted only a couple of years earlier and the power to coordinate and determine standards vested in the central government was a part of the consensus that had been worked out under the benign leadership of Jawaharlal Nehru. Not only was the *ethos* of political life more or less homogeneous in its approach and orientation, the same political party exercised power in all the states. Some of the subsequent contentions between the centre and the states of which one has been hearing a good deal during the last couple of decades were not heard of at that time.

The universities, however, reacted differently. They were vehemently opposed to the Bill. They advanced three main arguments and these may be described as follows:

(i)   It is for the universities themselves to regulate, maintain and coordinate their own academic standards.
(ii) For any outside agency to seek to undertake this job would amount to violating university autonomy.
(iii) If the standards were low it was mainly for lack of funds. Once adequate funds were made available, there would be hardly any problems.

At this meeting, speaker after speaker waxed eloquent on how the central government was planning to take away the autonomy of universities. The number of universities at the time was not particularly large, it was more in the neighbourhood of a quarter century than otherwise. More than 20 universities were represented at this meeting and amongst some of the luminaries who spoke the following may be mentioned: Prof. Hadi Hasan; Prof. A.C. Banerjee; Dr V.S. Krishna; Dr R.K. Shanmukhan Chetty; Mrs Hansa Mehta; Sir Navroji J. Wadia; Sir Vithal N. Chandalvarkar; Dr G.S. Mahajani; Dr V.K.R.V. Rao; Sir A.L. Mudaliar; and Sir A. Ramaswamy Mudaliar. On behalf of the Ministry of Education, Humayun Kabir was present. He described his presence at the conference as almost that of 'a culprit in the dock'.

All kinds of interesting things were said at this conference. Some of the remarks made at that conference may be reproduced here in order to convey a flavour of what was said:

(i)   We feel that no outside body should tell us how to coordinate our standards and how to determine our courses of study. I feel, therefore, Sir, that this Bill, if passed into legislation, will do untold harm and I am unable to see any good that it will do. It is true that a Central Council might do some good but only if it is made purely an advisory both and if it is constituted almost entirely of vice chancellors and other representatives of universities. (Sir N.J. Wadia, Vice Chancellor, Bombay.)
(ii) If the central government had begun to realise their constitutional responsibility in the matter of higher education, this Bill, instead of taking this shape, must really have taken the shape of a Bill to create a University Grants Committee and then to

define what the powers of the University Grants Committee would be and what the functions of the central government would be in regard to their responsibility. Because once you recognise that the central government must be the source of finance to the universities, then even the most ardent advocates of university autonomy cannot deny the implications of such a statement, viz., that if the central government which is responsible for finding the major part of the finances must have some voice, in some manner or other, for the way in which all this money is spent so that the whole basis of this proposed legislation must start from the kind of financial help that the central government is expected to give and what consequences regarding control of the central government would follow the grant of financial resources to meet the needs of the universities. Instead of doing that, the Bill has been shaped in such a manner that one is tempted to think that the central government is following in respect of education the example of non-democratic countries. (Dr R.K. Shanmukhan Chetty, Vice Chancellor, Annamalai.)

(iii) Let us confess frankly that standards vary from university to university but there is the constant attempt on the part of political bodies to lower the standards, to revise examination results, to have more percentage of passes than the university authorities think it's desirable, to give grace marks and in fact influence the universities in such a way that the number of first classes is more than the number of second classes. These are the obvious defects which the Inter-University Board can tackle, if it has only a little more power than it has at present. A fundamental difficulty of this Bill that has not been realised is the clash between the powers already existing and the powers proposed to be given to the new authority. It has ignored all the existing structure; it has ignored the Inter-University Board which has been in existence for 26 years and has done some little to put up standards of education. If in spite of that, here and there, standards are low, it is because sufficient powers are not given to the Inter-University Board. (Sir A. Ramaswamy Mudaliar, Vice Chancellor, Travancore.)

(iv) It is no use asking us to do this and that and not helping us at all with money. There was a Grants Committee appointed in the past, of which I was a Member, but we met once or twice and became defunct and there was no grant to distribute. If the Government of India thinks of raising standards, they must give financial assistance. (Mrs Hansa Mehta, Vice Chancellor, Baroda.)

(v) The question of standards is a question of finance. If the standards are low it is not because of the universities but in spite of them. (Prof. Hadi Hasan, Aligarh.)

(vi) Even supposing that the central government agrees that the Central Council should consist only of vice chancellors, I would very strongly put it to this body that we cannot allow any other body to issue directives. I can understand they can argue and try to persuade us but I am of opinion it is a complete breach of the very principle even if the Constitution is changed and it consists only of vice chancellors .... I therefore suggest that the government should take note of the views expressed by us regarding the constitution of the Grants Committee which would be an autonomous body and would disburse grants to different universities in India. The Grants Committee should advise the universities in all matters, but they should refer all such matters to a committee of vice chancellors appointed by the Inter-University Board or the Standing Committee of the Inter-University Board, which would act as a liaison between the Grants Committee and the universities. (Dr V.K.R.V. Rao, Delhi.)

Clearly, the universities were opposed to the idea of any agency other than themselves to regulate standards. Quite a number of them felt that if the Inter-University Board had more powers than it exercised at the moment they could perhaps do the job equally well. In any case the one over-riding concern was to get additional funds from the central government. Several of them suggested the establishment of a Grants Committee on the lines of the UGC in Britain. Indeed some of them harked back to the pre-1947 days when an informal Grants Committee had been established in the Ministry of Education and did dole out some grants. Some of the well-known vice chancellors were even associated with it. Both Lakshmanswami Mudaliar and Hansa Mehta referred to their association with this Committee but obviously there was very little money to disburse and so the Grants Committee either did not function or became defunct.

Humayun Kabir who was present at this meeting in his reply made the following points:

(i) The government did not for a moment want to encroach upon the autonomy of the universities.

(ii) If the Inter-University Board could suggest some machinery for improvement in standards, the government would be glad to consider those suggestions.

(iii) Uniformity in standards and attainments was all that was contemplated and not necessarily uniformity in courses and syllabi.

(iv) There were some slighting references to the amount Rs 25 million in five years which was to be made available to the universities from the American Wheat Loan. But Humayun Kabir informed the conference that even in the First Plan the Planning Commission had provided Rs 120 million for the universities.

(v) He conceded that the use of the word 'direct' was unfortunate. What was intended, according to him, was to draw the attention of the universities to certain matters. May be the word 'direct' could be replaced, he said.

(vi) He assured the vice chancellors that if this Bill was passed it is not the central government that would assume these powers. These would be exercised by a body which would be autonomous in its Constitution and working. In fact he said that it would be a statutory body and all the members would command the confidence of the universities. 'It will not be department of the government, but it will be a statutory body where the university interests will be fully represented', he affirmed.

III

All this happened in September 1952. For the next year or so the matter continued to be debated within the government. Once the confidential records of that period are made public, and studied in detail, it would be possible to study the points of view expressed by various persons connected with this matter. Perhaps the two persons who were actively involved in the whole thing were Maulana Azad and Humayun Kabir. Both of them passed away some years ago and neither of them has left a record of the conflicting pulls and pressures experienced by them. It is only from the records of the government that it would be possible to reconstruct the details of the arguments which must have been advanced at that time. On the one hand was the desire of the Ministry of Education, as expressed through this Bill, to regulate standards. On the other hand was the vociferous and persistent opposition of the universities to the proposed Bill principally on the ground that it would rob them of their autonomy.

In retrospect, one can see that while the universities were robbed of their autonomy in any case, this did not happen in the interests of high standards. Before 1947, universities were certainly much more autonomous than they are today. It was indeed a distinguished man who was selected to be the vice chancellor of a university. Once selected, nobody breathed down his neck, nobody whispered anything into his ears, there was hardly any wheeling and dealing and, what is more important, nobody's tenure was cut short because at some point or other be became unacceptable to the powers that be. Universities then were truly sub-systems of the larger system and there was hardly any attempt to run the sub-system in a manner so as to make it subservient to the larger system. If most of the university representatives assembled in this conference protested against the attempt to take away their autonomy, it is but reasonable to conclude that they were thinking of the kind of autonomy that the universities had enjoyed till then rather than of the kind of autonomy which the universities enjoy now-a-days.

Those were the days when the universities were on the whole left free to manage their own affairs. More or less as a concomitant of this attitude, they were hardly given any financial assistance. The universities were expected to have a surplus from the examinations that they conducted and this was used for running the establishment and may be a few university departments as well. Except for unitary universities, the rest either did not have any departments or they somehow managed to exist. This was the general situation and the demand for financial help was therefore a genuine demand.

In this situation, the Ministry of Education found it difficult to work out a clear course of action for itself. If it established a Central Council, as visualised, and vested it with the powers to issue directives and penalised those universities which did not implement the directives, it would perhaps be violating the autonomy of the universities. And yet if such a central body was not established and the universities were left to their own devices, the standards would continue to be uneven, indeed unsatisfactory, and the obligation cast upon the centre to coordinate and determine standards would remain undischarged.

How was this issue to be resolved? Universities which were starved of funds (and almost each one of them was) required help through the agency of a Grants Committee. A Grants Committee had fitfully functioned for several years. The University Education Commission presided over by Dr S. Radhakrishnan had also recommended such a body. The planning era was about to begin in Indian economy and it was proposed to help the universities with funds from the central government. The obvious agency for such a large scale flow of funds could be a body like the Grants Committee. Clearly, the establishment of such a body would meet the needs of the universities. In the Indian context, such an agency had to be statutory in character. What was easier than to describe it as the University Grants Commission? It could always be referred to as the UGC, a name which corresponded to the UGC in Great Britain. The British model was all the time in the background and nothing appeared more natural to the decision makers than the fact that the agency created in India should also be called the UGC.

To establish a Central Council as envisaged in the Bill and to have to defend the government against the charge of violating university autonomy would have been awkward. All that the Ministry of Education was doing was to concretise one of the provisions in the Constitution, yet this would not prevent the universities from repeating, day in and day out, that something had been imposed on them from above and that they were no longer as autonomous as they used to be. To combine both the functions in one body, the function of disbursing grants to universities as also the function of advising them on how to improve their standards of performance seemed to be the natural thing to do. What was more, the Constitution did not come in the way of adopting such a course of action.

Today it seems natural and indeed obvious that the two functions should have been combined in one body. But let it not be forgotten that there was no precedent for it in any country of the world. Federal funding to universities is a fairly widespread practice. It is to be encountered in several countries and on the whole everybody seems to be happy about it. Universities are chronically short of funds and it is rarely that any university refuses to accept a grant from any quarter unless it is of a highly suspect character. But in no country of the world does the grant-giving agency have the power to sit in judgement upon the quality of performance of a university.

IV

Two other things require to be dealt with here. One is to analyse the UGC Bill as adopted in 1956 and see its relationship with the 1951 Bill which was discarded. The second is to examine whether the changes made were such as were calculated to improve standards and indeed to what extent the experiment of combining both the functions in one body had yielded good results.

The 1951 Bill vested the central government with the power of approving or not approving a university established by a State Legislature. The exact wording of the Bill was as follows:

> No University established or incorporated after the commencement of this Act by or under a State Act shall be deemed to be a university unless the Central Government, by notification in the Official Gazette, has made a declaration to that effect.

According to the Constitution, education was and is a state subject. It was only in respect of coordination and determination of standards that the centre had been vested with powers. It was in pursuance of this obligation that this particular clause had been inserted. In view of the outcry against the 1951 Bill however, this clause was deleted from the UGC Act passed in 1956. To what extent this was a step in the right direction or not should be apparent from one fact. In 1956, the number of universities was almost one quarter of what it was in 1972. There is a good reason why 1972 has been mentioned here. It was in the 1972 Amendment of the UGC Act that the following clause was introduced:

> No grant shall be given by the central government, the Commission, or any other organisation receiving any funds from the central government, to a university which is established after the commencement of the University Grants Commission Amendment Act 1972, unless the Commission has, after satisfying itself as to such matters as may be prescribed, declared such university to be fit for receiving such grant. (Section 12A)

Two things may be noted here. One, even when the UGC Act was amended in 1970 (the first amendment after 1956), this particular provision was not inserted. In other words, the central government continued to be cagey in respect of what the states would say in the matter. Second, even when in 1972 the Act was further amended, the provision inserted was not as categorical or as far-reaching in its implications as it had been in the 1951 Bill. The 1951 Bill refused to recognise a university as a university unless a declaration to this effect was made by the central government. The 1972 Act (which is still in force) merely empowered the central government and its agencies to withhold the release of grants to a university. Which is only a way of saying that a university could nevertheless come into being; only that it would not receive any central assistance. True to pattern, this did not prevent, a few years later, half a dozen universities from coming into existence without clearance from the central government, though it must be added in all fairness that the central government did not give them any grant. But clearly the centre even in 1972 was not prepared to go as far as it had chosen to go in 1951.

Another provision in the 1951 Bill was that it would be open to the central government to declare any institution of higher education other than a university to be a university. The existing provision in the UGC Act in respect of an institution 'deemed to be a university' is only a variation upon the original provision. Some of the other provisions were either repeated or slightly modified. For instance, it was stated in the 1951 Bill that no institution other than a university would have the right to confer a degree. This was repeated in the 1956 Act. Similarly, one-third of the membership of the Central Council was to consist of vice chancellors. The proposal to this effect made in the 1951 Bill was retained in the 1956 Act. This provision has however been whittled down step by step both in the 1970 and 1972 Amendments to the UGC Act. During the last few years only one or two vice chancellors have served on the Commission. They may be members of the Commission. There is nothing to bar them, but there is no mandatory provision as it existed until 1972.

It was in respect of two other provisions however that the real whittling down was done. One was in respect of directing the universities to take such action as may be specified and the second was in respect of the derecognition of degrees. The first proposal was altogether dropped. As to the second one, the precise proposal made in the 1951 Bill was as follows:

> If any university fails within a reasonable time to comply with any directions issued by the Council under Section 7 or Section 8, the Council may advise the central government to refuse to recognise any degree conferred or granted by such university for the purpose

of employment under the central government or for any other purpose.

This particular provision made no concessions of any kind. The central government gave unto itself the right to derecognise degrees given by a particular university on the recommendation of the Central Council. That was the only qualifying clause. For the rest the central government had the absolute power to derecognise any degree. This was more or less in line with the power given to the Medical Council of India. The Medical Council Act was passed before the UGC Act was passed. Despite the lapse of so many years the Medical Council still has that power. The power has never been used. Only on one occasion was a particular university threatened with the use of this power. Even there, all that the Medical Council could have done was to have recommended to the central government that the degrees of that particular college should be derecognised. By itself it could not have done anything more. But the fact remains that the Medical Council does have this power and on the whole this fact has had a salutary effect on medical education.

V

It should not be difficult to see that the issue is more political than legal. Legally speaking, the centre laid down in the 1951 Bill that no state university would be recognised as a university unless the centre approved it. Furthermore, if a university did not carry out a directive issued to it, the government would have the power to derecognise its degrees. Today, to quibble about whether the centre has this power or not, as is sometimes done, is beside the point. Under the Constitution, the centre has the power. That is why the centre introduced these provisions in the 1951 Bill. Nobody objected to this power on legal grounds. All the objections were on grounds other than legal.

If in the UGC Act of 1956 the centre chose to delete these provisions and did not re-induct them in any of the subsequent amendments, the meaning is clear. The centre hesitates to take any decision which would dilute the powers that the states have enjoyed all these years. In 1976, when the 42nd Amendment was adopted and education became a concurrent subject, it had hardly any effect on the centre-state relationship in respect of higher education. Higher education was already more or less on the Concurrent List. In terms of the power to coordinate and determine standards, the centre could enforce whatever it wanted to enforce. The 42nd Amendment simply put other sectors of education also on the Concurrent List. The significance of this particular Amendment was not that the centre acquired more powers in respect of higher education. Those it already had. Its significance lay in the fact that even in respect of other levels of education the centre now could legislate and this legislation would have precedence over state legislation.

Can one link up the argument with the different points of view held by different political parties? The evidence is not decisive enough to do so but a couple of pointers do exist. It was the Congress Party which sponsored the 42nd Amendment and got it accepted. To that extent the Congress Party may be said to be in favour of a greater role for the centre. On the other hand, one can see that there has been no follow up legislation of the 42nd Amendment so far and the situation therefore virtually remains what it was. In regard to the Janata Party, there is an interesting tell-tale piece of evidence. The UGC Review Committee suggested that the UGC be given the power to derecognise the degree of any university. This was nothing but a reiteration of what had been provided for in the 1951 Bill. When the report of this Review Committee came to be processed by the Janata government, then in power, this particular recommendation was not accepted. The moral is clear and need not be made explicit.

The fact of the matter is that the centre-state relationship over the decades has developed in such a manner that no political party would find it possible to take a strong line vis-à-vis the states. In 1951, the situation was qualitatively different. The Constitution had been adopted only recently. Different kinds of pulls and pressures had been exerted during the years the Constitution was being hammered out. The Constitution as it finally emerged, in a sense, represented a consensus. In the vision of future India that Jawaharlal Nehru and Maulana Azad had, education was to play a very important role. There is evidence of Maulana Azad urging 'central guidance, if not central control, on provincial progress' in the field of education. Pandit Nehru's mind also worked on the same wave-length and that is how the centre came to have the power to coordinate and determine standards in respect of higher education.

To have made the constitutional provision, as described above, was one thing. To have created agencies and instruments for the purpose was another. The 1951 Bill sought to establish an agency for the purpose. It was vehemently opposed by the universities and after a year or so of soul searching and mutual consultations, the Ministry of education eventually established the UGC in late 1953. For the next two and a half years it functioned as an ad hoc agency till such time as the 1956 Act gave it statutory standing.

Today, it is legitimate to ask to what extent the UGC has utilised the powers of coordination and determination of standards vested in it. The simplest answer would be that had these powers been put to use even partially the situation in higher education would not have been what it is today. This statement as a matter of fact needs to be qualified. To that extent that the situation today has been shaped by the economic and political forces at work (which is what makes the centre hesitate to use the powers at its disposal), the UGC could not have done anything to change the situation. But there was a role for the UGC to play and it was the role of an agency acting in the interest of higher standards. In plain words, it could have played the role of a professional body. To quite an extent it did not play this role and, indeed, it allowed itself to be swamped by the economic and political forces at work. These forces cannot be contained even by the centre. Without question there are elements at the centre which would like to control and contain them but they feel thwarted and outmanoeuvred by these forces that are too powerful for them. To expect the UGC to have stood up to these forces is to be both naïve and unconvincing.

VI

However, there was one way in which the UGC could have offered resistance and that was to act as a professional body. This is precisely what the Medical Council of India (MCI) has done. It can be nobody's contention that the MCI has acquitted itself with glory. At the same time one can see that the situation in medical education would have been much much worse, but for the restraining and professional role played by the MCI. Can one say the same thing about the UGC? The answer, sadly, is in the negative.

It would be best to illustrate this point of view with one or two examples. As of today something like 50–60 per cent of the colleges are substandard. They have an enrolment of not more than a couple of hundreds and what happens in the four walls of those colleges can hardly be described as education. Now there was no way of regulating the proliferation of these colleges. The colleges were being established because of a certain conjunction of interests between the politicians and educational entre-preneures. The whole thing was rooted in the reality of political life and even the state governments found it difficult to resist these pressures. The stark fact today is that more than 50 per cent of the colleges in India are intellectual and social slums and they are as difficult to take care of as it is difficult to convert slums into habitable areas in a city.

All this is undeniable but what justification is there for the fact that, after nearly 50 years of existence, there is no set of rules covering the establishment of colleges? Even though some 'norms' have been developed by the Commission, there should have been no difficulty in convening a meeting of principals and vice chancellors and laying down a certain set of ground rules to govern the establishment and affiliation of colleges. Even the Central Advisory Board of Education would have eventually accepted most of them, though in the process quite a few of them would have been watered down. And yet it was left to the Review Committee (which submitted its report in 1977) to suggest that a set of ground rules ought to be prepared. Even years after that report was submitted, the item is still to be put on the agenda of the UGC.

In another illustration, the UGC Review Committee suggested that standards of performance at the Ph.D. level called for some regulation. Now this is purely a professional matter. The rules and regulations can be laid down with regard to this matter and how the evaluation of a thesis is done are matters which are totally professional and do not admit of any other consideration. Even in this respect however an adequate initiative by the UGC has not been taken.

The point made here is that it is only as a professional body that the UGC can continue to function and be effective to some extent. If it ceases to be professional or allows its professional judgement to be influenced by political considerations, sooner or later its effectiveness as an instrument of coordination and determination of standards would decline. This is precisely what has happened and this is precisely what ought not to have happened.

Indeed one criticism often made with respect to the UGC is that it acts only as a grant-giving body and has seldom given serious attention to the problems of coordination and determination of standards. The illustrations given above point in this direction. But there is a prior question to be asked here. Is this mode of functioning by design or by accident? Unless the history of the last half-century can be wished away, it would seem that this is hardly an accident. Over the years the UGC has made a virtue of leaving the universities to act on their own. Not only that, non-intervention has been elevated into a principle. It can be nobody's contention that the UGC ought to lay down the law as far as the universities are concerned. Such a policy would ultimately inhibit the growth of universities and that is why this policy should be eschewed. At the same time, it is equally wrong to let every university function as if it were a law unto itself.

This philosophy of functioning (or shall we call it non-functioning?) is at variance with what the founding fathers of the Indian Constitution had visualised. There is enough evidence in the Constituent Assembly debates and other papers connected with the framing of the Constitution to show that the centre visualised a positive and forward-looking role for itself in respect of higher education. That is precisely why Entry 66 in Schedule VII was inserted. If the centre were to play only a passive role and everything was to be left to the universities concerned, there would have been no need to provide for coordination and determination of standards by the centre.

At the 1952 meeting of the vice chancellors who opposed the 1951 Bill, almost every single speaker argued that it was for the universities themselves to regulate their own affairs and that it was unthinkable for any outside agency to issue directives to them. Representing the centre, Humayun Kabir argued, rather weakly, that it was no one's intention to interfere from the centre and all that was being done was to create a Central Council which would be an autonomous body and would function in close collaboration with the universities. Humayun Kabir argued along these lines but there was hardly any body of precedents for him to assure the universities that their fears were unfounded and that all that the centre meant to do was to be helpful. If the Ministry of education had been more resolute about their original intention, the situation could have been distinctly better than what it is today. But it appears that both Maulana Azad and Humayun Kabir allowed themselves to be persuaded against their better judgement.

VII

How does one strike the balance-sheet? One thing is definite. No government in the foreseeable future would be able to adopt the posture that had been adopted by the central government in 1951. In plain words, even though the Constitution permits the centre extensive powers in respect of higher and professional education (the right to derecognise degrees for instance), those are not likely to be exercised today. They could not be exercised even in 1951. In 1981 the situation has undergone almost a sea change.

At that time opposition to the powers sought to be assumed by the centre came from the universities. Only one state government was opposed to it. Today almost every state government would be opposed to it. As to the universities, even though they are battered day after day by the state governments, not many of them are likely to take the unqualified stand that the last word should be with the central government.

What is to be done in this situation therefore? To treat the UGC mainly as a grant-giving body, as has been the practice hitherto, would be to circumscribe its functioning. Indeed such an approach cuts at the roots of the unique experiment launched by India in 1950. This must not be allowed to happen. At the same time one has to be realistic and understand the parameters within which academic change can be brought about. The UGC can function as a body which determines and coordinates standards provided, and this is an important proviso, it is protected as well as insulated against political pressures. To the extent that this requires some kind of self-abnegation on the part of political parties, one may not be too sanguine about it. But to the extent that the UGC itself can function as a non-political organisation, this is perfectly feasible. Perhaps the right way of putting it would be that the UGC should function as a professional body. Even when there are pressures exerted on it those should be met on the professional plane.

There would be limitations, nevertheless. The analogy of the MCI is correct but upto a point. The composition of the MCI is, on the whole, professional in character. Over the years, however, this character of the MCI has got rebooted though other obstacles have arisen. In the case of the UGC the professional element is almost absent and all said and done the UGC is treated as a limb of the government. Notwithstanding this difference in composition and, by implication, in its outlook, the UGC deals with a sector of activity where its effective functioning depends upon the extent to which it can be professional. If it is professional in its orientation and programme of work, there is no reason why its performance should fall short of its promise.

As stated earlier, the issue is political rather than legal. In legal terms, the utmost power that the centre has given to the UGC is to withhold grants but there are many more powers which the centre could have given. This has not been done for reasons which are entirely political. Universities functioning on their own cannot fight these political forces. By the same token and more or less for the same reasons the UGC with its limited powers is obliged to come to terms with these forces. It would be an over-simplification however to assume that the battle is lost. This is not so and that is for two reasons. For one thing, over the years the UGC has acquired a kind of standing in the country which can always be put to good use. For another, what the UGC has to do is to function as a professional body. Once it does so it would have enormous leverage with everybody concerned. The important precondition however is that it must function as a professional body.

II

OTHER PROFESSIONAL BODIES*

How the UGC was established has been discussed already. It would be helpful, however, to look at how the Indian Constitution went about doing the job. Apart from enumerating three central universities (Aligarh, Banaras and Delhi), the National Library, the Victoria Memorial and some others, the Union List provided for union agencies and institutions with respect to professional, vocational and technical training, promotion of special studies or research organisations (like the Survey of India, the Geological, Botanical, Zoological and Meteorological Surveys), and 'co-ordination and determination of standards in institutions for higher education or research and scientific and technical institutions'.

As even this rough enumeration of the powers of the union would show, the centre had a wide reach which covered an extensive range of activities and there was no legal impediment of any kind. A note proposing the establishment of a coordinating agency in respect of higher education prepared for the cabinet on 28 August 1950 explains that 'the ministry of

---

*This is a revised and updated version of an article entitled 'Coordinating Agencies in Higher Education' which was published in Higher Education Reforms edited by Philip G. Altbach and Suma Chitnis in 1993. The subsequent article (Problems of Coordination) was detached from the main article and has been expanded into a separate piece for use in this book.

law which has been consulted agreed that the proposed legislation was within the powers of Parliament and generally suitable'.[1]

What happened after this note was submitted and what turns and twists the proposal to set up a coordinating body took are not matters to consider at this stage. That concerns the history of the UGC primarily, rather than the role of this body as a coordinating agency. What needs to be noted is the fact that the initiative to establish such a coordinating agency was taken soon after the promulgation of the Indian Constitution in 1950. At that time, the Ministry of Education was already handling technical education. From 1946 till 1988 (when the All India Council of Technical Education [AICTE] was given a statutory status), this body continued to function as a part of the Ministry of Education. The proposal to give this body a statutory status was mooted on quite a few occasions but was never really pushed through till 1988.

Two other bodies which had been in existence earlier must be referred to specifically. One is the Medical Council of India (MCI) which was set up as a statutory body in 1933. The Indian Council of Agricultural Research (ICAR) was also established before 1947. Both these bodies met important needs and have performed useful functions.

After 1947, a number of coordinating agencies, besides the three referred to above, were established. Amongst those that need to be mentioned are: the Indian Nursing Council (1947), the Pharmacy Council (1948), the Dental Council (1948), the Bar Council (1961), the Council of Architects (1968), the Central Council of Indian Medicine (1970), and the Homoeopathy Central Council (1973). Three others which function somewhat differently may also be referred to here. These are the Institute of Chartered Accountants (1949), the Institute of Cost and Work Accountants (1959), and the Institute of Company Secretaries (1980). Each of them is a statutory body and deals with a professional field where both training and professional practice are important in their respective ways.

Apart from the statutory bodies enumerated above, there are a number of non-statutory bodies also. Each of them has played an important, supportive role. They have represented the profession with which they are concerned in a variety of ways and have sometimes exerted pressure upon the government also. This has happened partly on the professional plane and partly in order to get certain concessions from the government. Hardly any one of them has really confronted the government as that does not seem to be a part of the ethos in which they operate.

THE MEDICAL COUNCIL OF INDIA (MCI)

It was in 1822 that two medical schools were established at Calcutta and Madras respectively. In 1833, these were raised to the status of colleges. In 1845, the Grant Medical College was started in Bombay. When the universities were established in the Presidency towns (Bombay, Calcutta and Madras), the colleges were affiliated to the respective universities. In 1860, a fourth medical college was established at Lahore.

What needs to be noted is that after the First World War, some kind of a confrontation developed between the General Medical Council of Britain and the medical profession in India with regard to the recognition of degrees. In 1930, the General Medical Council of UK withdrew recognition from a medical college in Calcutta making it imperative to review the arrangements concerning medical education within the country. In 1930, a conference of provinces and university representatives was convened and this led to the establishment of the MCI. A Bill to that effect was adopted in the Central Legislature in 1933 and the Council was constituted in early 1934. The following shows how the Council was instituted:

1. Both the states and the universities were involved right from the first day. In the beginning the balance was very much in favour of the universities which had 25 representatives in the Council. A total of 13 persons were nominated by the states (or provinces as they were then called), eight by the central government and 14 by registered graduates. While the first president was nominated by the central government, after four years it was open to the Council to elect its own president and vice-president: this practice is followed to this day. This system of election gave birth to certain problems in recent years but those need not be elaborated here.

2. Among the functions that were allocated to the MCI, three crucial ones must be enumerated. One was with regard to recognition of degrees, both within and outside the country. Second, MCI was empowered to send inspectors and visitors to medical colleges to report the adequacy or otherwise, of standards of medical education under heads like staff, equipment, accommodation, reliability of examinations, training and other facilities. The third power vested in MCI arose from the second power given to it. In

certain situations it could move for the derecognition of the degrees if already recognised. This could be done by the Council only after following a certain procedure in which a proposal (if mooted by it) would be sent to the state government concerned, its response secured and all the relevant documents then submitted to the central government for appropriate action.

How has the MCI performed over the years? In the course of its actual working, certain inadequacies came to light and an amending Act was passed in 1956. It was again amended in 1992. It was in the fifties that a new problem arose. Earlier, almost all colleges were run by the government and there was hardly any problem of mismanagement except of the kind that bureaucratic control brought in its wake. As a result of reservation for certain categories of students, however, it became more and more difficult to ensure admission to talented students, especially if they came from the upper castes. This led to the establishment of a private medical college in Manipal in 1953.

For colleges run by the government, grants came from that source. In the case of non-government colleges, someone had to meet the relatively high cost of education, and the students were asked to do so. This was the beginning of the system of capitation fees.

Following the example of Manipal, a number of medical colleges were established, particularly in the state of Karnataka where Manipal is located. By now such colleges in the state of Karnataka and elsewhere number several hundreds, around half of the total number of colleges. Most of them are run on commercial lines. The promoters charge large sums of money for admission to these colleges. In a few cases the facilities are satisfactory and the arrangements are professional, but in the majority of cases this is not so. Consequently, a lot of resentment and public criticism was voiced.

Owing to limitations in its structure, the MCI could not cope with this problem. The MCI Act provided for a chapter in each state and these were vested with certain powers. One of them was the right to recognise the medical qualifications of those graduating from colleges in that state. In such a situation, all that the local promoters of such colleges had to do was to persuade the state council of the MCI and the university concerned. The MCI could, and was in practice, bypassed.

The capitation fee system led to undisguised commercialisation of medical education and resulted in a decline in professional standards. In the mid-eighties, an attempt was made to remedy the situation. An amending

Bill was presented to the Parliament, but the lobby in favour of the capitation fee colleges forced the referral of the matter to a select committee. This led to some avoidable delays.

The situation got somewhat dramatised when on 30 July 1992 the Supreme Court gave what may be described as a landmark judgement when it held that the charging of capitation fees was illegal. This concerned a case which had occurred in Karnataka. While certain issues arising out of that case and a subsequent judgement given in 2002 led to a redefinition of certain issues, one thing stands out clearly. Commercialisation of professional education had gone so far that it had to be stopped. The professional councils had failed to do so and the Supreme Court, therefore, stepped in. Since the law on this subject is still to be given a definite shape, it would be premature to comment upon a transitional situation with any degree of finality.

However, one thing has already happened and as such requires attention. As a response to the 1992 judgement of the Supreme Court, the president issued two ordinances empowering the Medical Council and the Dental Council respectively to withhold or reject the sanction of any proposal to set up a medical or a dental college unless the conditions prescribed were fully adhered to. In plain words, the delay in amending the MCI Act which, in the opinion of most people was deliberately manoeuvred, was now short-circuited by the social and legal pressure generated by the judgements of the Supreme Court. Altogether, professional education is being given the dignity and prestige it is entitled to.

What is being done in respect of medical and dental education would also have to be done for other branches of professional education. How soon and how effectively it is done is another matter altogether.

OTHER MEDICAL BODIES

In addition to the MCI, two other medical agencies were established by the centre. One is the Central Council of Indian Medicine, established in 1970. The second is the Homoeopathy Central Council, established in 1973. Both of them are more or less modelled on the MCI. They have the powers to prescribe minimum standards of education for courses in Indian systems of medicine, for instance, Ayurveda, Unani, Siddha as also homoeopathy. As in the case of the MCI, they too can prescribe standards of professional conduct and codes of ethics to be followed by the practitioners of these systems.

If these councils are not as visible as the MCI, this is largely because these systems of medicine do not attract much talent. In China the traditional system of medicine is used extensively. In terms of coverage, it reaches out to more than three-fourths of the population. The Indian response has been not to worry about those living in the countryside or in inaccessible areas. In the urban areas it is the allopathic (western) system which is most widely patronised. No wonder it also attracts much more talent.

This is evident from the way the Indian Council of Medical Research (ICMR) has been organised. This body traces its ancestry to the Indian Research Fund Association, which was established in 1911. In 1949, however, it was reorganised with the principal objective of promoting medical research. To start with, the Indian systems of medicine were left out but, with the passage of years, the situation has changed.

The ICMR maintains two dozen or so permanent research centres, half a dozen regional centres and three times as many centres for advanced research in universities and colleges. All aspects of medical research like communicable diseases, reproductive biology and fertility control, maternal and child health, nutrition, and environmental and occupational health are covered.

The ICMR does not have any direct impact on teaching or classroom instruction. But to the extent that research support is made available to universities and colleges through this specialised agency, it is important in this analysis.

THE ALL INDIA COUNCIL OF TECHNICAL EDUCATION (AICTE)

The All India Council of Technical Education was established as an advisory body in 1946. During World War II, India saw a considerable boost in her industrial power. As soon as the war ended, there was an unmistakable drive to expand technical education. What came to be called IIT, Kharagpur, was first established as a strong engineering college in 1946. This was consequent upon the report of a committee which had gone into the post-war scenario of technical education.

It was in this ferment of expectations and planning that the AICTE was established and continued to function as such until 1988 when it was given statutory status.

In the early eighties, a Bill to give it statutory status was drafted. Among other things, a provision was made to prescribe the norms and guidelines for charging tuition and other fees. But the UGC was not in favour of the AICTE being given statutory status, an instance of unconcealed rivalry. Through a sleight of hand, the UGC Act was amended in 1984 and one of the powers vested in it now was to prescribe fees for courses including those in engineering and technology. In addition, the UGC was also empowered to ban any kind of unauthorised educational charge or gift.

True to form, however, the UGC did not evolve a set of rules and procedures which would regulate the fee structure of the various courses. Meanwhile, the educational policy was reviewed in 1985–86 and one of the outcomes was the decision to give statutory status to the AICTE.

While the immediate impulse for giving statutory status to the body dealing with technical education might have sprung from the need to curb the system of capitation fees, the overall thrust of the Act seeks to emphasise three main areas. One is to promote technical education and make it as thoroughly professional as possible. The second is to integrate planning with development both at the state and central levels, and, also, to ensure coordination between the two. The third is to regulate the imparting of technical education in such a manner so as to serve both the objectives listed above as also to take care of some of the immediate abuses that have crept into the field of technical education.

Of the three objectives, the last one seems to have claimed much more attention during the first few years. This is because, during recent decades, technical education has become commercialised to a large extent and it seemed urgent to put things on the right rails before the other two objectives could be suitably and appropriately fulfilled. Among the powers enumerated in the Act are those to fix norms and guidelines for charging tuition and other fees and to 'prevent commercialisation of technical education'. A couple of decades from now, when some of these things will have been, hopefully, taken care of, clauses like the ones referred to above may look somewhat incongruous. But as of this moment, they are contemporary and relevant.

The performance of the AICTE since it became a statutory body does not inspire much confidence, especially with regard to the prevention of 'commercialisation of technical education'. Some of the decisions made during the first few years had been of a kind which went against this objective. The situation with regard to some of the underhand practices in some of the technical institutions around the country is not particularly favourable. Colleges which charge capitation fees have had almost a quarter of a century to develop into some kind of a parallel system of education. It will be years before this system can be rationalised.

Over the years, the system has however became commercialised with the result that the Supreme Court has had to intervene thrice, once in 1992, then again in 2002 and 2003. Professional colleges were permitted by the Supreme Court to fix their own fees. The state governments had different ideas in the matter. Unavoidably almost, the matter went up to the court again. Even though the court verdict seeks to balance different forces, two things will eventually ensure the right kind of functioning.

One will be regulating the conduct of those promoters who are commercially rather than academically inclined. This category of promoters have not yet been put in their place. Their accounts must be rigorously examined every year and any attempt at manipulation, if detected, must be severely punished. However, it is only the emergence of the consumers as a force that will ensure their eventual marginalisation.

Consumers operate at two levels. At one level, there are students seeking admission to colleges and universities. If the system of admission can be regulated better than is happening today, things will change. But there is another role that the consumers can play and that brings us to the second point.

Industry is the biggest employer of those who pass out after completing degrees. If organised industry was to evolve a new method of recruitment, the situation would change decisively with industry playing a positive role. For obvious reasons, industry would like to engage students who have given evidence of having performed well and also show promise in respect to creativity. Other things being equal, it should select those candidates who come from institutions which are known for being professional rather than commercial. In plain words, if a choice has to be made between two candidates, preference should be exercised in favour of those who were educated in 'professional' rather than 'commercial' institutions.

Once this starts happening, word will go around that 'commercial' institutes which wish to make money out of education are not welcome. In consequence, the other category of 'professional' institutions will gain higher ratings. If a promoter wishes to make money, he should go into industry rather than promote an institution which claims to be like any other academic institution but is really a money-making proposition.

It is such an approach on the part of the employers that will eventually drive out those black sheep who have found their way into the establishment of institutions where the focus is on commercial rather than professional considerations. This would be in the long-term interests both of professional education and industry.

WORKING OF AICTE

Three other aspects of the AICTE's working need to be discussed here. One is its dealings with the states. Partly because of the general ethos and partly because the centre is trying to prescribe certain guidelines or rules which the states should follow, the common perception is of 'we' and 'they'. The states feel that they are being told by the centre to do or not to do certain things. Second, during the decades that the AICTE was functioning as a non-statutory body, certain other statutory bodies were established. Three of them that can be readily referred to are the IIT Council, the Council of Architects and the Pharmacy Council. Once established, they developed a certain rhythm and momentum of their own. In statutory terms they had the same authority as the AICTE had but the powers vested in the AICTE were so extensive that what these various councils did could also come within the overall jurisdiction of the AICTE.

Consequently, one of the issues that arose quite early in the history of AICTE as a statutory body was how to deal with this problem. Without being too formal or rigid about it, the AICTE rightly took the view that as long as these various statutory bodies were functioning within the limits laid down by their respective Acts and there was no conflict of interest or jurisdiction, they should be permitted to function without anyone breathing down their neck. And this is how it has worked during the last few years.

Third, one of the tasks entrusted to the AICTE is to set up a National Board of Accreditation to evaluate and assess all technical programmes and grant recognition or withhold it as and when advised. This is a specific responsibility vested in the AICTE. Unfortunately, this job has not been attended to with the earnestness it deserved.

In terms of the circumstances of its establishment and also its charter, the UGC was established in order to fulfil two interrelated functions. One was to coordinate and determine standards and the other was to make grants available towards the furtherance of those objectives. In actual practice, as stated earlier, it is the grant-giving function which has received all the attention and the other functions of coordination and determination of standards have not been stressed. In order to partly mask this inadequacy, the UGC itself took the initiative to set up a separate National Assessment and Accreditation Council to do the job which it was required to do.

In other words, having failed to do the job entrusted to it, the UGC set up another substitute body which would perform the functions that it should have performed in the first place. The difference between the two situations lies in this fact that the AICTE has been specially charged with the job of setting up a National Board of Accreditation whereas the UGC was expected, in addition to providing grants, to modulate their disbursements in such a way that the basic objectives of coordination and determination of standards were fully and properly met. Before moving to the next issue, two other things need to be said. First, the job of accreditation in the AICTE has been handled much more slowly than can be defended publicly. Second, some kind of a working relationship with NAAC needs to be developed.

It may also be helpful to underline another crucial difference between the UGC and the AICTE. The first function of the UGC as given in the Act is to 'enquire into the financial needs of the universities' and second, to 'allocate and disburse grants to them'. Other academic functions are enumerated a little later. In the case of the AICTE the first function is to undertake surveys in the various fields of technical education in the country at all levels and the third, is to allocate and disburse funds. Was it an instance of learning from experience? Or was it an instance of the circumstances in which the UGC was established (in the early fifties) that determined the priorities?

That apart, there is another dimension of the problem which has not received the attention it should have. Partly owing to the impact of commercialisation and partly owing to its own lack of professionalism and administrative weakness, the AICTE has come under considerable criticism over the years.

Perhaps nothing hurt its reputation more than the fact that, unlike the MCI, it failed to evolve a detailed set of criteria in regard to its norms of functioning. Even when the facilities available were downright unsatisfactory, institutions were given provisional permission to enrol students. In certain cases, abandoned workshops, even discarded stables were used for conducting classes. If the promoters wanted something done, they always found a way of doing so.

Apart from engineering, business management too was within the purview of the AICTE. Equipment was not so important in this case as it was in the case of engineering. Even though, the teaching personnel of the required calibre was available for no more than one-fourth of the institutions in existence, another three-fourths were 'provisionally' recognised. This did immense damage to the standing of the AICTE. Recently, some steps have been taken in the right direction. Hopefully, things will improve but it is too early to say anything more specific than that. There are many more things of this kind that can be said but it is not necessary to go into details.

Two things have saved the situation somewhat. One was the decline in the number of applicants for engineering. It was the classic situation of the market forces asserting themselves. Second, the intervention of the Supreme Court helped to a certain extent.

As against these somewhat favourable developments, the AICTE has all the time to come to terms with the legacy of the Ministry of HRD having handled technical education for a long time. Unlike the UGC which is on the whole free from intervention by HRD, the AICTE deals with a sector of education where public interest is relatively strong. In consequence, the AICTE has not been able to develop a stable tradition of autonomous functioning.

The AICTE also provides funding to technical institutions and universities but this is not perceived to be its primary function. Regulation of standards seems to be the most important consideration in terms of its performance. What is more, the AICTE over the years has at least to some extent lived up to this particular reputation that it has acquired. While eventually the AICTE will perhaps disburse grants in much the same way as the UGC does, this has not yet been implemented.

THE BAR COUNCIL OF INDIA

Legal education was one of the last sectors of higher education to be given attention. Why that should have been so should not be difficult to understand. Legal education has not been generally regarded as professional in character. The usual mode of entry into this profession is to do a Bachelor's degree generally in the humanities and then go on to the

LL.B. degree which, until recently, was a two-year course. In fact, in certain universities it was possible to do a law degree at the same time as one was doing a Master's course.

What is referred to as postgraduate education in law—the LL.M. degree—was so little emphasised before 1947 that not more than a handful of universities had even instituted the degree. Legal learning has so many branches and sub-branches and the amount of literature published even within India is so large, that it is quite surprising that it was neglected for so long. In this connection, it may be appropriate to recall that one of the key factors in ensuring a stable social and cultural base for British rule in the nineteenth century was the imposition and widespread use of the legal system that the British introduced in India. Indeed, the legal system, along with the continued role of the English language, remain the two most enduring legacies of British rule in India. The current legal system is by and large the same as was introduced in the first half of the nineteenth century.

It was in 1961 that the Advocates Act was adopted. It deals with a wide range of issues, only one of which relates to legal education. Among other issues which have received detailed attention are the establishment of the Bar Council of India as also the State Bar Councils, enrolment of advocates, the rights and obligations of advocates to practise their profession and the manner in which the advocates are to conduct themselves and so on. Consequent upon the passing of the Act, the Bar Council prepared detailed guidelines with regard to standards of professional conduct and etiquette and several allied matters. There is also a provision in the Act for disciplinary action which can be initiated by the Bar Councils against erring individuals.

As far as legal education is concerned, it took the Bar Council some time to move in the matter. One of its initiatives was to lay down that the LL.B. degree be awarded not after two but three years. To start with, several universities found it difficult to adjust to this demand made upon them. A university is a statutory body as much as the Bar Council is. Some of them chose to assert their right to act autonomously without being given specific directions by another statutory agency. However, it was not long before they came to see the logic of what the Bar Council was insisting upon and fell in line with its thinking.

While universities deal with all branches of knowledge, most of them perform two functions. One is to promote and disseminate knowledge and the other, is to train professionals in their chosen field of specialisation. With regard to the latter, the professional bodies, wherever they exist, are in a position to lay down the norms. This is particularly so when the body is statutory in character. The Bar Council was one such body and what the Council said, therefore, had to be accepted by the universities.

A few of the other proposals made by the Bar Council may be referred to here. They illustrate its concern with higher professional standards. The Council, for instance, insisted that a law college should be located only at a place where there was a district court or at least a circuit district court. Similarly, legal education may be imparted through full-time colleges and the definition for that is that they should work for at least five and a half hours continuously on every working day with four teaching periods of one hour each and the remaining one and a half hours are to be devoted to contact programmes, library work and so on. With regard to the rest, the success has been at best partial. There are other requirements like a student–teacher ratio of 1:40, provision of a suitably equipped law library (with details about how much to spend in the first year and the subsequent years) and others. In these matters, success has been partial.

LEGAL EDUCATION AND PROFESSIONALISM

One of the problems encountered in every university is that, for about a century, legal education has been regarded as a course which anyone could take up and it was not considered academically rigorous. While at the higher levels, say, the High Court or the Supreme Court, intellectual ability is indispensable, at the lower levels political skills matter more. To change this image of the legal profession has been an uphill task and it cannot be said that the Bar Council has succeeded in this job in any significant way.

In this connection, reference may be made to a proposal which the Bar Council mooted in the beginning of the eighties. It suggested a five-year course for LL.B. after the pre-university test. In other words, instead of a student joining any of the other faculties—for instance arts, science, commerce—he or she was expected to join the law course immediately after school. In the first couple of years the student would study disciplines like history, economics, political science, sociology and also receive a strong grounding in English which was to be the medium of instruction ordinarily. After this foundation course, he or she would be ready to undergo legal training.

This new structure has been adopted by less than a quarter of the universities so far. Almost three times as many are still continuing with the old structure—a three-year degree course and then a three-year law course. Incidentally one of the issues that came into the open when the duration of the law course was extended from two to three years was that the Bar Council conceded the right of the universities to award a law degree after two years. It asserted, however, that such persons would not be entitled to practice in the courts. If they wanted to practice, they had to study for three years. This clinched the argument, so to speak.

The universities came to appreciate the force of the argument of professional requirements and, before long, accepted the requirement laid down by the Bar Council. However, the success of the National Law School at Bangalore and the establishment of almost a dozen law universities around the country has changed the situation somewhat.

The comparative inability of the Bar Council to make an impact upon the university world is related to the perception of the universities with regard to legal education more than anything else. Despite heroic efforts made by this Council, there is a reluctance to concede to legal education, the status of a professional faculty.

It is not as if the universities alone are responsible for not treating legal education as a professional field. Public perception is equally responsible for it. If standards of legal education are not improving to the extent that they should, the explanation is not the absence of statutory powers vested in the Bar Council but the other factors referred to above.

The Indian Council of Agricultural Research (ICAR)

The ICAR, established in 1929, still continues to be a registered society. It was originally known as the Imperial Council of Agricultural Research but after 1947, it was renamed the Indian Council of Agricultural Research. In the mid-sixties it was reorganised radically and given the form it now has.

Though agriculture, including agricultural education and research, is a state subject, the centre has had a great deal to do with it in terms of Entry 66 of Schedule VII referred to earlier. Unlike most other areas of activity, the centre has given considerable attention to agriculture. At one stage, foodgrains had to be imported but that is no longer necessary.

The Green Revolution has been a spectacular success in certain areas and the total agricultural output has gone up considerably.

Another factor that has helped the centre to play a role even at the state level has been the amount of funding that has been made available through the ICAR. Since the mid-sixties, for instance, the amount has gone up 10 to 15 times. A part of it goes towards payment for running the 50 or so research institutes and farm stations established by ICAR and some of it goes into promoting research conducted under the auspices of agricultural universities which, as of today, number more than two dozen. Altogether, the interventionist role of the centre has been more marked in agriculture than in several other sectors of activity. This in turn has led to increased food production.

In the several decades of its existence, the ICAR has not only expanded in terms of its research, reach and activities but has also modified its structure in keeping with the changing times. Though its legal status is that of a registered body, in actual working it is closely allied to the ministry of agriculture. For instance, the president of the ICAR is the minister in charge of agriculture in the union cabinet. The minister of state holding that portfolio is the vice president and other ministers handling finance, planning, science and technology, education and commerce are also its members. Similarly, junior ministers in the Ministry of Agriculture are also members. Ministers who deal with agriculture, animal husbandry, fisheries and others at the state level have been members, more or less from the beginning. Among the new additions are members dealing with agriculture in the Planning Commission and the secretary of the Commission, the chairman of UGC and the Atomic Energy Commission.

In addition, the president has the right to appoint any person as a substitute member in case some member of the the ICAR is unable to attend a meeting. The director-general of the ICAR, who is the principal executive officer, is ex-officio secretary to the Government of India. It may be added here that he deals only with agricultural research which is one of the functions discharged by the ICAR. Other functions which are quite extensive in character are handled by other officials. The president has such far-reaching powers that not only does he have the right to periodically review the work of the society, he can also appoint committees and commissions to enquire into the affairs of the society and pass such orders as he may consider appropriate.

Since the ICAR maintains a number of institutions, powers have been delegated to these institutions in a variety of ways. In the case of the

Indian Agricultural Research Institute, Pusa, to take one example, which has the status of 'deemed to be university', the powers delegated are of an enhanced character. In the case of the rest, however, decisions taken by the respective managing committees have to be brought to the notice of the secretary, ICAR within one week of the meeting. The director-general has the right to review, or cause to be reviewed, any decisions which are not in consonance with the general practice or priorities of the council though the director of the institute concerned has the right to make a representation against such a decision and its enforcement is held in abeyance till a final decision is taken.

A notable feature of the ICAR is the provision for a Norms and Accreditation Committee presided over by the director-general. Among its members are five vice chancellors of agricultural universities, the deputy director-general in charge of education and the chairman of the UGC. This committee determines the norms of accreditation of agricultural universities, lays down the norms of their functioning and assesses their performance. To what extent this committee is functioning satisfactorily is open to question. Most agricultural universities are not performing as well as they ought to. What is more, there are no external experts on this committee and the whole thing is managed and controlled by the director-general—a kind of inside job—with the result that the kind of objectivity of decision making or professionalism—to put it another way—which ought to prevail does not do so.

Both in terms of its constitution and working, the ICAR is so closely linked to the government that any autonomous working can be more or less ruled out. To put it plainly, the ICAR is a limb of the Ministry of Agriculture and functions as such. While every statutory body is dependent upon the government in one way or another, in certain cases the dependence is more direct than indirect. Wherever for instance the chief executive is to be nominated by the government, there are occasions when decisions are not taken on time and the work of the concerned body suffers. The ICAR is an example.

There has hardly been any instance of a state being non-cooperative because eventually they stand to gain by what is done by ICAR. But, in certain instances, delays do take place. Such delays affect the rate and degree of coordination between the centre and the states and sometimes have an adverse effect too. The issue has occasionally come into the open but has seldom taken the form either of confrontation or of total lack of alignment between the two. As stated earlier, the intervention of the centre has been so beneficial to the states that, unlike other sectors of activity, there is no real clash of interests. Actually speaking, there is no clash of interest even with regard to the sector of education. Sometimes, however, the states opt for short-term gains and neglect long-term considerations. In the case of agriculture, however, such mistakes are not likely to occur except through mischance and therefore, it seldom leads to conflict or confrontation.

The work of the ICAR was reviewed in the late eighties. Some of the recommendations have been implemented while others are either in the process of implementation or will continue to be ignored, as is usual in such cases. A certain measure of decentralisation, if carefully promoted, would definitely be good for it and improve its working and performance.

However, the biggest failure of the ICAR lies in its failure to project the cause of agriculture both at the planning and funding levels. While it cannot be said that agriculture has been seriously neglected, the plans implemented so far have not given it the degree of importance it requires. Even in the last few plans, the situation has not registered any significant or marked improvement. It is widely acknowledged, for instance, that the rural areas ought to be given much more attention than has been the case so far. Since agriculture is the mainstay of the Indian people, more should have been done for it. For a hundred years or more, the top professions have been medicine and engineering. Law has been a close third. Of late, management and IT have emerged as new favourites. Superior services have always had a place of their own. But one profession which has failed to attract high quality talent is the field of agricultural research.

With over three-fourths of Indians dependent on agriculture, it is of vital importance that much more attention be paid to agricultural research than has been so far. This is not to say that new fields like nuclear energy, space science and petrochemicals have to be given less attention than they are receiving at present. But it must be admitted that the country will never prosper unless agricultural yields are significantly improved and the bulk of the people living in rural areas get a better deal.

LESS POPULAR PROFESSIONS

So far no reference has been made to some of those bodies which deal with relatively less popular professions. The numbers involved are not large and neither is the degree of public support that they enjoy particularly high. This, however, should not be taken to mean that the professions are unimportant—only that those who follow them are small in number.

Nursing, for instance, is one of the less well regarded professions in the country. Even the proportion of nurses to doctors is less than half of what is internationally acceptable. There are many reasons for this state of affairs but some of them are obviously more important. One is the social prejudice against nursing. While no firm data is available, perhaps half the nurses in India come from Kerala. In that state, literacy among women is high and they are expected to work as much as men do. Nursing seems to be one of the more popular professions in that state.

The Nursing Council was set up in 1947. The Act empowered the Council to ask for information regarding courses of study, training and examinations. It also empowered the Council to send inspectors to visit the institutions and report back to it. After following due procedure such as reference to the state government concerned and so on, the Council has the right to withdraw recognition. It can also decide to restrict its recognition within a particular state. In other words, all-India recognition can be denied but local recognition may be granted.

In course of time, the Council framed detailed regulations with regard to courses, inspection, examinations etc. To what extent these are being followed is difficult to say. For one thing, there are not many colleges to teach nursing and, for another, most institutions are below the college level and give training on a plane where universities do not enter the picture.

A year later in 1948, a Pharmacy Council was set up. At the time it was set up, pharmacy was not a distinctly defined discipline in most universities. Only a handful ran courses in pharmacy and most of what was done under the auspices of this Council was related to operations at the lower levels as well as the dispensing level. From the latter point of view, the passage of this Act in 1948 was particularly useful. But for the powers which came to be exercised in consequence, it would have been difficult to regulate dispensing at any level. Now only a properly qualified person can undertake this job. This is usually preceded by some kind of training. Universities are not particularly involved because the kind of training imparted is below the university level.

With regard to the educational aspects, however, the Pharmacy Council has been empowered to regulate the nature and period of study; the mode of practical training, the equipment and facilities to be made available; the subjects of examinations and standards to be attained therein; conditions of admission and such other matters. Other powers relate to the sending of inspectors, evaluating the facilities, reporting to the Council, asking the states for their point of view and ultimately taking appropriate action including withdrawal of recognition. The constitution and composition of state councils was an important provision and, in certain cases, inter-state agreement with regard to various matters were also visualised. Unlike the Nursing Council, however, for which there was no such provision, the central government was authorised to appoint a commission of enquiry in order to go into the work and functioning of the Pharmacy Council. The usual visitorial safeguards were provided. In terms of actual functioning, the Council has performed more or less on the same level of competence and regulatory control as the Nursing Council.

The year 1948 also saw the establishment of the Dental Council with more or less the same provisions as were provided for the Pharmacy Council. State councils were also an integral part of the set-up. In addition, like the MCI, the Dental Council was authorised to prescribe standards of professional conduct and etiquette.

Another similarity with the Pharmacy Council was that a commission of enquiry could be appointed to go into the working of the Dental Council. This provision did not exist in the MCI Act and was not introduced even in the 1956 Amendment. However, it found place in both the Acts of the Pharmacy Council and the Dental Council.

It was 20 years later, in 1968 to be precise, that the Architects Bill was introduced. It was preceded by a good deal of discussion and debate about who qualifies as an architect. Till then, civil engineers could also claim the right to design buildings. When architects insisted on being defined as a distinct professional category, they were opposed by several others, most notably by civil engineers. Eventually a kind of compromise was worked out and the Bill was adopted.

As in the case of various similar statutes, the Council of Architects was authorised to prescribe standards of architectural education as also standards of professional conduct. Those approved as architects had their names included in the schedule laid down for the purpose and anyone falsely claiming to be registered could be penalised. Though not entirely satisfied with the provisions of the Bill as finally adopted, on the whole the architects were gratified. They had now been recognised as a distinct profession. Over the years, the Council has acquired a certain degree of prestige partly because of the system of regulation introduced in 1968 and partly because the profession has grown in numbers as well as stature.

Three other professional councils which are not a part of the university set-up also need to be referred to. The earliest of them is the Institute of

Chartered Accountants of India (1949). The next is the Institute of Cost and Works Accountants. This was set up in 1959 when, more or less simultaneously, the Act setting up the Institute of Chartered Accountants was slightly amended. The third body is the Institute of Company Secretaries (1980).

Each one of them conducts its own examinations and regulates its own affairs. When the Company Secretaries Bill was moved in 1980, several members raised the question of why it was not possible to do what was being done in medical education. That is, the syllabus, standards of attainment and such other matters were laid down by the MCI but instruction, clinical training and examinations were conducted by the universities. This point of view, however, was not accepted.

The concerned minister went out of his way to make it clear that while the government was retaining the right to issue directions conducive to the discharge of the functions of the Council, it had given an independent status to the Examination Committee and did not propose to interfere with its working.

It may also be added here that unlike the other two institutes, in the case of the Institute of Company Secretaries, the government took over the power to dissolve it in case such a step was called for. In the case of the other councils, there was no such provision. They had been given autonomy to conduct their own affairs in the manner that they thought best, provided they were consistent with the maintenance of professional standards.

National Council of Teacher Education (NCTE)

Two other issues must be raised here. The first one relates to the National Council of Teacher Education (NCTE). By itself this body does not cover a large range of activities. Legal education, for instance, is more wide ranging and has perhaps a greater impact on national life. But there is one thing about the NCTE which marks it out as a professional body which made an early impact.

Established in 1994 and empowered in a variety of ways, the NCTE started by taking note of something outrageous which had been happening for the preceding few years. One university in the south and another in the north had started enrolling students for the B.Ed degree through correspondence on a large scale. As a theoretical proposition, there is nothing about this arrangement which can be regarded as inadmissible or impracticable. If other branches of knowledge can be taught through correspondence, B.Ed could also be handled in the same way. However there was one notable difference.

The B.Ed degree course covers both the theory of pedagogy and its practice. While the theory part could be imparted through correspondence, practical teaching required preparation of lessons according to a prescribed plan and classroom teaching in order to ensure a certain measure of actual teaching experience. It is a comment upon things that, in regard to both, the performance of all the universities, including the two referred to above, was by and large in serious default. The whole intention was to make money and defraud the students. What the students wanted was a degree and that is what was offered to most of them.

In their anxiety to enrol students right away and in larger and larger numbers, students were admitted in thousands. Though the students are physically absent, the minimum that a university which enrols them has to do is prepare good teaching material. Even that was not done in every case. When it came to practice teaching, the whole thing was a colossal hoax. Something was done here and there but it did not cover even 5 or 10 per cent of the students in terms of arrangements made for actual classroom teaching. In less than a decade, the two universities referred to above are reported to have grossed more than 500 million rupees.

This amount was paid by the students in order to meet the expenditure on the facilities which were to be arranged for them. Facilities were however not offered and that is why the word hoax has been used. Had some students taken the matter to the Consumer Court, they would have perhaps got a good deal of their money back. Furthermore, the concerned universities could have been fined for having misled and exploited the students. But no one took the initiative. Even the UGC which could have taken action did not do so.

It must be said to the credit of the NCTE that, through patient and steady follow up, it managed to persuade these two universities to discontinue the system of B.Ed through correspondence. There was a minor argument between the NCTE and IGNOU on study through the distance mode. The former was not in favour of what the IGNOU had proposed: B.Ed through correspondence. But the IGNOU was within its rights to have insisted upon using the distance education mode; the university had been set up for that very purpose. In any case, to equate some of the other universities, which were operating through correspondence, with the IGNOU was not exactly right.

The IGNOU has a large number of study centres where students have the opportunity to meet their tutors and have their doubts, if any, removed. There is a good deal lacking in these arrangements. As a matter of fact, the Regional Study Centres as these are collectively known, are the weakest links in the IGNOU set-up. But that issue need not be taken up here.

Meanwhile what needs to be noted is that as a result of discussions between the IGNOU and NCTE, a via media was worked out. Now the IGNOU too has started B.Ed under its own auspices in accordance with the norms worked out between these two bodies. In addition, norms in regard to other universities which operated only through correspondence have also been worked out. Further, these norms are being implemented by and large. One only hopes that the NCTE has not fallen into the trap of laying down the norms and then not bothering about their implementation. Unless the follow-up is also ensured, at least some of the universities can lapse into non-performance on that front.

Altogether, the NCTE made a good start. After that however, things have been fouled up. Some of the NCTE regional offices did not take their job seriously enough. There were a few instances of allegedly fake institutions being given permission to enrol students and so on The situation is much too murky and obscure to permit a clear analysis. The fact, however, remains that the original intervention of the NCTE came at a time when it could, and did, make a significant difference.

IGNOU AND DEC

The second issue relates to the overlap of jurisdiction between the UGC and IGNOU. When some of the universities started conducting a large number of courses, either largely through correspondence or through the distance education mode, nobody was clear as to whose responsibility it was to maintain proper standards. Was it the UGC's responsibility or was that job to be done by the IGNOU? The law was not all that clear. Therefore an understanding was worked out between the two bodies leading to open universities becoming the exclusive charge of the IGNOU and correspondence courses continuing to be under the charge of the UGC.

Unfortunately neither of the two bodies has performed the job as well as they should have. To take the UGC first. Something like 50 universities work through correspondence courses. There is no clear line of demarcation laid down. Sometimes they call it 'distance education', sometimes 'correspondence'. In any case, with the popularity of IT courses becoming a fact of life, one single technical university established something like 100 centres all over the country. Scores of them were set up by other open universities too. It became a mad house of jurisdictional claims and counter-claims, to put it mildly.

For its part, the IGNOU was equally negligent. When one technical university established 100 centres as referred to above, the issue arose: could it do so? No clear cut answer was forthcoming and meanwhile 100 centres were established. In this case, students might or might not have been exploited directly but those who undertook to set up these centres did exploit the students. They charged heavy fees for providing facilities which they reneged on. In the bargain, thousands of students got cheated.

What did the UGC and IGNOU do in the matter? The former issued a circular in mid-2002 AD disapproving of some of these activities; so did the latter within a few weeks of the UGC doing so. Neither of them followed up the matter with the result that nothing got done. Since the issue of coordination amongst these various bodies will be taken separately, no more needs to be said about this particular matter except that what is called the Distance Education Council (DEC), set up by the IGNOU, is on the whole a body which has made no impact whatsoever upon the situation that arose in the wake of a large number of universities venturing into other states and hundreds of study centres being established by entre-preneurs on behalf of certain universities under a system of franchising instituted by some of them.

The situation is so chaotic that the only thing one is obliged to ask is: was it the right thing to have given charge of the other open universities also to the IGNOU? In the less than two decades that the IGNOU has been in existence, it has hardly given 10 per cent of its attention to the DEC. Rules in regard to how other open universities are to be dealt with, what kind of information is to be asked for, whether directives issued by the headquarters have been implemented or not and what financial aid is to be given to an open university, are all issues that have remained un-decided for years together. Ad hoc decisions are being made all the time. Certain universities are helped and others are not. In other words, whoever is in office takes decisions as he wishes to and this is how it goes on. The IGNOU's true focus of attention is its own campus and little else.

It is not suggested here that the DEC should be made into a separate body. But it is clear that to have clubbed it with the IGNOU was not the right thing to have done. There are only two choices that can now be made. One is that it is set up as a separate body and the IGNOU has nothing to do with it. The second is that it is merged with the UGC and is made into an independent sector of activity even under the UGC. In either case, the matter needs to be discussed in fuller detail.

The truth of the matter is that distance education learning is a new and burgeoning field. Even as it is, 15–20 per cent of the total number of students are enrolled in distance education mode. According to Tenth Plan projections, the proportion of such students is estimated to go up to 40 per cent. Perhaps that will not come to pass but presumably it will range somewhere between 25 and 30 per cent. That being so, the issue of its reorganisation is an important issue and needs to be attended to on a priority basis.

Note and Reference

1. Ministry of Education file No. F.29-29/50, 03, Part II, p. 36 in the National Archives of India.

III

Problems of Coordination

With so many professional councils at work at the same time, problems of coordination amongst them are bound to arise. While this issue will be taken up a little later, one obvious question to be asked is: to what extent are the powers of these bodies comprehensive in character and insulated against non-professional intrusions?

It is difficult to discover one pattern of functioning common to each one of them. Except for the ICAR and the ICMR which still continue to be registered societies, others enjoy a statutory status that clothes them with the requisite powers. In most cases the powers are circumscribed so that while the councils are in a position to act in certain respects, the power of derecogniton, which in a sense is the ultimate power, cannot be exercised by any one of them.

The Central Council of University Education, as visualised in the 1951 Bill, had two powers which were deleted in the UGC Act as finally adopted in 1956. These two were the power to recognise or refuse to recognise a university, whether already existing or proposed, and second, the Council could derecognise degrees awarded by any university. Both these powers were withheld from the new body, now rechristened the University Grants Commission. In consequence, the UGC found it difficult to ensure compliance with its priorities or directives.

In all such situations, the power to enforce compliance stems from two sources—one being the statutory kind, the other the power of the purse. The former was denied to the UGC. As far as financial strength is concerned, there was never enough funding available to the UGC at any stage. In its early years, the experience of most universities was that funding were relatively liberal. The number of universities was fewer and the prices were not what they are today. Therefore, the universities received much more help from the UGC than has been possible of late. Similarly, the number of colleges has multiplied almost 20 times in about five decades and not much help can be extended to a large number of them.

What has complicated the situation markedly is the fact that the volume of central responsibilities has been growing. As compared to three in 1950, the number of central universities today is six times that number and the number of 'deemed to be universities' has already crossed 80. The claim for funds that the central universities make upon the UGC does not leave much for state universities. This issue has been discussed in some detail separately.

Maintenance of state universities is always met by the concerned state: it is only development funding which, according to the UGC Act, can be provided by the UGC. With the inexorable shrinking of funds, there is not much left for them and, on average, an average state university gets Rs 10 million or so in a plan period by way of a development grant. Some of the bigger universities, especially those in metropolitan towns and a few others, get more but this figure represents about the general average.

The AICTE does not have much to distribute though it must be conceded that the per capita cost in engineering and technology is much higher. The AICTE, however, has one advantage. Colleges often charge much higher fees and by and large rely on their own resources. To that extent, the number of claimants gets reduced. In any event, funding for technical education has never been as constrained as for the general stream of education. A comparative analysis of the amount of work done both by the UGC and the AICTE would show that one of the problems from which the former suffers is excessive staffing at the lower and middle levels. In consequence, the UGC is crushed under the weight of too many people of questionable calibre who are expected to do jobs for which they are neither well-equipped nor well-trained.

The ICAR is a large operation and though its funding could be larger than what it is, the overall ethos is not one of niggardliness. The research institutes, which are under the direct charge of the ICAR, are fairly well-funded. In the case of agricultural universities, grants that are given could be somewhat larger but they are not inadequate. The main problem with the ICAR is excessive centralisation and day-to-day control by the Ministry of Agriculture.

The Bar Council does not have funds to give and to that extent it feels handicapped. The same is true of the various other councils including such a high powered body as the MCI. Funding for medical education comes either from state governments or from student fees. The centre has not taken on the obligation for providing financial support to medical education (what is provided for research through the ICMR is another matter). Demands for doing so are occasionally voiced but so far there has been no progress in this regard. And the same may be said about the various other councils also. Most of them do the job of regulation without the supporting arm of funds being available to them.

ROLE OF THE CENTRE

The second issue which arises is concerned with the nature and extent of the relationship between the central government and the various agencies. While a good deal has been said on this issue earlier, it must be restated that none of the councils has the power to derecognise any institution or degree. This power is vested in the central government and can be exercised only by the centre after the concerned council has gone through the established procedure and requested the centre to exercise it.

In the early seventies, the MCI wanted one particular medical college in a politically important state to be derecognised. The centre, however, dragged its feet over the issue and the matter was sought to be taken care of by adopting other, less drastic, modes of action. In a soft society like ours, the path of least resistance is generally preferred. In any case, the power of derecognition has a strong bearing on the relationship between the centre and the states.

As stated in the beginning, any large country is faced with the problem of how to allocate responsibilities between the union and the states with regard to a matter like education. Even if the 42nd Amendment which made education a concurrent subject was not to be taken into account, the centre has far-reaching powers in respect of a whole variety of matters concerned with education.

It is not only technical education which comes under the purview of the centre. Vocational education is also a part of its responsibility. This mainly refers to education and training at the pre-university and even lower levels. Evidently the centre cannot handle the activities directly and the participation of the states is both unavoidable and necessary. In other words, the relationship between the centre and the states has to be defined in such a manner that the states do what the centre would like them to do. And at the same time, the states should not feel that they are being dictated to or made to do things which either go against their interests or their wishes. The whole battery of coordinating agencies is partly calculated to serve this purpose.

Perhaps because of the resistance offered to the 1951 Bill which eventually led to the establishment of the UGC, the centre became somewhat cagey with regard to what the states felt about the initiative taken by the former. While public opinion is for the most part not in favour of over-centralisation such as has been witnessed of late, the disregard of professional opinion falls in another category. The real issue here is whether we stand for professionalism or not.[1]

DEVALUING PROFESSIONAL OPINION

Third, the relationship between the centre and the states is crucial for the successful working of these bodies. Quite a few of the functions entrusted to them cannot be discharged effectively unless both governments cooperate with each other and indeed operate on the same wave-length. In this connection, the role of the first education minister of free India might be recalled. Maulana Azad, who was in charge of education at that time, in a letter to Pandit Nehru specifically referred to the example of China. When the communists took over in 1948, they tried to establish a strongly centralised state. In respect to education, too, they had far-reaching powers. Influenced by that example, Maulana Azad expressed himself in favour of the centre having a dominant role in regard to education.[2] Entries 62 to 68 in the Union List of Schedule VII of the Constitution are the direct outcome of that thinking.

When it came to logically working out the provisions thus made, the states felt that what was proposed was not to their liking. In consequence they started resisting the centre's proposals. The controversy about the 1951 Bill illustrates that process at work. In addition to the sensitivity of the states, another strong contributory factor was the resistance offered by academic opinion and the universities. Both these factors combined to weaken the initial thrust of a strong role by the centre in education.[3] Such a role is not necessarily good. It can even be negative in certain cases. But to have a situation where, unlike in most other areas, the centre's writ does not run in the case of a nation-building activity like education is certainly anomalous.

A better way to accomplish the same purpose would be to make the professional councils more effective than they are today. No council is authorised to adopt the ultimate sanction of derecognition of a degree or an institution. All such cases have to be referred to the centre for a final decision. At one level this was in line with what had been provided for in respect of the Medical Council in 1933. At another level the fact that the British had left in 1947 and that the situation was now no longer what it was before 1947 was overlooked.

Another way of saying this would be that whether it was so intended or not, it amounted to devaluing professional opinion. While the implications of centre–state relations cannot be disregarded, the issue is which of them is more important. It is difficult to give a categorical answer. Both are important. The centre, however, gave prime importance to the political angle rather than to professional judgement. Had professional judgement been given greater importance, each one of the councils would have been much more effective than has been the case.

Some kind of a safeguard could have been built into the powers vested in the professional councils. For instance, the exercise of such powers could have been made subject to review by the centre both in terms of the grounds to be stated and the views to be recorded. This would have meant that the initiative would always have been with the professional councils and the centre's role would only be to moderate that power.

In actual practice, now the states are able to pressurise the centre. Not even in one instance, has the centre taken strong action, for which there are provisions and which it has contemplated in certain cases. In plain words, the power of regulation by a professional body has been diluted, if not negated, because of political considerations. It should be clear to anyone that this is a development in the wrong direction. But to what extent it can now be reversed is a question for which it is difficult to find an easy answer.

As stated more than once, the nature and extent of relations between the centre and the states is crucial for the successful working of these professional councils. Today the councils dealing with medical education, nursing, pharmacy and several other professions have their counterparts in the states. They function within the terms laid down in the respective Acts. There have not been many instances of clashes between the state units and the concerned central councils. But this is largely because most of the powers are vested in the central councils and the state units, by and large, conform to the regulations laid down by them.

In the case of the AICTE, there are zonal offices and, by and large, they have functioned successfully over the years. In fact one reason why the AICTE has functioned somewhat effectively is because of the support provided by the regional bodies. What would happen if the State Councils of Higher Education, as contemplated by the 1986 Policy, are established in all states? The issue has not been seriously debated so far. But sooner or later it is bound to come up.

When that happens, it should be possible to work out an appropriate relationship between the two. All that needs to be stated today is that this is an issue which cannot be brushed under the carpet. On the contrary, it has to be faced and sorted out in a manner so as to preserve and ensure the initiative of the states and the professional primacy of the UGC.

Financial Support

The issue of financial support made available through the various councils cannot be overlooked. While some of these bodies do provide financial support, others do not. Is that the right thing to do? How much support, if at all, can be made available? Can the issue of financial support be coupled with the issue of the coordination and determination of standards? There are a number of issues involved and these would have to be taken care of.

Since the Supreme Court has permitted professional colleges to fix their own fees, this issue will find its own level in due course of time. There is one problem, however. Neither the state nor the entire range of private philanthropists has so far devised a system to help the poor but able students. In most other countries, universities and colleges raise funds from the public and their alumni. Unless something of this kind begins to happen in our country, the situation will continue to be difficult.

REFORM, INNOVATION AND COORDINATION

In the end, it is important to raise the question to what extent, if at all, this spectrum of coordinating agencies has helped in the task of reform and innovation. In a sense, an answer has already been given. These bodies have undoubtedly helped. But for their interventionist role, the situation would have been much more adverse.

At the same time, it must be recognised that their powers are circumscribed and each one of them has to operate within certain constraints. These do not have to be specified all over again. What is, however, frequently overlooked is the flawed character of Indian federalism. In terms of law, the centre has overriding powers with respect to education at all levels. In terms of coordination among these bodies, the situation is ambivalent and far from consistent. No single agency at the centre is responsible for what is happening or not happening.

It may not be out of place here to therefore refer to one particular recommendation made by the 1986 Policy. It was to set up a National Council of Higher Education so as to advise the government on policy matters, coordinate the activities of the various professional bodies, encourage interface among different areas, allocate resources in terms of national needs and manpower planning, and establish and manage common infrastructure and institutions. Nothing, however, was done by way of a follow up. All kinds of jurisdictional issues were raised and no firm decision was taken.

The matter continued to hang fire for half a decade and was commented upon in critical terms even by the Estimates Committee, 1988–89. However a curious twist was given to it by the Ramamurti Committee in early 1991. This Committee recommended a somewhat different approach. It is not possible to go into details here but one thing should be clear. While coordination among different agencies of the central government is crucial, it is no less crucial to seek to ensure the primacy of professional opinion over other considerations. This is not happening today. Nor is the federal dimension particularly effective. And this, if one may say so, is a source of considerable weakness.

Owing to the fact that these councils were set up at different intervals, some discrepancies were bound to creep in. There is also another angle to it. In the enthusiasm to set up a new council, its powers were sometimes defined in such a way that care was not taken to harmonise the powers vested in the councils which are already in existence with those being set up now.

An example may be given. The Bar Council of India has one thing to say about the nature of work and responsibility of the teachers. The NCTE has projected a somewhat different picture. On top of it, the UGC, which was the first to be established in terms of chronology, deals with the issue differently. Each one of them has a different definition. The variations are minor but they do exist. And as explained earlier, these arose because decisions were taken by different authorities at different points of time and no attempt was made to harmonise things.

There is a further angle to the issue which also needs to be taken into account. The first body to be established in terms of the power to maintain standards as mandated by the Constitution was the UGC. It was set up in fulfilment of the mandate to coordinate and maintain standards.

For quite some years, the UGC continued to be the leading actor in the game. One by one, the other councils started coming up. And as could have been anticipated, some of the powers which were exercised by the UGC had also to be exercised by the other councils. Since no attempt was made to straighten out things in the beginning, some of these variations came to assume greater salience than might have happened otherwise.

As already stated, for reasons which do not have to be repeated, the UGC looks upon itself as the senior most of these professional councils. In any case, it deals with about 80–90 per cent of the students as well as the bulk of teachers. Ordinarily speaking, the UGC could have been treated as the senior most council or commission, if that description is preferred, and other councils could have been expected to fall in line with what the UGC said. But two things got in the way.

After the 1986 Policy, when the idea of National Council of Higher Education was mooted in the Programme of Action, one awkward fact came in the way. While the UGC chairman was appointed by the Ministry of HRD, the minister of HRD himself had become the chairman of the AICTE at the time it was given the statutory status. To ask the chairman of the UGC to preside over the National Council was therefore not feasible. Though the minister was the chairman only for the first five years and now the chairman is an academic, as in the case of the UGC, the initiative did not get off the ground and no one has chosen to take the initiative again.

Another factor in the situation was that some of the councils had started asserting themselves and told the universities that, as per their statutory mandate, theirs was the last word and the universities did not have the kind of untrammelled autonomy which they had enjoyed earlier. In a couple of cases, the matter went up to the courts. The judgements given were in favour of the universities insofar as, within their limited range, the councils could lay down the norms but, for the rest, it was the universities which were incharge of the show.

In any case, no one at the centre was all that interested in education. Another proposal informally mooted was that this National Council be presided over by the prime minister and the minister for HRD should be its vice chairman. It should not be forgotten that ministries other than HRD are involved in the working of the various councils. The Ministry of Law for example deals with the Bar Council and the ministry of health deals with the MCI and so on. To have the prime minister as chairman seemed to be something which would not create any controversy. But nobody is taking any initiative in the matter and it is difficult to anticipate whether, without considerable public pressure, the central government would move in the matter.

This bit of a digression brings us to another dimension of the problem. Not only are there disputes about the jurisdiction of the various councils (some details about the UGC and IGNOU have already been given), the fact remains that the centre is cagey about asserting its rights more than is minimally necessary. An act of the state of Chhattisgarh has however brought things to a boil. This state passed an Act where, amongst other things, it took over the power to set up universities through a gazette notification. Indeed 50 such universities were established within a matter of months.

What has complicated things further is the immense popularity of IT courses where private initiative has played a notable role. But then, the different players in that game were now desperate to get a legal fig leaf. This was given to some of them either through the umbrella of open universities or the newly established university in the state of Chhattisgarh. Altogether, a situation has arisen where the centre is feeling outmanoeuvred by the initiatives being taken by different states. Had relevant legislation been passed by Parliament in time, this situation would not have arisen. Foreign institutions too have penetrated the Indian market quite extensively. In the upshot, it is the UGC which is feeling isolated and somewhat defensive.

Is it not time to invoke the powers of the centre given to it by Clause 66 of Schedule VII? Since the centre has the power to coordinate the working of the universities and both define and determine the standards of teaching and research, the existing UGC Act itself can adopt a number of regulations wherein these powers can be taken over by the UGC. So far the UGC has hardly paid any attention to these issues. Under the impact of some of these developments, it will now have no choice except to adopt those new regulations and take over powers which were implicit but had not been spelt out or exercised. If these regulations are challenged in a court of law, there is every reason to believe that the Supreme Court would go with the centre rather than with the states.

NOTES AND REFERENCES

1. For further details, see Marina Pinto, *Federalisms and Higher Education: The Indian Experience* (Bombay, Orient Longman, 1984).
2. M.S. Ramamurti, 'The Constitutional Framework', in Amrik Singh and Philip G. Altbach, (eds), *The Higher Learning in India* (Delhi, Vikas, 1974).
3. For details, see the article on 'Foundation and Role of the UGC' in this book (Chapter I).

IV

THE CENTRE-STATE BUSINESS

I

The relationship between the centre and the states in regard to education is a perennial topic of discussion. Every now and then someone raises the issue. As would be recalled, in 1976 the 42nd Amendment was adopted and education was made a concurrent subject. Higher education has virtually been a concurrent subject since 1950 when the Indian Constitution was adopted. The 42nd Amendment brought other sectors of education also under concurrency.

Not unexpectedly, little has been done since 1976 by way of any follow-up action. The situation remains exactly as it was which is however unlike the situation say, in respect of forests! Forests too had been brought under concurrency in the 42nd Amendment. Due to the linkage between forests and environment, there has been some follow-up action. The same concern however has not been shown in respect of education.

It is not intended to refer to the statutory issue any further. My contention is that, regardless of whether the centre takes any initiative or not, the real problem lies elsewhere. This contention can be illustrated best of all by saying that the scene of action lies essentially in the states and even if the centre were to assume greater powers than it exercises today, the situation would not undergo a qualitative change. For such a change to occur, we must, recognise above all that, as already stated, the scene of action lies in the states and, in consequence it is at the state level that new initiatives must be taken.

This is for the simple reason that more than 95 per cent of educational activity is controlled by the states. The central sector consists of a dozen and a half central universities, the IITs and IIMs (half a dozen each), less than 20 Regional Engineering Colleges which have been upgraded into National Institutes of Technology and a few other institutions which cannot be enumerated here. For the rest, everything is handled by the states. How the states perform is, therefore, a matter that cannot be treated as of secondary importance as is generally done. How the states function should be a matter of deep concern to all those who are concerned with education.

Between one quarter and one-third of the budget of each state is spent on education. There are some states which spend an even larger proportion of their budget on education: Kerala is one such example. In terms of priorities however, 'education' is not the portfolio which most ministers prefer. Amongst the officials also, the department of education is not looked upon as glamorous enough. In terms of the number of persons who work in any area of operation, the largest number belongs to the sector of education. Despite these unmistakable factors in favour of a higher priority to education and educational management, education is still virtually treated as a poor relation. Nobody disowns it but nobody is prepared to put in hard and dedicated work in its favour. This is the sad situation as it obtains on the ground.

Two other factors complicate the situation somewhat. One is the financial clout that the centre has. The centre has much more funds at its disposal than the states can command. Apart from the mechanism of the Finance Commission which is appointed every five years in order to devolve funds from the centre to the states, there are all kinds of other channels through which funds are made available to the states by the centre. Occasionally there is controversy in the National Development Council as to the relative spheres of operation of the centre and the states. Notwithstanding this fact, by virtue of varied sources of revenue which the centre can mobilise and draw upon, the centre is the giver and the states are the recipients.

In this situation of an unequal partnership, the centre likes to suggest all kinds of innovative things to the states. Some years ago, the number of Centrally Sponsored Schemes was much higher than it is today. Even if this particular channel has somewhat dried up now, the capacity of the centre to influence the states in different directions remains undiminished. For one thing, it has funds at its disposal and, for another, it can also project certain new ideas. Ideas are not the monopoly of either the centre or the states. Over the decades however, the centre has given greater evidence of being able to produce and project new ideas.

Owing to a variety of reasons, including the experience of the past, the centre is somewhat more professional in its approach to problems than the states. So whether it is agriculture or health or education, the centre is able to project new ideas and introduce them into the body politic of the country. While some of the states certainly have shown initiative in appointing committees and commissions in respect of matters dealing with education, for the greater part the initiative has been with the centre. In any event, the ideas and schemes projected by the centre have received much greater attention than those projected in or by the states.

What does it all add up to? Briefly speaking, the centre has funds as well as ideas but the scene of action is in the states. It is only when the centre is able to persuade the states to take up those ideas and actually implement them that the role of the centre will become something to be proud of. As it is, despite all the advantages in its favour, the centre gives the impression of being an ineffectual bird fluttering its wings in a void, though some people would describe this as a piece of exaggeration. It is however true to quite an extent.

But the situation on the ground is not always in consonance with the wishes, both expressed and unexpressed, of the centre. Whether this fact is openly acknowledged or not is another matter. The states accept guidance from the centre to the extent that it suits them. In any case the states are much more subject to the pulls and pressures of local politics and ever so often they are unable to do what they are expected or required to do.

II

Is there any way of dealing with this situation? In my opinion, it needs to be acknowledged that whatever be the statutory position, the role of the centre cannot be more than marginal. Once this limitation is accepted, the role of the states will be seen in a new light. In addition, the focus of attention would, to some extent, at any rate, shift to the states as it perhaps ought to. Towards this end, the following three steps may be considered relevant.

First, since the unit of operation is the state, it is for each state to decide what it should or will do. In other words, each state should be required to prepare a plan for education. Each state does prepare a plan for development which is discussed with the Planning Commission every year. What I am suggesting is a sub-plan dealing with education which in turn should be discussed with the Ministry of Education. This should be done before it is merged into the State Plan for subsequent discussion with the Planning Commission.

The Ministry of HRD should advise each state in regard to its priorities and programmes. In doing so, this particular ministry should draw upon the expertise of the various professional bodies established by the centre. These would not be only the UGC or NCERT and so on but also bodies like AICTE, ICAR, the Bar Council, the MCI and so on. If the plan dealing with the development of education leaves out important sectors of professional education, it is flawed right from the beginning and this pitfall has to be avoided. Preparing an integrated educational plan and involving various professional bodies would give a different kind of thrust to what is today programmed by each state.

The weakness of the present system lies in not treating education as one of the more important sectors of development and furthermore in not giving it that professional touch which only professional bodies can provide. If this line of approach is accepted, that which has been happening over the years will not happen any longer. This refers, for instance, to funds being diverted to higher education though these were originally earmarked for elementary education. The states usually insist upon a broad allocation under the heading of education. They are generally not prepared to earmark funds for any particular sector. As a result of local pressures usually, it is higher education which gets preferential support and elementary education gets neglected. This has been apparent in most states for 25 years, if not longer.

While it would be too much to claim that this kind of thing will altogether stop if the new mode of operation is adopted, it would certainly minimise the dangers of it happening. This would be for the simple reason that if proposals are discussed each year with the Ministry of HRD which in turn would seek the advice of various professional bodies, the diversion of funds would become more difficult. This however is one of the minor advantages that would accrue in the proposed scheme of things. The real advantage would be that planning would become more systematic, more detail-based and more professional.

Second, if the states have to prepare a plan for development in respect of education, the states would have to create the capability for doing so. As of today, most of them do not possess this capability. Furthermore, hardly anybody takes an integrated view of education. This deficiency would also have to be repaired. To put it another way, most states would have to become more professional and more integrated in their approach and more down-to-earth in their planning. This would be a distinct gain and cannot be treated as marginal in character or unimportant.

At the same time, it must be recognised that such a thing is easier said than done. At the central level, the professional councils would be able to contribute in a meaningful way for the simple reason that each one of these councils either already has or can mobilise a good deal of professional, talent. The states for their part would find it difficult to do the same. Planning, if it is to be creative, cannot be a top-down operation. Schemes and ideas must emerge on the ground and not be imposed in any manner. This indispensable requirement can be met only if greater cooperation of those actually engaged in the task is ensured. The indifference of most academics to these issues is a serious handicap. And yet, things will have to be changed.

Third, in order to make state level planning effective and meaningful, it is necessary to involve academics also in the process of planning. Today planning is a totally bureaucratic affair. Not many non-officials are involved in that process. But if state level planning, particularly in the sphere of education, is to acquire greater capability and thrust it is not possible to completely ignore academics. The question of whether academics have lacked professional commitment or the bureaucracy has been unwilling to make use of their services, need not become a subject of controversy. Whatever the truth, it lies somewhere between these two extreme statements.

The fact remains that either planning is not done as it should be or there is hardly any demand upon academics to rise to the challenge of planning in the state in which they are working and the profession to which they belong. In any case there would be a distinct gain as far as the planning of education at the state level is concerned if academics are involved. Once the quality of planning improves, it is reasonable to believe that the quality of implementation will also improve. Or is it hoping for too much?

III

While the centre is reasonably well equipped to discharge its function, the same cannot be said about the states. Apart from the UGC, a number of other professional bodies have been set up during recent decades. Each one of them has been assigned a distinct job. During the last 50 years, more than a dozen professional bodies have been established. And one problem that has arisen in consequence is how to coordinate their working. This is not the occasion to go into that issue. But the point that is being made is that as education has become more and more diversified and professionalised, different agencies have been set up and each one of them has a specific task to do.

What about the states? According to the Indian Constitution, all education, including higher education, is a state responsibility. If one chooses to be specific, one can say even at the risk of repetition, that 95 per cent of the job is done at the state level. It is only a small segment which is looked after by the centre directly. For the rest, the centre is expected to provide leadership, project new ideas and support, generally in financial terms, various kinds of initiatives etc.

A question which needs to be answered is how the states are going to fulfil that part of the responsibility which has been assigned to them. If so, what organisational mechanism has been created by them or for them. In almost every state, the annual budget for education is fairly high because the number of teachers who are paid from the government exchequer, whether directly or by way of assistance to private institutions, is fairly high. The organisational set up however is approximately the same as in the case of the other departments. As in the case of the other departments, the department of education has one secretary and some supporting staff. In a couple of states, there is an additional secretary also and there is a kind of division between higher education and other levels of education. The plain fact is that the state department of education is organised on the same lines as it was before 1947. The area of operations has meanwhile multiplied 20–30 even 40–50 times in certain cases. But there has been no corresponding reorganisation or significant strengthening of the department of education.

Some two decades ago, an attempt was made to set up a Council of Higher Education in a number of states. Something like a dozen states have established such councils. In terms of power and responsibility however, everything is managed and controlled by the secretary of education as before. That is to say, the secretary of education is the one person who operates the entire machinery and there is hardly any delegation or sharing. In almost all states, the chairman of the state council is the minister for education and it is the vice chairman who has some kind of an academic background and does the actual job. But as experience in most states has shown, things are tightly controlled by the secretary of education. It suits both the minister for education and the secretary of the department.

Contrast that with what obtains at the centre. The UGC is a fairly large and influential body and handles a good deal of work with respect to higher education. Similarly, the All India Council of Technical Education handles a considerable quantum of work. In addition, there are more than a dozen other professional bodies, each one dealing with different categories of professional education viz., architecture, accountancy and several other such specialisations. Most of them deal with ministries other than education, and to that extent, the Ministry of HRD does not have to carry that much of a load. This in turn has other important implications. But that issue will not be discussed here. In most cases, the chief executive of the professional body is nominated or elected by the body itself. There is some degree of coordination with the government and that is undertaken as and when necessary.

The question to ask is: if the state governments are to do the job as assigned to them by the Constitution, was it not incumbent on them to reorganise their own set-up and working? Nothing of that kind has happened and the department of education continues to function in the same ad hoc way in which it has been functioning for over half a century. Meanwhile the scale of operations, as described above, has expanded to an unbelievable extent.

Not many people realise that till the fifties, a considerable proportion of school education was handled by district boards. When prices began to rise and it became necessary to upgrade the pay scales of school teachers, the district boards could not cope with the task. They just did not have the requisite financial resources. In state after state, therefore, this job was taken over by the department of education. More specifically, the schools were 'provincialised', to recall the phrase used more commonly during those days. Consequently, the department of education got overloaded but there was no mechanism for distributing that load.

In one state someone I had known earlier was appointed as secretary of education. I asked him after a couple of months how he was finding the new job. He told me that there were several hundred legal cases before the courts filed mainly by disgruntled school teachers and he was helpless as well as unhappy about the whole thing. Before long, he managed to get out of that job and got himself transferred to the centre. Since I had known him for a long time, he readily confessed that that was the least satisfying assignment which he had handled.

The fact of the matter is that not even in one state in the country has the department of education been reorganised. The structure has remained the same though the quantum of work has increased. Earlier, the Director of Public Instruction mainly looked after school education. Once district board schools were taken over by the government, the DPI alone would not handle the job. Therefore, in most states, there was one DPI for primary education and another one for schools, i.e., the secondary schools. During these very years, new colleges started coming up. If they were not private in character and the colleges were government-run, this meant more work for the department of education. Therefore the job of the DPI (colleges) was also created. Each one of them however reported to the secretary of education who for obvious reasons could not attend to everything.

Alongside, medical education and technical education were taken out of education. But one thing that was not done was to divest the secretary of education of some part of his responsibility. Even when the State Councils of Higher Education were set up, no one thought that, as at the centre, these councils would be delegated responsibility on the lines the UGC and other professional councils were functioning. Though not ideal in every respect, this was a kind of model which could have been conveniently duplicated in the states. What is generally called misgovernance is also a refusal to share power with others, if it may be said.

When it comes to asserting their rights vis-à-vis the centre, the states are ready to fight. They do not wish to share their turf with any one else. But when it comes to doing the job, the whole thing gets mishandled.

To put it another way, there are two sets of problems here. The problem at the centre is that a large number of professional bodies have been established and the centre is unable to coordinate their working. At the state level, no corresponding mechanism has been created. The department of education continues to function in an overloaded and unprofessional way, more or less as it used to before 1947. But the quantum of work has grown immensely and what we get is either confusion or nonperformance.

On top of it, the number of times the secretaries of education get transferred is unbelievable. There are instances where an individual does not last for more than a few months. This makes the working of the department even more difficult and the result is what we see. Clearly, without a restructuring of the department of education at the state level, things will never improve.

IV

What has been said above can be described as the perception of the centre about how things happen at the state level. To be fair, the states have their own perception of things and it differs from how the centre sees the issue. Therefore it would be in order to say something from the point of view of the states as well.

The states are faced with a double problem. The first one is that the UGC deals with the universities directly. To quite an extent, therefore, the state government is not in the picture. From the central point of view, this is defensible. It is on a professional plane that this contact between the two is established. To put it provocatively, the centre is not conspiring against the state government in any way. On the contrary, the centre does so in order to help. The help is extended not only in respect of professional matters but also with funds.

And the second one is that the state government finds it difficult to accept a situation in which it pays for the universities but is unable to influence their working except marginally. This is more a matter of perception than an actual fact. Having established a university as per the statutory powers vested in the state, the latter is bound to support as well as promote it. What is required in this situation is mutual adjustment rather than a division of powers between the centre and the states.

For their part, the universities too are acutely aware of the fact that they have to prize and uphold what is called university autonomy. Right from the pre-1947 days, university autonomy has been something which has been talked of a great deal, time and again. More than that, it is a legacy which has come down with a baggage of hopes and expectations and is regarded as something which is valuable and worthy of preservation. The universities therefore do whatever they can to cherish and treasure it.

In the set-up in which the universities function, they are by and large left free to decide things on their own. Quite some matters certainly go to university bodies like the executive council where nominees of the state sit as full fledged members. Not only that, the state government has nominees on various other university bodies like the Finance Committee or the Planning Board and even the Court or the Senate. Grants come from the state government in any case. Universities have, for all practical purposes, a certain vaguely defined measure of internal autonomy. But when the chips are down and there is some kind of a confrontation, the slogan of university autonomy is invariably raised and, generally speaking, some kind of a compromise is worked out.

Altogether, the state governments are aware of the fact that they can ask the universities to do certain things only up to a point. The vice chancellor who is the chief executive has some kind of a public status. If he chooses to confront the state government, he can do so but only in a limited sense. Consequently when the state government deals with the universities, it is not like dealing with the State Transport Authority or something equivalent. All these bodies ultimately draw their authority from the state. Hardly anyone of them can go against the wishes of the state government. But the universities are differently situated, and rightly so.

When it comes to grants from the UGC, certain decisions are made in which the state government is involved but not all that directly. In any case, the fiscal situation of almost each state has been tight of late. This in turn strengthens that kind of outlook which leans in favour of university autonomy. It would not to be far wrong to say, therefore, that by and large there is some kind of an unspoken tension between the state government and the universities.

The latter are not financially autonomous. The bulk of their support comes from the state government. A quarter of century ago, UGC grants constituted one-fourth or one-fifth of the budget of most state universities. Owing to certain unwise decisions taken at the UGC level and the growth in the number of university-level institutions, there has consequently been a strain on central funding and the situation has undergone a qualitative change. The universities have therefore become more dependent upon the state than they were some decades ago.

In this state of unexpressed tension, the state government finds it difficult to push the universities beyond a point. If it is contended, as it has been in the earlier part of this argument, that the UGC should have a greater say in the running of the universities, the response from the state government generally is that they already do what they wish to do. And to some extent this is not untrue.

Having said all this, however, two things will have to be conceded. The state of tension and the uneasy relationship between the states and the universities does make things somewhat difficult. In this background, to seek to empower the universities further would generally be seen as an inroad into the authority of the state government. This is the situation today when, for the most part, universities are seen as some kind of a drag upon the state. It would be in order, however, to visualise a situation in which the universities begin to play a leadership role and bring lustre to the state.

Those universities which have been identified as possessing potential for excellence by the UGC are a case in point. A good deal of what causes tension today flows from the fact that universities are not performing as well as they were expected to. This state of heightened frustration, leads to misunderstandings between the two bodies who can, and indeed do, help the universities. In the process, however, there are some red faces all around. In the years to come, this will hopefully undergo a change for the better.

There is a second string to the bow also. Universities have quite some say as far as the university functions as a unit. When it comes to colleges, the state government is much more assertive. It gives substantial financial aid to colleges. On the other hand, even though the universities do have some say in regard to colleges, it is at best marginal. Therefore to make the point that the colleges are not as much guided by what the UGC would have liked, would not be an unfair statement to make.

Instead of going on with this somewhat circular argument, it would be quite in order to say that a way should be found to make most decision making about the universities tripartite in character. This will enable the UGC, the state government as also the local university to take such decisions as are acceptable to each one of them. This should not be particularly difficult to ensure.

At the moment, the UGC and the university do not have any role in the establishment of new colleges. If a system of advance planning and mutual consultation could be worked out, it would work entirely in favour of better rationality and better productivity. Quite a few colleges get established for reasons other than the academic. Given some mutual consultation and more rational planning, things could be handled differently.

Later in this chapter, a new formula will be proposed. This would ensure a fair deal both to the universities and the colleges in terms of which the state governments will understand the UGC and the university point of view in a more positive way and have a better sense of participation. Details of how this is proposed do not have to be given at this stage.

V

If the states are not taking the necessary initiative, it is for the centre to raise this question with the states. In order to be more concrete, it would be in order both for the Ministry of HRD and the UGC to look at the way colleges get established. In certain states, Maharashtra and Andhra Pradesh for example, more than in other states, growth in the number of undergraduate colleges has been phenomenal during the last few decades. This process of expansion is also accompanied by the introduction of self financing courses in certain cases. This system began with engineering and medicine. Gradually it spread to some of the science courses as also, and more particularly, the IT courses. The problem has reached such a dimension that only a few months ago the Supreme Court, in its minority rights judgement, chose to say a good deal about professional colleges.

All this confusion arose because neither the Ministry of HRD nor the councils working under it helped the Supreme Court to work out the right kind of balance. It is to be hoped that, as a result of the 2002 judgement of the court, there will be fewer mistakes made now. Properly speaking, these decisions had to be made by the educational institutions. But in the absence of clear and cogent thinking on the part of those who decide at the university or the HRD level, difficulties arose and those are now in the process of being sorted out.

In plain words, the Ministry of HRD can be faulted for not having put forward an academically progressive and socially viable scheme for admission to these professional institutions. And that is what led to the repeated intervention of the courts.

If the centre has been fumbling on its own, can one expect it to be able to guide the states? The fact of the matter is that, in 1950 when the Constitution was enforced, a delicate kind of balance was struck between the powers of the centre and those of the states when all education, including higher education, was vested in the states. The centre was given the power to coordinate and determine standards. It is in terms of that power that, as stated earlier, the UGC and the various other professional councils have been set up. But these bodies themselves are not performing as well as they were ex-pected to with the result that, apart from the legal tangle that arose at the level of the Supreme Court, the centre has not been able to help the states in any way to reorganise their mode of functioning and the job of administrative reorganisation.

VI

Perhaps nothing illustrates this state of confusion more graphically than the manner in which foreign institutions have been coming into India during the last few years and entering into all kinds of dubious collaborations with some Indian institutions. The whole thing has become a racket. Indeed it has become so unmanageable that it will be quite some time before things are set right.

In this connection, to repeat, a couple of serious slips made by the Ministry of HRD need to be referred to. Since they have a bearing on how the UGC functions, something may be said here about the former too. The first one relates to the Private Universities Bill which was moved in Parliament in 1995. It was not passed and the matter is still pending. The Bill was not so defective as some people would like to imagine. It was wrong to have called it the Private Universities Bill. The Bill should have been more appropriately titled the 'Self Financing Universities Bill'. That apart, the fact that so many years have gone by during which the Bill has not been redrafted and the situation has been allowed to drift, shows one thing clearly: the centre's sense of priorities is not right.

Another example already cited, in 1997 an assurance was given by the Ministry of HRD to Parliament to put an end to the system of fake universities. The whole thing was linked to amending the UGC Act. After half a decade, things are still pending and problems have multiplied. So much so that by now the situation is almost unmanageable.

To say no more about these issues which concern the Ministry of HRD more than the UGC, it is time to return to the important issue raised earlier: how do the states function within their own jurisdiction and, second, how does the UGC influence educational thinking and planning in the states?

Throughout the five decades of its existence, the UGC has not even once insisted that a state government must prepare a plan of action in respect of both universities and colleges. Such an exercise is either not done at the state level or done casually, as already described, as part of the State Annual Plan which is then discussed with the Planning Commission. Even in that Plan, the claims of one sector of education as against another sector are hardly defined.

In a few cases even when the Planning Commission wanted the state governments to be precise about their estimates, the latter were unwilling to be pinned down. In some instances, the allocation to higher education was raised while that to elementary education was cut down. Public pressure, apparently, was the reason! Therefore the states prefer an arrangement wherein they are free to change budget allocations and, by implication, their priorities, as it suits them at a particular point of time.

While it is for the Ministry of HRD to protect—as happens every now and then—the allocations are made, then altered and sometimes not even made in the first instance. The honest truth is that nothing is planned in order to fulfil certain specific targets, and indeed even the targets are not fixed in each case. Most decisions are made in an ad hoc manner, quite often in response to the pressures mounted at that particular point of time when the decisions are being formalised. Were this system to change, it would create problems for the state governments.

It is for the Ministry of HRD to worry about sectors other than higher education. As of today, the centre has yet to arm itself with the requisite statutory powers. As is known, the issue has been hanging fire since 1976. It was open to the centre to adopt follow-up legislation in respect of concurrency of education. But the centre did not choose to do so. In the case of higher education, the centre has always had powers; only those have not been invoked through the agency of the UGC, as they could have been.

At this stage, it might be legitimately asked: under what authority does the UGC send out visiting teams to the universities every five years? The answer is to be found in the UGC Act. Citing the Act, the UGC has decided to exercise the power of sending out visiting teams every five years. It is equally open to the UGC to ask each state government to send it a plan of development for higher education every year. After their plan has been scrutinised, it would be equally in order to fix a date for mutual discussion at the UGC headquarters.

Whether the secretary of education attends this meeting or the chairman/vice chairman of the State Council of Higher Education does so is a matter of detail. Instead of responding in an ad hoc manner to the various issues raised by each university individually, the whole operation would have to be planned in advance. To put it no more strongly, the entire functioning of the university and college sector in each state would undergo a drastic change. Today things get decided as and when they arise and in response to day-to-day pressures. Then, everything would have to be planned in advance according to an overall design.

As a matter of fact, there is much more to it. At this meeting convened at the UGC headquarters, all communications to universities and colleges.

wherein issues had been raised and quite a few of them have remained unattended, can be gone into. Now this job is done after every five years—if at all. By then, most of the problems have either got resolved or been left to smoulder. Once the exercise is undertaken every year and not every five years, the shape of things will begin to change and so will the pace and direction of decision making.

As argued earlier, the states have no organised system of decision making. If what has suggested above can be put into effect, the situation would undergo transformation even at the state level to a substantial extent. The issue is worth examination, if it may be added. In addition, this might put new life into the working of the State Councils. Either they do not exist or they do not function as well as they are capable of. Hopefully this will change. Equally important, such a step will also oblige the UGC to reorganise its own functioning. Not a small gain, it may be said, by way of a conclusion!

VII

What needs to be reiterated is that the mode of functioning in respect of education needs to be drastically changed at the state level. The centre is by no means a model of good governance. But on the whole it has managed to perform better than the states do. In any case the argument advanced here is that the centre needs to exercise those powers of coordination and determination of standards which have been on the statute book since the Constitution was introduced in 1950. Not to have done so is a failure of governance for which there is no justification.

If through the exercise of its powers, the centre can ensure one thing, it would be a considerable step forward. There has to be a certain amount of advance planning in respect of universities and colleges at the state level. That is not happening today. Further, there is no attempt to involve teachers in that process. This can happen only up to a point because the teachers themselves are victims of their own apathy. Still, some individuals can be involved and deserve to be involved in this job. To put it another way, the State Councils which are phoney bodies at present, can be brought to life and even given teeth. In order to achieve this objective, to which the UGC is committed, it too can play a useful and effective role. Equally important, it would be well advised to do so.

Even after having said it, one indisputable fact must be acknowledged. Almost every single state suffers from the ills of misgovernance and undergovernance. Obviously, it is not possible to go into those issues here. One thing is clear however. As far as the limited area of higher education is concerned, the situation would significantly improve were two things to be done. One, the UGC should so arrange things that instead of a five-yearly meeting, there is an annual interaction with the states. Second, the department of education needs to be radically reorganised as suggested. As an important by-product, the State Council of Higher Education would move into the centre of things in a manner which is not happening today. It is time to understand these interconnections and work out a more imaginative and more productive model of work at the state level.

V

The Reconstituted University Grants Commission*

One of the important recommendations of the University Education Commission which submitted its report in 1949 was the establishment of a University Grants Commission for the country. Informally the UGC started working towards the end of 1953 but the Act giving it statutory existence was passed in 1956. Since its establishment it has played, as intended, a leading role in the field of university education. In the course of a review of its working in 1964 (Report of the Committee of Members of Parliament on Higher Education under the chairmanship of P.N. Sapru), certain difficulties and deficiencies came to notice and the recently amended UGC Act of 1970 is the logical culmination of the review that was undertaken in 1963–64.

It all started with a Member of Parliament moving a resolution at a meeting of the Informal Consultative Committee of the Ministry of Education in March 1963 to the effect that university education should be made a union subject. This was a matter of fundamental and far-reaching importance, and the Ministry of Education appointed a small committee from among members of the Consultative Committee to consider 'the constitutional provisions in all its aspects relating to the coordination

---

*Originally published in the *Economic and Political Weekly*, August 15, 1970.

and determination of standards for institutions for higher education including research, scientific and technical education'.

The Committee took approximately a year to report and went through
the usual rounds of issuing a questionnaire and meeting a large number
of people. The main issue before the Committee was whether higher education could be included in the Union List. As a result of exhaustive discussions, the Committee came to the conclusion that this was not possible.
Since the Government of India Act of 1935, university education had
been handled by provinces and the central government had only played
a supporting role. The University Education Commission (1949) had also
not advocated such a course of action. It had only recommended that
university education be placed in the Concurrent List. The Constituent
Assembly did not choose to accept that recommendation and inserted a
few entries relating to education in the Schedule VII of the Constitution.
One of these entries, Entry 66 of List I, vests in the central government
powers in respect of 'coordination and determination of standards in institutions for higher education or research and scientific and technical institutions'. Evidently, this arrangement had not worked very satisfactorily
and that is why it had been proposed that university education be made
a union subject.

The Sapru Committee felt that this would be going too far and that
the purpose would be served by including university and higher education
in the Concurrent List. One of the members of the Committee argued
that in the existing constitutional set-up it was more advisable for the
central government to seek to influence policies at the university and
professional level through more effective use of the powers that accrued
to it under Entry 66 than had been done hitherto. It was said that these
powers had not been exhausted yet and that it was possible for the central
government to make much more extensive and effective use of the resources and standing of the University Grants Commission. Almost inevit-
ably thus, the Sapru Committee was led to a detailed discussion of the
role and working of the UGC.

At the time the Sapru Committee was engaged in its deliberations, the
UGC had been functioning for almost a decade and it seemed an appropriate time to review its functioning and performance.

The Sapru Committee gave high praise to the work of the UGC. In
order to make its functioning more effective, it made a number of suggestions, some of which have been embodied in the new UGC Act. One of
its principal recommendations was that the size of the Commission should
be enlarged. Instead of nine members, the strength of the Commission

should be raised to 15. Instead of only one full-time member, the chairman, there should be five whole-time members. The Committee also recommended that, as in the United Kingdom, serving vice chancellors should be debarred from becoming its members.

Another problem that had come to the attention of the Sapru Committee was that while the UGC was empowered to give grants to the universities for development purposes, the same could not be done in respect of their maintenance. This had caused all kinds of problems in respect of state universities and the Sapru Committee therefore recommended the removal of this bar.

Several other recommendations of a detailed nature were also made and most of them have been incorporated in the recently amended UGC Act. There was one important recommendation, however, which was not taken note of. In the words of the Sapru Committee 'professional education cannot be completely divorced from general education'. It therefore recommended that professional education including medical (basic), agricultural, engineering and law should also come within the purview of the University Grants Commission.

II

Before the provisions of the new UGC Act are analysed, it seems important to draw attention to the time that the Government of India has taken to amend the UGC Act. The Sapru Committee was appointed in 1963 and reported in 1964. A Bill to amend the UGC Act of 1956 was introduced in the Rajya Sabha in April 1966. It was passed by the Rajya Sabha in August 1966. The third Lok Sabha however could not consider it before its dissolution a few months later. Between 1966 and 1970, for reasons not known publicly, the amending Bill was not taken up. In other words, difficulties as well as deficiencies in the working of the UGC which had been brought to light by the Sapru Committee were not removed for a period of approximately six years. Considering that the initial impulse for this entire exercise came from a feeling that the union government did not have adequate powers in respect of higher education, this seems surprising, to say the least. To make the UGC operate on a reduced level of efficiency after the reasons for it have been identified indicates a slackness of functioning which is not untypical of the way things have been happening in the country for some years now.

III

As stated above, the initial impulse for the amendment of the UGC Act came from a feeling held by some and possibly shared by the Union Ministry of Education that the centre ought to have a greater voice in the field of higher and professional education. The proposal to put higher education on the Concurrent List did not eventually get accepted. Given the political situation in the country, this was not an entirely unexpected development. Consequently, the situation today in this respect is what it was in 1963 before the Sapru Committee was appointed. As a matter of fact, the only good thing that came out of the recommendations of that Committee was its proposal to streamline and strengthen the UGC. The new UGC Act seeks to achieve this twin objective. In order to see to what extent these objectives will be achieved, two issues need to be considered: (i) the composition and functioning of the UGC in terms of the amended Act; and (ii) the social and political situation in the country in which the UGC has to operate.

The main features of the new UGC Act are:

(i) The number of members of the Commission will be increased from nine to 12, out of whom not more than three may be appointed as whole-time members.

(ii) Serving vice chancellors and heads of institutions which are entitled under the Act to receive grants from the Commission will be excluded from the membership of the Commission.

(iii) Provision has been made in the Bill enabling the members of the Commission to elect a vice chairman from amongst themselves.

(iv) The term of office of the chairman will be five years and the term of office of the other members of the Commission will be reduced from the present six years to three years with eligibility for re-appointment for a further period not exceeding three years so, however, that the total period for which a member may hold office shall not exceed a period of six years.

(v) The Commission will be empowered to give assistance to the non-central universities for the maintenance of their special activities like the advanced centres.

(vi) The Commission will be empowered to withhold grants to any university established without the previous approval of the Commission and the central government.

(vii) The Commission will be empowered to give grants to institutions deemed to be universities in pursuance of a declaration made under Section 3 of the Act for their maintenance in special cases, development or for other specified purposes.

(viii) The Commission will be empowered to make regulations regarding delegation by the Commission to its chairman, whole-time members or officers of its power of general superintendence and direction over the business transacted by or in the Commission including the powers with regard to the office expenditure and other matters relating to the internal administration of the Commission.

This summary is taken from the Statement of Objects and Reasons appended to the UGC (Amendment) Bill 1968, as introduced in the Rajya Sabha. While other points would be taken up for consideration a little later, one of them may be referred to here. The Sapru Committee reporting in 1964 recommended the exclusion of vice chancellors from the membership of the Commission. The Education Commission however recommending in 1966 expressed itself in favour of the vice chancellors continuing to be members. As the Education Commission argued, 'At least one-third should be from the universities and we should not rule out vice chancellors being included'. But the Bill, as introduced in the Rajya Sabha in 1966 as well as in 1968, provided for the exclusion of vice chancellors. The exact language used was as follows:

provided further that no person who is Vice Chancellor of a University or the head of an institution which is eligible under this Act to receive grants from the Commission, shall be chosen to be a member of the Commission.

The qualifications for membership as provided for in the Bill were in general terms. Except for two officers of the central government, the rest were supposed to be persons representing (1) industry, commerce and agriculture; (2) legal, medical or other related professions; or (3) person who are educationists of repute or who have obtained high academic distinctions. This was presumably regarded as unsatisfactory by the Rajya Sabha and it inserted the provision that the Commission shall consist of 'not less than five members from among the officers or teachers of universities'. The other provision that serving vice chancellors would be excluded from the membership of the Commission was allowed to stand.

The Lok Sabha however went a step further and deleted the word 'officers' so that now only teachers of universities, not less than five in number, are eligible for the membership of the Commission. It goes without saying that this is a bold innovation in the Indian context and will significantly influence the outlook and working of the UGC.

The Sapru Committee had not made any specific reference to the inclusion of teachers. It had only recommended the exclusion of serving vice chancellors. The Act, as now amended, has introduced a new emphasis. For one thing, only teachers of universities are eligible. Whether this includes teachers of colleges also or not is a moot point. In certain universities, teachers of colleges are recognised as teachers of universities also. In certain other universities, in fact in the majority of them they are not. For another, along with vice chancellors principals of colleges have also been excluded. Since the number of colleges today is in the neighbourhood of 3,000, this excludes quite a considerable body of those involved in the process of higher education. It is difficult to say if all these implications were visualised at the time the Bill was drafted. The significant thing to note however is that, as now reconstituted, the UGC (with serving vice chancellors and principals excluded and approximately half of the strength consisting of teachers of universities) would consist of active academics.

IV

If, however, anyone believes that replacement of serving vice chancellors by teachers of universities is *per se* going to lead to far-reaching changes, he is bound to feel disappointed. Judged in terms of their respective casts of mind, there is no significant difference between a vice chancellor and that teacher of a university who is regarded to be suitable enough for the UGC. To draw a distinction between these two categories is an exercise in semantics. The real distinction to draw is between people who have vision, an unwavering sense of realism and a deep commitment to excellence and those who are not similarly endowed. What has plagued higher education in India in recent decades is the absence of such people in any significant numbers. In almost every institution, college or university, a few people who fit this description are to be found. But either they are too few or through a combination of circumstances they are rendered singularly ineffective. Whether such people are found in the ranks of the vice chancellors or of teachers is a matter of detail. To the extent that the amended UGC Act excludes serving vice chancellors from the membership of the Commission, it is not a good provision. Some of the serving vice chancellors would fit the above description admirably and to exclude them just because they are in office is to deny the benefit of their participation to the UGC. That some of them would have to become ex-vice chancellors in order to become eligible for membership is indeed a measure of the mechanical thinking that has gone into the drafting of the new Act.

The proposal to appoint whole-time members in addition to the chairman who is in any case a whole-time member is a step in the right direction. Their number is not to exceed three and they are to be appointed only if the judgement of the central government such appointments are called for. The work of the Commission in recent years has increased to such an extent that it has been necessary to enlarge the staff of the Commission considerably. While it would still be necessary to continue to have the required complement of secretarial staff, it would be an advantage to strengthen the decision-making apparatus of the Commission by including several whole-time members. In his speech introducing the Bill in the Lok Sabha, the minister for education said, for instance, that one full-time member might be made responsible for looking after the students' welfare, students' activities and students' problems in the universities and another whole-time member might be put in charge of colleges. This administrative model is being followed in the Railway Board and a few other organisations. To adapt it to the needs and problems of an organisation like the UGC should not be difficult.

It terms of the Constitution, the state governments have the right to establish new universities. If developments in the last two decades are any guide they have exercised this right generously indeed. In a few cases the establishment of new universities was not looked upon with favour by the UGC but this did not inhibit the said governments from going ahead with their plans. The powers of the UGC, as laid down in the 1956 Act, went no farther than to 'advise any authority, if such advice is asked for, on the establishment of a new university or on proposals connected with the expansion of any activities of a university'.

In the amended Act, these powers have been made a little more specific and the new provision runs as under:

> provided further that the Commission shall not give any grant to any university which is established after the commencement of the University Grants Commission (Amendment) Act 1970, without the previous approval of the Commission and of the Central Government.

The power to withhold grants was vested in the UGC even in the 1956 Act (Section 14). In empowering the UGC to withhold grants after the commencement of the UGC (Amendment) Act 1970, the new Act does not mark any advance except in one respect. Now it is laid down that previous approval for the establishment of a new university, both of the UGC and of the central government, has to be obtained before it becomes eligible for grants from the Commission. Why the central government should have been specifically mentioned is difficult to see. Does this not introduce a new element in the situation? Does it not, in a manner of speaking, weaken the professional character of the UGC?

The central government may, in a given situation, tend to take a somewhat politically expedient view. But the UGC, in terms of its intentions and constitution, should not be obliged to take any other view except that of a body of profes-sionals who are concerned with coordination and determination of stand-ards in higher education. There is a whole host of issues here which in the ultimate analysis may impinge upon the autonomous working of the UGC.

V

There is another aspect too of the grants given to universities by the centre.

The centre–state relations in recent years have neither been a model of rationality nor of lucidity. To allow them to be further complicated in any manner would be unwise. In a particular situation, the UGC may withhold grants of a university for genuinely academic reasons. Yet, such a step may be described as punitive by a state government. The said government may argue that the withholding of grants to a university run by it is denying to that state its due share of financial aid from the centre. Whatever may be the nature of the centre–state relationships, as defined in the Indian Constitution, one fact is unmistakable. The centre has more resources than it can utilise for its own purposes. The surplus, as is well known, is channelled to the states through the Finance Commission which is appointed every five years. The trend in recent years on the part of the states has been to attract more and more funds towards themselves and to that extent qualify the financial overlordship of the centre. At recent meetings of the National Development Council, several schemes which till recently had been operated by the centre were transferred to the states at their instance. The trend is clear even though some of the details might be confused or amorphous.

The UGC funds also fall in this category. What the UGC gets from the budget of the Ministry of Education is basically a part of that surplus which the centre has at its disposal and which it transfers to states either indirectly through the mechanism of the Finance Commission or directly through agencies like the UGC. There would be nothing surprising therefore if the withholding of grants to a state university becomes a political issue one of these days.

What has been said above is not fanciful or fantastic. There is a fairly vocal section of public opinion which is not in favour of the centre exercising the kind of overlordship which it has done during the last two decades: One Member of Parliament (Susheela Gopalan) for instance, said in the course of discussion about the UGC (Amendment) Bill that she was opposed to the whole concept of the UGC. She felt that the entire amount earmarked for education should be given to the states according to the proportion of the population and there should only be a coordinating centre to look into the affairs. This sentiment is not all that uncommon as to be overlooked completely; with passage of time it can grow and perhaps will grow. The UGC in its dealings with state universities therefore must, of necessity, give due consideration to political complications that might arise should it, at any stage, decide to withhold grants to a university.

Does it follow therefore that the UGC must all the time look over its shoulders and not do anything which would offend the susceptibilities of the state governments? If the answer to this question is in the affirmative, the UGC might as well not have been established. The model before the UGC might have been the University Grants Committee in UK but, as visualised in the 1956 Act, its scope and functions are much wider and unmistakably more academic. The British UGC is only a grant-giving body. To the extent that grant-giving is linked up with academic questions, it concerns itself with them. For the rest, academic leadership is provided by the Committee of Principals and Vice Chancellors which has a close and creative relationship with the UGC in UK.

The UGC, as visualised in India, is different. It has two primary functions. One is to inquire into the financial needs of the universities and allocate and disburse grants to them. The second function which is elaborated at considerable length in the 1956 Act relates to the academic leadership which the UGC is required to provide to Indian universities. It has, for instance, the power to recommend to any university measures for the implementation of university education. It can advise the central or any state government on the allocation of any grants to universities for any general or specified purpose. It can advise the central government or any state government or university on any question which may be referred to it. It can require a university to furnish it with such information as may be needed relating to the financial position of the university or studies in the various branches of learning undertaken in that university together with all the rules and regulations relating to the standards of teaching and examinations in that university in respect of each branch of learning. What has been stated above is quoted from the UGC Act 1956. The chapter dealing with the powers and functions of the Commission concludes with an omnibus clause which empowers the Commission to perform such other functions as may be prescribed or as may be deemed necessary by the Commission for advancing the cause of higher education in India or as may be incidental or conducive to the discharge of the above functions.

The UGC thus is both a grant-giving body and a body charged with important academic responsibilities. The unique strength of the UGC in India derives from the fact that the two functions have been linked together in statutory terms. That is to say, in discharge of its academic obligations, the UGC is empowered to give grants to universities, central as well as state. So far it could give only development grants to state universities. According to the new Act, these grants can be given 'for the maintenance, or development or both of any specified activities of such universities'. In this respect, the capacity of the UGC to show the carrot has been considerably enhanced.

VI

In terms of the analysis given above, it is much easier for the UGC to show the carrot than to wield the stick. The political climate has been changing rapidly in recent years. The increased number of colleges and universities and the virtual doubling of the student population in the last decade are significant pointers in this direction. The democratic pressures for access to higher education are so strong that no state government dare resist them for long. That is why, one by one, old values of academic functioning as well as governance have been collapsing. This was almost inevitable. What is more, these pressures are likely to grow stronger every day and all aspects of planning, including those relating to education, must be based on a hard-headed recognition of this fact.

All that professional bodies like the UGC can hope to achieve is to moderate the intensity of these pressures. To seek to achieve anything more than that would not be realistic. As a matter of fact, the situation in the last decade or so has become more and more vulnerable to these pressures. Professional standards have come increasingly under strain. To reinstate them as the basis for academic judgement, which in essence would be the task of the reconstituted UGC, is not going to be a simple matter. There will be resistance from the state governments who have got used to a certain style of functioning. Educated unemployment is growing at such an alarming rate that it is beginning to generate peculiar pressures of its own kind. Then there is financial stringency which almost every state has to contend with. Universities are proliferating but sources of financial support are not growing at the same rate of expansion. The situation is certainly not beyond redemption but it is fair to admit that it is difficult.

How best to deal with this difficult situation is a matter which does not admit of a straight answer. Pressures leading to dilution of standards are bound to become stronger and stronger everyday. To fight them successfully may not always be possible. What, however, is within the bounds of possibility is that in the contest between professional standards and pressures to undermine them, standards do not always lose. The only hope in this situation lies in the UGC giving itself a greater professional standing. The more firmly its professional character gets established the easier it would be to meet and, in certain cases, sidestep politically motivated pressures. The UGC Act of 1956 is fairly specific on the powers that the UGC enjoys and the functions that it should perform. These were amplified in a meaningful manner in the report of the Sapru Committee 1964. The said Committee drafted a statement and asked the attorney-general of India to respond to it. The statement of the case made out for the opinion of the attorney-general is a fairly extensive one and is given as an annexure to the Sapru Committee Report. The following brief extract contains six explicit questions to which the attorney-general has also given equally explicit answers:

... The Committee has desired that the advice of the Attorney-General should be obtained on the question of the extent of the implied powers of Parliament to undertake legislation under Entry 66 of List I of Schedule VII to the Constitution, and in particular, the extent to which such implied powers include the power of Parliament to provide by legislation:

1. *That in the interests of co-ordination and maintenance of standards in universities the president of India shall have Visitorial powers.*

    The powers will have to be specified. It will have to be considered in this connection whether the UGC has not all the necessary powers. Those powers are, of course, with references to the grants made and to be made by the UGC and I think it is desirable to enumerate and consolidate the powers of coordination and maintenance of standards in one person such as the visitor to the extent it is possible.

2. *That chancellors shall be persons of eminence either in educational world or in other spheres of public life of the country and shall have such powers as may be specifically delegated to them but that they shall not be vested with any Visitorial powers.*

    The connection of this item with Entry 66 appears to me to be extremely remote.

3. *Regarding minimum standards of fitness for admission to universities or to technical and professional institutions including medical, engineering and agricultural institutions.*

    This seems to me to be well within Entry 66.

4. *Prescribing the procedure for the appointment of vice chancellors.*

This seems to have little or no connection with Entry 66. No doubt an efficient vice chancellor is better than one who is not and an experienced one better than one who is not, but since the visitor will have the necessary powers to give directions and see that they are carried out, it does not appear to me that this item has any reasonable relation to the needs of Entry 66.

5. *Regarding the right to direct inspection of colleges and other institutions in order to ensure that proper standards are maintained.*

   Item (e) appears to me to be well within Entry 66.

6. *Regarding the fixing of qualifications as also the method of selection of members of (a) the teaching staff and (b) other members of the community to various governing bodies, such as, the court or the senate, the executive Council or the syndicate, the academic councils, appointments or selection boards, examination committees for bringing out results and other similar University bodies.*

   (i) General directions could have a relation to the maintenance of standards.

   (ii) This to my mind is far too remote. The method of election to the various bodies etc., are obviously within the functions of university itself and if these are all taken over, one may well ask what is left to the university.

Of the six questions asked, the attorney-general is emphatically of the opinion that at least in respect of two of them any action taken by the UGC would fall clearly and unambiguously within the meaning of Entry 66 of List I of the Indian Constitution. If the UGC were therefore to prescribe minimum standards of fitness for admission to universities or to technical and professional institutions, it would be entirely within its rights. Similarly, were the UGC to direct inspection of colleges and other institutions in order to ensure that proper standards are maintained, this too would be perfectly in order. It requires little effort to see that the academic landscape of the country would undergo a profound change if these two powers were to be exercised by the UGC. Universities which today have to surrender to political pressures in respect of establishment of new colleges, standards of admission and such other matters would have their hands immeasurably strengthened if in their response to such pressures they had the directives of the UGC to fall back upon. Considering that the pattern of developments over the last two decades has followed a certain inexorable course, this sounds too good to be true. To continue to follow existing policies and not to reverse the gear would, however, be a disaster. And, as argued above, the only agency which can fight, so to speak, a rearguard action is the UGC. Now that it has been reconstituted and given a new orientation, its charter of work is quite clear.

What the attorney-general did in his opinion quoted above was to indicate the limits within which the UGC can operate. To operate beyond these limits would be politically risky and constitutionally untenable. To operate below the limits would compromise the professional character of the UGC and render it ineffective in the long run. The task which the reconstituted UGC now faces is how to operate within these limits without sacrificing either efficiency or integrity.

PART II

Other
Related Issues

VI

The University Grants Commission and Accreditation

I

Was it necessary to establish a separate body called the National Assessment and Accreditation Council or NAAC as it is popularly known? Some people might regard this way of putting things as an act of impertinence. My reason for posing the issue in this manner is that, as I understand, accreditation was a job which was to be done by the UGC itself rather than by any other body created by it.

In this connection, it is important to recall why the UGC was established. This issue has been discussed in the very first chapter of this book. Unlike the British UGC on which it has been somewhat modelled, the Indian UGC had a different set of objectives. The British UGC was certainly a grant-giving body and was attached to the treasury and not the department of education and science. In India, the initials were taken over. That could have been lived with. Unfortunately the resemblance between the two is much greater than ought to have been.

As I see it, the job of the Indian UGC is to get the universities to assess themselves and prepare a plan of financial assistance to them. If it is a central university, the UGC is responsible both for its running and its growth. If it is a state university, the situation is somewhat different. (This issue has been discussed in the Chapter IV.) Basically, it is for the concerned state to fund the university but the UGC also has a role to play.

A quarter of a century ago, before the UGC started leaning more and more in favour of the central universities and the number of state universities was not as high as it is today, most of them received something like 15–20 per cent of their funding from the UGC. Since then, the situation has changed a great deal for reasons into which it is not necessary to go here.

Did the UGC go about its mandate as given to it? Here the answer, sad to say, is in the negative. Instead of asking the universities to analyse how they were working and preparing a plan for financial assistance, the UGC started floating a variety of schemes. Most of these schemes were academically sound, even progressive. Even if they had not been progressive enough, the state universities would have been happy to receive support for the simple reason that they were in need of money and were not very choosy about their priorities. Therefore funding was welcome from whatever source it came.

As an illustration of what is involved here, one has only to look at a self-study report which is prepared by each university when it applies to the NAAC for purposes of accreditation. This report holds up a mirror to the university. It required the intervention of an organisation like the NAAC to make a university analyse its own working. Properly speaking, this would have been done had the UGC gone about discharging its basic function of the determination of standards in the way in which it had been originally mandated to do.

Over the decades, the UGC started functioning like a government office. For the first few years, things had not settled down. Once they did, questions like what is meant by standards were asked. It so happened that even when a Committee on Standards was appointed in 1962, it took over three years to submit a report. And even then, no clear cut formulation was forthcoming. In the meantime began a big boom in student expansion at the undergraduate level. For details of what was happening and how the UGC got derailed under the pressure of numbers, one can refer to J.N. Kaul's study, *Higher Education in India: 1951–1971*.

The only constructive response which the UGC could make to the growing proliferation of colleges was to set up departments of advanced study. It was a good initiative and helped some select departments in the universities to protect themselves against being swamped by numbers. By the early seventies when the UGC tried to pull up its socks, so to speak, it was too late. What is worse, the introduction of the revised scales of pay a little later put the college teachers in the seat of power. Since then, almost all decisions, whether by the government or the UGC, have been taken in line with what suited the undergraduate teachers and what they preferred.

In terms of the decline of standards, the last couple of decades have witnessed a steep fall. Even the report of the V.S. Jha Committee submitted in January 1977 hardly made any impact on the situation. None of the UGC chairmen could help to change the direction of developments. Since grant-giving had become the accepted mode of functioning and no alternative pattern of work had been forthcoming, several alternatives were now explored. One of them was to introduce the system of accreditation. Had the UGC stuck to its original mandate given by the Constitution in 1950, it would already be doing what was now being proposed. Over the years, the UGC had got so used to the procedures it was following that the notion of setting up an independent body appeared to be attractive. It was a conceptual vacuum in which the seed of the NAAC was planted.

In the Programme of Action of the National Policy on Education in 1986, the following observation was made:

> Excellence of institutions of higher education is a function of many aspects: self-evaluation and self-improvement are important among them. If a mechanism is set up which will encourage self assessment in institutions, and also assessment and accreditation by a Council of which these institutions are corporate members, the quality of process participation, achievements etc., will be constantly monitored and improved.

In the wake of this recommendation, the UGC set up a committee in 1987 to look into the matter. This committee submitted a report which also recommended that:

(i) the report be widely circulated among the academics,
(ii) regional seminars and a national seminar be convened to discuss the report, and;
(iii) the comments of the academics along with the recommendations of the seminars be placed before the Commission.

Most of this was done but the Commission did not move in the matter as decisively as it should have. It was eventually in 1994 that the body called the NAAC came to be established. The proposal went through largely because of the push given by late Ram Reddy who, after having retired from the chairmanship of the UGC, became the first chairman of the NAAC. Unfortunately he died within a few months of its establishment and this was a kind of a setback. One of the important setbacks was that the UGC decided to make assessment and accreditation of colleges and universities optional whereas the original proposal was that every university and college would get accredited within a specific time frame. The UGC however chose to be cagey in the matter and adopted an over-cautious position.

In the course of the various turns and twists between 1987 and 1994 when the NAAC was finally established, its concept had undergone several changes. For instance, in 1986, it was visualised that institutions which are assessed would be its corporate members. That important dimension was not found very workable in the Indian context. To cut a long story short, the NAAC received strong support from the Ministry of HRD in its new incarnation. In a swift changeover of policy, it took the position that every institution would have to submit itself to assessment and accreditation. Following that lead, the UGC also changed its position. It should not be necessary to provide more details. Once the support to the NAAC came ungrudgingly, things started happening and the pace of activities quickened.

II

After a good deal of preliminary work and considerable hesitation, the NAAC took a plunge in 1996. Between 1994 and 1996, rules of assessment had been laid down after a good deal of consultative work. The experience of other countries was analysed and those things which were found to be applicable to our situation were adopted. To take one example, originally 10 criteria of assessment were laid down. Experience however soon showed that those could be abridged and these were reduced to the following seven:

1. Curricular Aspects
2. Teaching, Learning and Evaluation

3. Infrastructure and Learning Resources
4. Organisation and Governance
5. Research, Consultancy and Extension
6. Student Support and Progression
7. Other Healthy Practices

When all this was being implemented, there was an unexpected break in the tenure of the first director who left in order to join his home university where he was appointed as its vice chancellor. There was some kind of a legal tangle about his successor. For a period of almost two years, the chairman of the NAAC doubled as the director also. At that time, in those circumstances, there was no other course of action open.

Even then, things were vigorously pushed through. A large number of universities and colleges were visited and they were assessed. The response was fairly positive and in two years something like 200 colleges and universities were visited and assessed. For reasons which it is difficult to understand, a curious kind of distortion entered the process of assessment at this stage. Due to the defective mode of measurement, a number of universities which could not have been given a high rating were given five stars. Was it done in order to attract universities to get themselves accredited or was it done in order to pander to our national habit of not calling a pot black even though it is black?

During the last few years, there has been considerable activity and several hundred institutions have been assessed and graded. While other things proceeded satisfactorily, there was dissatisfaction with the practice of giving five stars to some institutions. To put it no more strongly, this approach was seen as an instance of the triumph of hope over experience. Even though the NAAC persisted with this act of indiscretion for some time, the UGC saved the situation somewhat. At this stage, it must be added that when there were arguments about the appointment of a new director, the occasion was utilised to redefine the status of the NAAC as an inter-university centre.

In consequence, the UGC was in a position to take part in reviewing NAAC's activities. In a prolonged two-day discussion, the rules of measurement were significantly tightened and refurbished. Earlier, all those who got a score of 75 per cent or more got five stars. In the revised scheme of measurement, the basis of calculation became more precise. If an institution obtained the 75–80 per cent score it fetched only a B+ grading. Beyond B+, now there is the B++ grade and this implied a 80–85 per cent score. For every additional five marks, it earned an A, A+ and an

A++ grading. Today thus, the situation is much better than what it used to be a couple of years ago. Even then, because of the earlier legacy there is an undisguised hankering after securing five stars for the university. It will take several years before the situation is decisively rectified.

III

In addition to the direct intervention of the UGC, the Ministry of HRD also played a strong, supportive role. The earlier over-cautious posture that going to the NAAC—and an institution may or may not opt for it— for assessment was a voluntary act was now reversed. The Ministry of HRD supported the revised decision and so did the UGC. Seeking ac-creditation was no longer a voluntary act and every institution had to get accredited. It is another matter that only a part of the job could get done and the target as laid down was not achieved.

In this connection, it needs to be noted that what worked in USA could not work in our situation. Accreditation in USA accomplishes two things. The first one is the need for legitimation. While anyone can estab-lish an institution without seeking anyone's permission in that country, legitimation can come only in the wake of accreditation. In our country, legitimation comes from the fact of the state granting recognition either by legislation—to set up a university—or affiliation to a university. The latter procedure applies more to colleges than to any other institution. In India, therefore, the institution could do without accreditation.

But the second part of the process of accreditation was also important— that related to grading. If asking for accreditation by the NAAC was im-portant, that was because, by doing so, the institution was able to earn a grade in terms of a recognised academic hierarchy. It is here that the then decision makers stumbled. Instead of being objective and upright, they pandered to the customary human weakness of conceding more than was expected or asked for. This gave rise to the system of giving five stars when it was not even expected. Doing it once gave a signal to others and they also demanded what had been, in their eyes, a kind of favour shown to some other institutions. The situation became indefensible and the whole system had to be reorganised. One only hopes that a lesson has been learnt and the mistake will not be repeated.

There is one additional snag to which only a partial answer has been found so far. But before long, a proper answer will have to be found.

Following the American example, it was said that accreditation would be valid for a period of five years. It so happens that the situation in our country is very different. As of today, approximately 500 universities and colleges have been accredited and the rest are yet to go through the process. Quite a number of them have applied and are at different stages of preparation for a visit by the NAAC. If things continue at the present pace of activity, during the next couple of years, the number would become almost double of what it is today. But even then, this would leave a very large sector of higher education outside the reach of the NAAC.

The NAAC as constituted today is not a large enough body to be able to cover more than the 300 university-level institutions in the country and more than 12,000 colleges which have already come into existence. It has taken quite some effort for the NAAC to recruit the right kind of people who possess the necessary knowledge and skills to be able to handle the growing quantum of work. Every year the number of institutions will keep on rising. As against this statement, it may be stated that while technical universities are covered by the AICTE and medical and agricultural universities belong to a different category altogether, the number of universities which have to be covered by the NAAC is almost within reach though it would require a certain amount of effort to cover all of them. A substantial number of colleges would still remain uncovered in any case. Approximately half of them have not been recognised even by the UGC so far. Even if they were to be covered by the NAAC which is extremely doubtful, this would not make much difference to the overall situation.

What about those universities and colleges which have been covered by the NAAC so far? Has that experience been positive? The answer to this question is in the affirmative by and large. As observed by the 1986 Policy, self-evaluation and self-improvement are two important engines of progress. So far, this mode of functioning was not being put to positive use. An outcome of this exercise in respect of a few hundred institutions was that, to start with, they were asked to prepare a self-study report.

The proforma for self-assessment is so comprehensive and so searching that every institution requires about three to six months of effort to fill it up. Our educational institutions have not been accustomed to analysing and cataloguing things. The proforma requires that to be done. Therefore, these institutions have had to undertake this exercise. In so doing it proved to be a useful learning experience for most of them. Questions that they had never asked themselves earlier had now to be answered. In the process, they learnt several things about their own working. This also helped them to envision a more planned future for themselves.

The point of saying all this is that when these institutions are visited the next time, whether after five years or after, their self-study reports will hopefully improve on their earlier ones. Another factor would also influence the situation. Institutions that were rated X in earlier visit would obviously like to register a better performance the next time around. They may not be able to do so for all kinds of reasons, including lack of resources or lack of personnel or some other valid reasons. But the desire to improve their earlier rating is bound to propel them into greater activity.

Whether that desire also leads them to qualitatively performing better is another story. Going by past experience, one can say that while most of them would probably work better than before, a few of them would only be able to keep up and not do better than that. That would be unfortunate. Perhaps it may help them if the NAAC revisits them not after another five years but sooner than that. Perhaps they could pay an additional fee for this special consideration and they would probably be willing to do so. Some of them might even come across better than before in this format. All these are matters about which one can only speculate and not be certain of one's answer.

However there is one more important issue. It has not been considered so far but it must be considered now.

IV

This is an issue to which the NAAC has also given some thought. Recently it decided that everything cannot be handled from the headquarters. Therefore, it is necessary to establish regional offices and gradually help them to grow. Steps in that direction are to be taken in the near future. So far so good, as they say!

The question which needs to be asked is: will these regional offices be able to perform as well as, within limits, the headquarters have been performing? It is difficult to answer this question. What if the experience of the regional offices established by the UGC, in respect of grants to colleges, gets repeated in this case? In other words, regional offices would by and large carry out the instructions given to them by the headquarters. Policies would be framed at the headquarters and they would be required only to implement them.

It may also happen that the regional offices are given more and more freedom to operate. For example, once a particular institution in that region has asked to be visited, the headquarters could pass on that request to the regional office which would in the ordinary course of things, deal with it. Alternatively, the said institution may write to the regional office directly and simply inform the headquarters, and sometimes dispense with even that. A number of variations are possible and it is difficult to anticipate what would happen.

The crucial question to ask is: how autonomous would the regional office be? For example, it can choose its own visiting team. But that would be in terms of the guidelines laid down by the headquarters. If, for instance, the headquarters lays down that the visiting team must consist of a set number of people of which a certain number must be from that region, the regional office would not be able to deviate from the guidelines. Or if the headquarters lays down that two members of the visiting team must belong to that region and two from a neighbouring region or other similar regu-lations, the regional office will be bound by it. By way of a contrast, it may be in order to cite what happens in USA—the country where the system of accreditation arose about a century ago.

One element of contrast may be noted right in the beginning. But it is not so crucial that that precedent would make it inapplicable to the Indian situation.

In USA, as stated already, no approval from any quarter is required to start an institution. In India this is not the case. Even a college cannot come into existence unless it is affiliated to a university. All kinds of elaborate rules have been framed in order to ensure that the first round of affiliation by a university and the second round of recognition by the UGC, steer the college in the right direction and they do not get stumped as has happened in many cases. Our situation is, therefore, different. No more need be said about this particular point. More might be said about it after the rest of the argument has been put forward.

There is another point of difference which makes our situation qualitatively different. In USA, because of the voluntary nature of the accreditation process, the initiative was taken by some groups and appropriate voluntary bodies were established. These bodies functioned in competition with one another. In course of time, procedures and guidelines were brought in line with one another. Indeed everything was eventually brought down to the same level of assessment at the time of performance. There was hardly anything significantly different between what was done in the north as compared to the south and so on.

India too is a vast country though not as large as USA is. The tradition of voluntary activity is however stronger in USA than in India. Therefore it would be too much to hope that in India any agency parallel to the NAAC would be set up by voluntary initiative. What is likely to work in India is something akin to what the NAAC is today; a UGC-sponsored body. It works under the overall supervision of the UGC but also works autonomously. The UGC nominates quite a number of persons who sit on the various NAAC bodies and in that sense it is a UGC-controlled body. Even then, the NAAC is autonomous for all practical purposes and will hopefully continue to be so.

To return to the argument, it is difficult to visualise a situation where the regional bodies being established by the NAAC will get launched on their own and would in course of time become policy making bodies in their own right. What is more likely to happen is that the regional office will continue to function under the overall supervision of the UGC. All attention must therefore be focused on how to make the regional offices function as autonomously as possible.

To add anything to what has already been said should not be necessary except that there should be a sense of awareness that unless the regional offices of the NAAC become more active and more autonomous, they will not be able to perform as well as they are expected to perform.

To be a little more specific, within a year or so NAAC will have to be expanded to approximately seven to eight times of its present size if it is to perform as it is required to. A way has, therefore, to be found wherein NAAC is able to give a much better account of itself than it has been able to do so far. One also hopes that meanwhile there are some amendments to the UGC Act and more and more colleges become autonomous. While this would in one sense add to the NAAC work load, in another sense, it would simplify that job to a great extent.

V

Of all the problems that face the NAAC, the most urgent is likely to be how to decentralise its operations and yet maintain unified functioning among the various regional offices. This particular issue, therefore, needs to be discussed a little further.

It is difficult to anticipate the shape of things as far as the colleges are concerned. In other words, the question to ask is: will the system of affiliation as followed at present be somewhat modified or will it remain as it is? If the system stays as it is and the present rate of expansion continues, by the end of the current plan, the number of colleges is likely to be close to 15,000. That about half of them will continue to be substandard is not all that unlikely. The plain fact is that colleges get established not because they always fulfil a genuine social or academic need but because, to a large extent, students do not know what else to do with themselves once they pass out from school and therefore college education provides an acceptable way of passing time.

Those of them who come from families that can afford to keep them at college do so, so that they can be kept out of mischief. As any one can see, it has a good deal to do with the state of employment in the country and also with the growth of the economy. If commercialisation of agriculture is promoted and both indusrialisation and services expand, that would be an opportunity for vocationalisation also to be promoted. In other words, the booming population of the country is a factor which is going to unsettle many things, including the educational sector of the country.

Yet another contributory factor which cannot be overlooked is the unsatisfactory quality of the new teaching staff. This has a direct impact on the quality of teaching. The country is simply not producing enough competent persons of the required calibre to meet all the demands that arise. The more competent ones opt for numerous new openings in the newer sectors of activity like management, IT and similar jobs. Despite the higher scales of pay as compared to what obtained a quarter of a century ago, teaching still fails to attract the right kind of talent.

There is also another alternative possibility. The existing system of affiliation is becoming more and more dysfunctional. Were the policy makers to become a little more assertive and were the growth and establishment of colleges to follow a more rational pattern of growth, we can have a situation in which, within the next few years, 4,000–5,000 colleges can become virtually autonomous. These colleges would have the potential as also the possibility of functioning for longer hours and many more days per year than is the accepted practice today. Another possibility is that vocationalisation at the college level may get promoted more extensively than is happening today and so the structure of college education may undergo some changes. Most of it is speculation. But the point to which attention needs to be drawn is: to what extent will this affect the functioning of the NAAC?

If the NAAC continues to function as it is functioning today and, even if it has four regional centres as visualised, it is difficult to envisage a situation in which all universities and colleges will be visited and accredited within the next three to four years. The more likely scenario is that while all universities would get accredited, in the case of colleges a large number would still remain uncovered by the NAAC. In this situation, it is for the NAAC to decide how to deal with this situation. And why only the NAAC? Even the UGC will have to find an answer to the situation where the performing sector will be smaller and the non-performing sector will be bigger.

In the case of universities and technical colleges, the AICTE, in the near future, might step up its accrediting activity. Which has a statutory National Board of Accreditation already in existence though it has remained somewhat inactive. The Medical Council might choose to undertake a similar initiative. The same thing can happen in regard to management and other similar courses. The upshot is that what will remain is the hard core of a large number of arts, social sciences and commerce colleges. They will present a problem. The UGC having passed off its problem to the NAAC, so to speak, can still stay untouched by it but the problem NAAC will find it difficult to escape its deadly fall out. No definite solution can be foreseen as of today. But one thing is clear, if the NAAC is to retain its credibility, it will find it difficult to function in a situation where it is partially active and partially inactive. To put it another way, it either covers the whole body of institutions or it will begin to lose out in terms of credibility. Since it would not like to lose its credibility, a way to deal with this problem will have to be found. It goes without saying that the NAAC will not be the only agency seeking a way out of the situation. The UGC too would have to be involved in finding a solution. But it needs to be recognised that unless all institutions are both visited and accredited, sooner or later, the NAAC will lose out in terms of its credibility. Having launched on this initiative therefore, the UGC owes it to the NAAC to help it maintain, if not enhance its credibility. To say anything more on this subject at this stage should not be necessary.

VI

Another related question (it has been raised earlier also) which is going to present a difficult problem for the NAAC is that, following the American model, every institution has to be accredited within five years and get reaccredited after an interval of every five years. In other words, the NAAC will retain its credibility only when its contact with the institutions, both universities and colleges, is a live and continuing one.

If the contact takes place only once and nothing more is heard about it for several years, it will look like a mechanical exercise which therefore would begin to suffer in terms of academic standing and credibility.

To put it bluntly, every other institution, including the state governments and those universities which affiliate colleges, can afford to take a relaxed attitude. They can afford to forget about the child they gave birth to. But the NAAC, unlike the UGC, cannot adopt this attitude of unconcern. Instead, it can do its bit to avoid any misunderstanding and even seek to sidestep the basic issue, though it would be difficult to do so. If this line of reasoning is correct, a way would have to be found to deal with the situation.

One way would be that while universities and autonomous colleges are dealt with by the NAAC as at present, the rest of the colleges are dealt with in another, less demanding, way. While the autonomous colleges will be visited like any university, the other colleges might or might not be visited with the same degree of rigour and thoroughness. Even a written statement (something like a self-study report) received every five years and verified, as and when convenient, might be looked upon as a kind of acceptable substitute. If this is not found acceptable, the number of regional offices might have to be increased. Today it is proposed to set up four regional offices but there is nothing to prevent the NAAC from deciding that, instead of four, it should set up six, seven, eight or even 10.

It may also happen that the bigger states have a separate office to look after the large number of institutions in that state and some of the smaller states are combined with each other and one office looks after two or even more of them. All this is looking too far ahead but these are problems which are not all that distant on the horizon. These problems will confront the NAAC within a year or two of its beginning to function through its regional offices.

As far as regional officers are concerned, it is taken for granted that they will maintain the same level of competence and attention to detail as the headquarters has been able to ensure so far. Whether the same level of performance can be maintained even in the regional offices remains to be seen. And going further, whether this operation can be extended while retaining the same level of competence and attention to detail is yet another question that will have to be addressed.

One thing has to be ensured. The regional offices, when they are established, will have to be manned by competent and committed persons. In the current set up at its Bangalore headquarters, the NAAC is performing reasonably well. One important explanation for this is that the strength of the staff is not too high and the dozen or so professionals who are functioning there, function like a team. Once this number expands to 60–70 and then to 100 plus, it will be difficult to ensure that the same standards of competence and responsibility are maintained.

To seek to follow the American model in respect of regional decentralisation will be difficult. In that country, private initiative is rated highly. In any case, the various regional set-ups in that country have had a history of more than half a century each. Over the years, they have given convincing evidence of being able to function at a fairly high level of competence and responsibility. To be able to repeat the same thing in India does not look all that easy. The UGC, once having sponsored the NAAC, will find it difficult to withdraw and leave things to it to function entirely on its own. And yet, if everything is left to it, it does not follow that the NAAC in consequence will perform better. There are a number of issues which arise here and these will have to be looked into.

At any rate, one thing is not likely to happen. The UGC, for whatever it is worth, will not agree to an arrangement where a body other than the NAAC (which it controls today) will be permitted to come into existence. In other words, the NAAC will not be permitted to convert itself into an independent enterprise. This, in turn, will put the responsibility on the UGC to involve itself more and more with the working of the NAAC. Even the Ministry of HRD's thinking will be along the same lines, it may be added.

VII

What is likely to be the\nature of relationship between the UGC and NAAC? This issue which could have been taken up earlier has been deliberately left over to be discussed last of all.

As of today, the UGC is not making much use of the findings of the NAAC. The UGC knows and remains informed of what is happening. But does this fact influence decision making in the UGC? The answer is more or less in the negative. Having developed, a certain mode of functioning over the years, the UGC finds it difficult to keep in step with the changing rhythm of things. Had the UGC, right from the beginning, linked financial aid to the planning and performance of each university, things might have been different. To expect the UGC to change its style of functioning now would require a virtual review of the UGC functioning. But can this be evaded?

Such a review will have to be undertaken one of these days. If only a column gets introduced in the UGC reports which would indicate the grading which that university or college was given by the NAAC and almost everything else remains the same, this would be an utterly inadequate response to the substantive work that the NAAC is doing. At the same time it would be in order to express the misgiving that for the UGC to expect to change its own style of work drastically is more unlikely than likely.

It is not realised today that this problem which lurks unrecognised in the background today, is likely to emerge as a serious problem within the next few years. So much will depend upon the quality of leadership of both the bodies. A vigorous and enlightened UGC should, properly speaking, work out a new plan of functioning for itself which it might adopt phase by phase. If the plan of reorganisation is pragmatic, it should be possible to envisage a situation where the UGC comes into the picture only after the NAAC has reported. In other words, the starting point would be the NAAC evaluation. Since it would be largely based on what a particular institution has said in its self-study report, its credibility would be difficult to question.

What can be questioned, and this will happen in several cases, will be the value placed on the NAAC report by the UGC. If the evaluation report is weak or loosely formulated or at odds with established facts, the matter can even be reopened. In a certain number of cases, this might come to pass. But the primacy of the NAAC evaluation will by and large stay. Today, the NAAC assessment is being ignored for the most part. Once the focus is readjusted, and this will have to be done, a new equation would emerge. In the ultimate analysis, the UGC judgement in regard to financial allocations will have to be based on what the NAAC had to say.

In this unintended and unplanned way, the character of the UGC decision making can undergo a significant change. So far, no university has raised such an issue but it can arise. A university or a college can question a decision handed down by a UGC official or the Commission itself. In that case, the matter would have to be argued out again and a good deal will depend upon what NAAC said in the first instance. Such a development will be strongly resisted. It can even happen that nothing gets done in a particular case but then a lesson would have been learnt for the future and, in the next case, both the NAAC and UGC would be more careful. Though yet distant, it is possible to visualise such situations emerging.

To conclude this part of the argument, the NAAC which is today regarded as the junior body can gradually emerge as a stronger player in the game. The UGC's unquestioned supremacy will begin to undergo a transformation once it is realised that any kind of interpretation is to a large extent determined by the facts of the case and those would be largely handled by the NAAC. If this line of reasoning is correct, what the NAAC will have to say will carry considerable weight. As of today, the NAAC is nowhere in the picture. In a few years, the balance might begin to change.

Once that starts happening, the NAAC will have to be much more careful in its recommendations, both in its verification of the data available and its interpretation. This can prove to be a major hazard in its own working. More particularly, when it is being expanded and, at the same time, its focus is being redefined. To say no more about it, both the NAAC and the UGC are entering a phase in their respective careers when they are likely to reexamine and redefine their respective roles within the next few years.

VII

POSTGRADUATE EDUCATION

I

As anyone involved in higher education in India knows, colleges were established first and the universities were established later. Even after the universities had been established in 1857, all that they did was to conduct examinations for colleges within their jurisdiction. As a matter of fact, right till the beginning of the last century, hardly any university engaged in any direct teaching. Their main activities were to draw up the syllabus, hold examinations and declare the results. The first university to take the initiative to undertake postgraduate education was Calcutta University.

In the early years of the twentieth century, Ashutosh Mukherjee became its vice chancellor. Gifted as he was with the quality of academic vision, he could see for himself that Indian universities were not discharging their basic function which was to undertake postgraduate teaching and research.[1] In the twenties, the Sadler Commission, which reported in 1919, also supported this proposal. In its wake, Calcutta established departments of postgraduate teaching. People like C.V. Raman, S. Radhakrishnan and several others were invited to be on the staff of that university and the University of Calcutta became a kind of a model for others to emulate.

During those early decades of the twentieth century, the academic leadership of the country was with Calcutta. This was in consonance with the fact that, even in economic terms, Bengal was the most industrialised state in the country. What happened after 1947, particularly after the outstanding leadership provided by Dr B.C. Roy, are matters that cannot be gone into here. During these decades, despite various handicaps, the University of Calcutta continued to be an important centre of postgraduate teaching and research. More or less simultaneously, a number of other universities came up and turned attention to postgraduate education.

Amongst them were Dacca, Benarus Hindu University (BHU), Andhra, Mysore, Lucknow, Osmania, Patna, Annamalai and several others. Some of the older universities like Madras, Bombay, Punjab and Allahabad among others also began to pay increased attention to postgraduate teaching and research. Whereas the newer universities, as enumerated above, did not have to break new ground, a relevant factor that might be noted here is that all these universities more or less survived on the income generated by conducting the matriculation examination in their area of jurisdiction.

Things started changing in the thirties, however. There was always a little surplus which went to pay for the university office staff. This became a problem with the passage of time. Funding for postgraduate departments was always difficult. The BHU and Aligarh were somewhat favourably situated as they had been able to raise some donations from the public. Quite often, the vice chancellors (generally High Court judges) worked on a part-time basis. There was not enough work to justify the appointment of a full-time person.

To go back a little earlier however, when colleges were established in the early mid-ninetieth century, some of them also established postgraduate departments. By the time the universities had established departments of postgraduate education, something like 20–30 of the colleges had started doing a reasonably competent job of providing postgraduate teaching. That there was no research back up to the Master's teaching need not be referred to here. For that matter, even the universities were deficient in this respect. Even when the universities took to postgraduate education in a systematic manner, this did not put the colleges out of business. No wonder, in 1950–51 for which period some data is available, 34 per cent of postgraduate students were enrolled in affiliated colleges and 65 per cent in university teaching departments or university colleges which amounted to the same thing.

In other words, one-third of the students that completed their Master's degrees were enrolled in colleges at that time. The situation started changing with the passage of time. In 1960–61, 40 per cent of the students were enrolled in colleges. By 1970–71, before the revised salary scales were introduced and undergraduate and postgraduate teaching were put at par with each other, the percentage had risen to 47 per cent. A more complete picture of the changing situation may be seen from the Table 7.1. It has been compiled on the basis of the data published in the annual reports of the UGC. Data for the first two decades is not exact for the simple reason that it took the UGC some time to evolve a system for collection of data. Even now, it is not exactly up to the mark but it is detailed enough to be able to study the trends and to judge which way things are going.

Table 7.1
Student Enrolment at Postgraduate Level in University Teaching Departments/
University Colleges and Affiliated Colleges (1950–51 to 2000–01)

Year	University Teaching Departments/ University Colleges	Affiliated Colleges	Total Enrolment
(1)	(2)	(3)	(4)
1950–51	13,115* (65.6)	6,877* (34.4)	19,992
1960–61	35,169* (59.7)	23,740* (40.3)	58,909
1965–66	48,424 (52.7)	43,406 (47.3)	91,830
1970–71	84,270 (52.3)	76,912 (47.7)	161,182
1980–81	125,242 (45.8)	148,095 (54.2)	273,337
1990–91	182,873 (43.5)	237,525 (56.5)	420,398
2000–01	262,402 (33.8)	512,902 (66.2)	775,304

Notes: Figures in parenthesis indicate the percentage of enrolment of that group (UTD/ UC or AC) to Total Enrolment.
*Estimated Figures.

II

Before the scales of pay were radically revised in the seventies, there were separate scales of pay for undergraduate and postgraduate teachers. For instance, in the Third Plan, the scales of pay were as in Table 7.2.

Table 7.2
Scales of Pay Introduced in 1968

Designation	Undergraduate Colleges	Postgraduate Colleges	University Departments
Principal	700–40–1,100	800–50–1,250	–
Professor	–	–	1,100–50–1,300–60–1,600
Reader	–	400–30–640–800	700–50–1,250
Lecturer	–	–	400–40–800–50–950
Lecturer (Senior Grade)	400–30–640–40–800	–	–
Lecturer (Junior Grade)	250–15–400	300–25–600	–
Tutor/ Demonstrator	250–15–400	250–15–400	–

Note: One-third of the Professors were to be in the scale of 1,600–100–1,800.

Since the scales of pay in postgraduate colleges were slightly higher, there was always a kind of competition among the colleges that aspired to have postgraduate teaching in different subjects. Even if the number of subjects taught at the postgraduate level was no more than two or three, it entitled the principal of the college to have a higher scale of pay. The preference shown for postgraduate classes was thus linked to some extent with the level of teaching in which the teachers were engaged.

This situation changed after the mid-seventies. Now there was no distinction between postgraduate and undergraduate teachers. Still, as the figures quoted above show, the percentage of colleges wanting to undertake postgraduate teaching kept rising so much that, in about five decades, the proportion of those engaged in postgraduate teaching now constitutes two-thirds of the total instead of one-third as it was half a century ago. This leads to the next related question: should postgraduate teaching be done in university departments or in affiliated colleges?

No one posed the issue in this manner at any stage. Instead more and more universities were established. Every new university wanted to have a certain number of postgraduate departments. Put another way, the newly established universities felt that there would be something lacking in their claim to be full fledged universities unless they had a few successful postgraduate departments under their direct charge. In actual practice, both the phenomena took place as parallel developments. More and more universities were established and, as a corollary more and more postgraduate departments were established. At the same time, increasingly the existing colleges, as also some of those which were now coming up, conducted postgraduate classes. There was no question of winding up these classes in colleges. In addition, some of the newer colleges also ventured into this field and the figures testify to the fact that they did so successfully.

In this connection, it must be stated that when Calcutta chose to focus attention on postgraduate teaching, it went about the job quite systematically. Some of the older colleges, Presidency College, Calcutta, for instance, had been teaching up to the Master's level for quite some time. Now everything came to be concentrated at the university. In addition, while the arts and social sciences departments held classes within the old premises of the University of Calcutta, a separate science college was established at some distance from the university headquarters. Almost all science departments were located there and they were both well staffed and well equipped.

Till the seventies almost, Calcutta University maintained a particularly high profile in respect of postgraduate teaching and research. Even when other universities were established in West Bengal, indeed a couple of them in Calcutta itself, this did not in any way bring down the standing of the University of Calcutta. Something unexpected happened also. Some of the better known teachers in Calcutta University were selected in the new universities. But they refused to join there. Several of them preferred to stay on wherever they were and even continued to be readers rather than move out and become professors. Over the decades, Calcutta had emerged as an intellectually alive university centre and this is what acted like a magnet.

At the same time, it must be added that once postgraduate teaching was concentrated at the university, none of the colleges in Calcutta was allowed to enrol students at the Master's level. Some of the teachers in the Calcutta colleges, however, did teach at the university. This very arrangement was duplicated in Delhi when, in the late twenties, the University of Delhi established some university departments. As a matter of fact, even B.Sc classes were taught at the university till the mid-fifties. It was only in subsequent years that science classes were decentralised in favour of colleges in Delhi.

The overall picture that emerged was that Calcutta and Delhi concentrated postgraduate teaching at the university level whereas Bombay and Madras did not. Even today, more than half a century later, in these latter towns, in addition to the university departments, in major subjects like chemistry and economics for example, there are a dozen colleges in each of these towns which conduct postgraduate teaching. The university departments also do the same. It goes without saying that on the whole the universities manage to perform better than the colleges do. That funding from the UGC also made a difference goes without saying.

What about towns other than the metropolitan ones? The situation varies from state to state. In Maharashtra for example, Pune, even before it got a university of its own, had postgraduate teaching in some of the colleges. The same phenomenon occured in towns like Madurai, Mysore, Bangalore, Trivandrum, Indore, Guwahati, Ahmedabad, Agra, Ajmer, Kanpur and a whole string of middle level towns. The continuing spread of postgraduate teaching in colleges is a testimony to what has been stated above.

Here also, the situation again varies from state to state. In Uttar Pradesh, for example, postgraduate teaching continues to be widespread and is found in a large number of affiliated colleges. In Bihar, on the other hand, this did not happen. This has happened in all the southern states as also Gujarat and Maharashtra as also in Punjab and Haryana and quite a few other states. There is no clear pattern that emerges. The only pattern which can be seen has been described above which, to repeat, was that Calcutta and Delhi concentrated postgraduate teaching at the university level and Bombay and Madras did not. During the last few years there have been some marginal change in Calcutta. For the rest, the pattern remains as it is.

III

One reason why the pattern did not undergo a change even after the establishment of the UGC in the early fifties and the rapid growth of the universities in the fifties and sixties was the absence of a clear cut and definite policy in regard to postgraduate education. The UGC had failed to formulate a policy on this issue. In 1964, for instance, the UGC convened a high powered meeting to deal with the issue of colleges. Since no college was prepared to give up postgraduate teaching and the UGC was not inclined to take a tough stand in the matter, as for instance Ashutosh Mukherjee has done in the earlier part of the century, the UGC stopped discussing this issue any further. This did not happen all that categorically. There is evidence (some of which will be quoted later) to show that there was a certain degree of uneasiness about where to locate postgraduate teaching—in university departments or in colleges?

By the early seventies, when there was a change of gears in the UGC leadership to some extent, soon thereafter came parity between undergraduate and postgraduate teaching. After that, there was hardly anything by way of a compulsion to insist upon postgraduate teaching being concentrated only in university departments. As a matter of fact, there have been instances, and those can be quoted, where some of the university departments did not attract as many students as the strength of the department as also its facilities justified. In plain words, the teaching staff was there but the number of students opting for the university departments was not all that large.

Quite a number of students still preferred to join colleges which, over the years, had developed some kind of a tradition of Master's teaching. Even today, as the figures quoted above show, university departments are not always preferred by students. Considering the fact that there are more than 150 affiliating universities now, the number of postgraduate departments in these universities is fairly large and still the situation remains what it was.

The basic explanation for this situation is three-fold. The first one is that owing to the rapid rate of expansion, even at the postgraduate level, the number of capable teachers was always limited. The tradition of good teaching coupled with research did not grow beyond a point. The research we see around us today is relatively recent and has a good deal to do with the availability of research funding for the purpose. The second factor was that, in some of the science subjects, as also some of the social sciences like economics, advances in the subject have been rather spectacular. Third, quite a few of the more able teachers in India chose to migrate abroad and the process of continued brain drain has most emphatically hurt the recruitment of talented teachers to Indian universities.

Yet another important factor in the situation has been the establishment of certain high profile institutions like the IITs and IIMs. They have attracted a good deal of talent and not much talent has been available for other universities. This led to a certain amount of dilution at the postgraduate teaching level even in the case of university departments. In the ultimate analysis, though, there was some degree of difference between university departments and postgraduate teaching departments in colleges, the difference was not all that notable. This is subject to one qualification. This is true in some but not in all cases. On the whole however, owing to poor standards of performance both at the undergraduate and postgraduate levels, the situation remains unsatisfactory.

One way of judging standards at the postgraduate level and above is the gap which a student is required to cover up if he goes on to do his Ph.D. There is such a wide gap between the two levels that, unless a student educates himself further and does so with some degree of depth, he finds it difficult to write his Ph.D. thesis. The truth of the matter is that, over the decades, we in India have evolved a very peculiar kind of deficit system. And oddly enough, this phenomenon is at work right from the primary to the university level.

For instance, even if a student chooses to drop out after his primary education, the least that he is expected to have achieved in five years is that he is literate. Does it really happen? Experience all over the country shows that it happens in less than 50 per cent of the cases. The same story is repeated at the upper primary and secondary levels. The difference becomes more notable at the higher secondary level.

Some 15–20 per cent of the students at this level are far ahead of their fellow students. They are the ones who generally get into professional colleges and go on to do well in life. The rest of them have the satisfaction of having completed their higher secondary course and the only choice they are left with is to join an undemanding white collar job after having finished their higher secondary course or college education. Had we been able to widen the area of the concentration of capability and take it to, say, 40–50 per cent instead of the existing 15–20 per cent at the higher secondary level, the situation would have been very different even at the school level.

In other words, poor teaching at every level contributes to this deficit phenomenon. The phenomenon does not terminate at the school stage but can be seen even at the undergraduate and the postgraduate stages. In a few universities—not more than 20–30 per cent of the total—undergraduate education is enriched by having what are called the 'Honours' courses. The course is enriched in such a way that the more ambitious students opt for 'Honours' courses and not the 'Pass' courses. Here also the situation differs from university to university.

Universities like Calcutta and Delhi have done a splendid job with this concentration on the talented students. Several other universities did the same but these two are being mentioned because they have established a successful tradition in this regard. What is required is that this system is extended to other universities also. This is a matter to which the UGC needs to pay urgent attention. The academic dividends, it should go without saying, would be much higher than most people can anticipate today. This would also significantly contribute to the improvement of standards even at the postgraduate level.

IV

That there was considerable uneasiness about how postgraduate education was being handled should become clear from two pieces of data which are taken from the UGC documents. The first one was an item for discussion which was reported to the UGC on 2 July 1971. Since there was a little history to this case, let that be described in some detail.

On 3 October 1969, the Commission had considered the report of a committee which had been set up by way of an indepth study of the non-professional colleges affiliated to Kerala and Calicut Universities. At this meeting, it was decided to refer the report to the state government and the concerned universities. Both the state government and the universities generally accepted the report. The University of Kerala however felt that the wider issue of the development of postgraduate studies in the university should be further discussed at a meeting of some principles of affiliated colleges, members of the syndicate and the heads of university departments. This meeting was held on 19 April 1971. Apart from the others mentioned, the additional secretary of the UGC was also present. The following items were agreed upon and these are reproduced below:

1. The university should not sanction the starting of fresh postgraduate courses in 1971–72.
2. It is desirable to fix an optimum number of admissions to the postgraduate courses. The optimum number for an arts course should be 20 to 25 and that for a science course 12 to 15. The colleges which fail to attract this number of eligible candidates should discontinue the postgraduate courses in the subjects concerned.
3. The minimum marks for admission to postgraduate courses should be raised. A first class in the subject or subjects concerned (with the usual 5 per cent concession to scheduled castes, scheduled tribes and other backward classes) should be insisted upon for admission to M.Sc courses. Colleges which do not get the requisite number of students with the above marks should

not offer the postgraduate courses in that subject in any given
year.

4. Special attention should be bestowed on the training and equipment of postgraduate teachers in the various subjects. The hard
core of postgraduate teachers in every college should be given
social encouragement and better facilities for improving their
competence as teachers so the they may put in their very best.
This may also be done by prescribing less hours of work or by
insisting on higher qualifications for postgraduate teaching and
some participation in research.

5. Refresher courses in selected disciplines, particularly in science
subjects, should be organised with a view to enabling postgraduate teachers to be better acquainted with the latest developments in their fields of specialisation. Special courses of longer
duration under the auspices of the university departments of
study and research may also be considered in order to give graduates in a new discipline over to postgraduate teachers of affiliated
colleges.

6. The possibility of centralised admissions for postgraduate courses
in private colleges may be explored with a view to ensuring the
admission of better candidates to postgraduate studies.

7. The number of colleges permitted to do postgraduate work in
any subject should be related to the demands of manpower and
also represent a fair geographical distribution in the university
area.

8. There should be adequate facilitates to produce the requisite
material for advanced postgraduate work in Malayalam.[2]

The minutes of this meeting which have been reproduced in full were
brought to the notice of the UGC once again. The UGC's response was
to note the minutes and leave it at that.

What do these observations indicate? Clearly there was serious dissatisfaction with what was happening in the colleges at the postgraduate level
and the issue was discussed in considerable detail because it was one of
those situations where the essence of the matter lay in how the details
were handled. Instead of merely noting the recommendations made by
this committee, the UGC could have gone further and circulated the
minutes to other universities so that they too in turn might learn from
the experience of an intensive study of the problem undertaken by a
particular university.

More precisely, these problems were common to all universities where postgraduate teaching was being done but there were no systematic attempts to ensure good standards of performance. To repeat, good standards could be ensured only through detailed and intensive analysis as had been carried out in this case. There was only one item missing and it was an important item. No reference was made at any stage to the quality of the teaching staff engaged at the postgraduate level. As stated earlier, teachers of the requisite calibre were and are just not available.

Each college was basically trying to engage the best person available (it seems safe to make this assumption) and there was no attempt to ensure high quality as compared to those who were working in university departments. If teachers of the right calibre were not available, this was mainly for two reasons. One, as already mentioned, a considerable proportion of capable teachers were leaving the country and settling down abroad. Second, the academic system was not producing men and women of the right calibre in the required numbers and the process had gone on for a quarter of a century. As a result of this dearth of talent, whoever was available (the assumption made earlier can be repeated again) was employed. Nobody realised this fact that the acquisition of a Master's degree qualified a student to be engaged as a teacher in a college. If the teachers were not of the right calibre, all that they would be able to do is to perpetuate mediocrity. And this is precisely what has been happening.

In this connection the second recommendation (as above) needs to be noted. Colleges were setting up new departments even when the number of students seeking admission was not all that large. Therefore, this particular recommendation held that it would be better to discontinue the classes than to admit unworthy students. The situation as depicted here was neither untypical nor confined to the state of Kerala.

It may be assumed that this issue has been discussed in the Commission periodically and that is why two other committees were appointed to go into this problem and come up with solutions. Even the right kind of solutions could have been identified but the UGC had no system of functioning in which it dealt with such problems nor had it evolved a system whereby if a measure was thought desirable then a way was found to implement it. Recommendations to that effect might have been made once in a while. Whether the UGC has ever acted upon these recommendations is difficult to ascertain. The UGC has not entered into that mode of functioning at any stage.

That this issue was considered in fits and starts should be evident from another UGC document. In 1987, the UGC issued a letter to the registrars of all affiliating universities laying down 'guidelines on terms and conditions of affiliation of colleges by a university'. A number of things in regard to this particular circular letter need to be noted:

1. The guidelines were issued almost a quarter of a century after the UGC had come into existence. All these years, there has been no formal document which could be held up as embodying a set of directives which the colleges were obliged to follow.
2. These guidelines were issued in the form of regulations which, in terms of the UGC Act, are binding on colleges. One of the statements made there is reproduced here for ready reference:

   While these guidelines are laid down for affiliation of new colleges, it is intended that the position of colleges affiliated to a university should be reviewed in the light of the conditions of affiliation now being proposed and the Regulations pertaining to the minimum standards for the award of the first degree already promulgated by the UGC.

   It is difficult to say whether this particular condition, which was laid down in the regulations, was faithfully implemented. If there was a follow up, it may be assumed that every college recognised by the UGC was following these guidelines. In that case, how did some of the discrepancies in the working of the affiliated colleges continue the prevail? As usual, the word was taken for the deed and the matter was left at that.

3. Without going into details, the important thing to note is that most of the headings under which the requirements are enumerated deal with issues like land, endowment fund, civic facilities, student hostel, staff quarters for teachers, library and laboratory equipment and things like that. There is hardly any discussion of those requirements which were identified by the University of Kerala while discussing the issues of postgraduate education as quoted above. In other words, the focus was on facilities and not on teaching or the quality of the staff.
4. Neither in the earlier document nor in this one was the importance of research brought out. At the university level, teaching and research generally went together. In the case of colleges, lecturing in the classroom was taken to be an adequate enough performance of the job in hand. The difference of approach in both cases underlines the point that is being made. At the

university level, either facilities for research had already been created or a case for doing so could be made. In the case of college, research was regarded as additional. This was not true of every postgraduate college. About 50-60 of them did manage to create research facilities as also the research atmosphere. Maybe, this number is understated. By and large, the link between teaching and research hardly existed in the colleges.

This about sums up the neglect from which postgraduate education has suffered at the hands of the UGC in the past decades.

V

The foregoing arguments suggest two points. The first one is that while postgraduate education is a real problem, the UGC has so far done precious little about it. Once in a while, it takes up some part of the problem, makes some observations and leaves it at that. As a result of the policy of drift, a situation has now arisen where two-thirds of students enrolled at the postgraduate level are enrolled in colleges. The colleges have poor facilities, unsatisfactory teaching staff and the overall situation is that those who instruct are not always up to the mark with the result that those who complete degrees year after year are not up to the mark.

Second, there is a problem here. There is no yardstick in terms of which one can measure satisfactory or unsatisfactory performance. Even if the students were not as well trained as they are today, they were still able to get their Master's degrees. Standards are notoriously difficult to define and this is a point which should not be overlooked. One minor suggestion was made earlier in regard to how to measure the performance of students. It was suggested that if someone who had completed his Master's course found it difficult to write his Ph.D. thesis, there was certainly something lacking in the training that he had been given. It cannot be said that this is a conclusive test. In any case, as noted elsewhere, in this book, even the Ph.D. degree in India is getting diluted.

Perhaps a more relevant thing to do would be to look at the calibre of the teachers who instruct the students. The only quantifiable way in which this little fact can be measured is the number and quality of their publications which teachers instructing at the Master's level are able to publish. Some kind of comparison with those working in university departments might also help. Then there would also be the additional problem of the quality of those journals where they publish and whether they went by the opinion of those to whom the articles were referred. The situation in regard to academic journals in India is so dismal that to pursue this issue any further should not be necessary.

Whatever the yardstick, there should be little doubt of the fact that the kind of teaching imparted at the Master's level in most colleges is far from satisfactory. And this is happening in a situation when, in more than 150 affiliating universities, each university has a reasonably well staffed department in most of the important branches of learning. In other words, we have created excess capacity and there are not enough students to avail of it.

Why is this happening? The problem is much too complex to admit of a simple answer. One element in the situation needs to be recognised. There is an insatiable desire amongst teachers to be known for their ability to instruct at the higher level of instruction. It boosts their ego. The whole thing is linked with the wider phenomenon where the concern for quality is minimal and the desire for recognition is enormous. This is a problem which has been around for a long time. Expansion has been taking place without any genuine concern for the maintenance of standards. And since standards are difficult to define, quite a large number of sub-standard colleges have taken advantage of this fact.

The job of the UGC is to coordinate and determine standards. In respect of postgraduate education, the UGC has so far not been able to evolve a set of guidelines which, if applied consistently, would lead to the maintenance of standards. Worse than that, the UGC has not defined standards even in respect of undergraduate education as precisely as could have been done. No wonder the number of colleges has been multiplying and now it has become difficult to even keep track of them. With so many of them also doing postgraduate education as the data quoted earlier shows, it only points to the fact that the UGC has simply been neglecting its job.

The minimum that could have been done should have been to regulate standards at the Master's level. As already stated, any one who does the Master's degree becomes qualified to instruct at a college. To have permitted relatively undertrained students to complete their Master's course and entitle them to become teachers in a college has led to a situation where the phenomenon, instead of being controlled, is getting out of hand.

VI

The minimum, therefore, that the UGC ought to have done was that it should have worked out procedures which, clearly and concisely, defined the terms and conditions which were to be applicable at the postgraduate level. One thing can be done right away.

Most of these colleges which run postgraduate classes are located in middle level towns. If there is more than one postgraduate college in the same town, one thing that can be done right away is to pool their academic resources. If they are imparting education in the same subject, some papers can be taught in one college and some in another one. In simple words, students can be asked to go to one college on certain days and receive instruction in some papers of the course. The same process can be repeated in the case of the second college. If there is a third or a fourth college, they can also be drawn into the network. By pooling to-gether the resource of different colleges, it would be possible to strengthen the teaching talent available for the purpose.

The second thing that can be done, and to some extent is being done, is to insist upon the teachers at this level to undergo systematic and repeated in-service training according to a plan which can be worked out in advance. Here again, teachers who are engaged for training should be of a high calibre and collected from far and near so that the trainees get to know much more about their own area of interest than would be possible otherwise.

The third thing to ensure would be that, in course of time, no one other than one who holds a doctoral degree is allowed to take part in postgraduate teaching. At first, there may be certain old and experienced hands whom it might be difficult to exclude and whose claim for continuance could be fairly strong. Therefore, a plan of action must be worked out, for about five years so that the change over can be effected slowly and systematically.

Fourth, the pooling of library and laboratory facilities is something that can be attended to. The UGC should insist upon it and also support it. Appropriate rules may be framed for the purpose and the universities can be asked to insist upon their observance.

If some of these things can be done within the next three to four years, the situation will get rationalised to some extent. And that would be the time to move to the next stage which would be really decisive. The UGC should lay down that only autonomous colleges should have the right to undertake postgraduate teaching. Today in states like UP and Tamil Nadu, the percentage of colleges handling postgraduate teaching is higher than the all-India average. While 20–30 per cent of the problem would be taken care of by taking the few steps suggested above, the heart of the matter would lie in whether the UGC can insist upon only the autonomous colleges alone undertaking this job.

This would not be so difficult to enforce as some people would be inclined to think. Most of the colleges which are autonomous today are doing postgraduate teaching in any case. Furthermore, several of them are good enough to be declared autonomous but there are all kinds of indefensible reasons why this process is being sabotaged. By insisting only upon autonomous colleges handling postgraduate work, that process will get expedited. And that is precisely what is required.

Having said this, the end of the matter cannot be said to be at hand. In a few odd cases, some of the colleges would be doing better than even the university-run departments. Instead of going by the label, the right thing to do would be to compare the situation in such cases and work out a solution so that by the end of it, no one is red in the face.

Two things have to be ensured. One, the system of postgraduate education has to contract to some extent. How this is done is a matter of detail. As of this moment, the scarce teaching resources are being spread out much too thinly. The highest priority, therefore, needs is to be given to reducing the size of the system. This would indirectly amount to a concentration of the limited teaching talent available.

I know about a couple of subjects but am not qualified to speak about all subjects. Indeed no one is. But most of us who have spent a whole life time in education do acquire a sense about these matters. Take a subject like economics about which I know something. There are not even 20–30 universities/colleges in India which are instructing at a level which would be internationally acceptable. And yet if the number of university departments and postgraduate colleges teaching economics were to be totalled up, it would come to a minimum of several hundreds. What is true of economics is equally true of a large number of other subjects.

In a certain state, a calculation was carried out which showed that, even if scholarships were given to some of the more promising candidates to move to bigger centres, it would work out to be cheaper than to engage substandard teachers in a large number of institutions and dilute the quality in a number of places. In plain language, those who have the requisite potential alone should be encouraged to join the course. To enrol all those who wish to join or can afford to join would be a perverse way of looking at things. The two basic things to ensure are that admission is regulated in such a way that capable students are not left out and are even financially helped, if necessary, and that the quality of teaching is not compromised. That these two things are not being done is precisely the mistake we have been making over the years. The sooner we can change the system and regulate it in the manner suggested, the better it would be.

VII

The thrust of this analysis points to two courses of action. One is that stand-ards at the postgraduate level are unsatisfactory and have been so throughout the last half-century. This should be accepted. Second, perhaps most people will accept this analysis but are not likely to agree with the solution suggested.

To suggest that some of the postgraduate colleges be asked to partially wind down their operations is to ask for the impossible, almost. Education is expanding. To seek to contract it in any way is to go against the prevalent trends. Therefore, this proposal is likely to be opposed not only by those colleges which would be directly affected but by quite some other quarters.

The only answer that can be given to these misgivings is that without contracting the system to some extent at the initial stage of the proposed plan of action, it will not be possible to improve standards. Since the existing system has been at work for over half a century and the pressure to expand was unremitting, expansion continued to take place without stop. No one, however, either raised the issue or went into the question of how and where to find the requisite number of competent teachers at the postgraduate level.

There is also a related question. The suggestion made here is that it is either the university departments which should handle postgraduate teaching or this should be done by autonomous colleges. All other colleges should be asked step by step to discontinue postgraduate teaching. This is easier said than done. The fact of the matter is that expansion at the postgraduate level during this last half century has been so much a part of the curve of normal growth that, instead of the colleges shedding postgraduate teaching, the numbers doubled from one-third to two-thirds. In terms of proportions, this was not right.

What is really disqueting however are the exact numbers. In 1950–51, 6,872 students were enrolled in colleges. By 2000–01, the number had risen to 512,902. In terms of sheer numbers therefore, the increase is about half a million. By any standards of reckoning, this is a formidable figure.

Somebody can turn around and say that if the percentage of those doing the Master's degree is not even 10 per cent of the total enrolment, this figure is low in any case. Therefore this figure should be doubled very soon, if not raised higher than that. It would be difficult to refute this argument. The Indian economy is expanding and most of the people who pass out with a Master's degree manage to find a job. There is hardly any data available regarding unemployment at this level though, as we all know, it does exist to some extent. At the same time, a number of new professions have emerged and quite a few of them require people who have done a Master's course.

This creates a situation which is in the nature of a double bind. On the one hand, we need to increase the number of people who are doing Master's degrees. On the other hand, a substantial number of them are seriously undertrained. To certify them as having done their Master's course also raises questions in regard to the mode of testing being followed today. Were a more scientific mode of testing to be followed, a large number of them would not pass. Therefore the issue is much more complex than it appears to be.

Even on further reflection and while taking into account the difficulties involved in restructuring the system, it is not possible to get away from the fact that what is happening today is plainly unsatisfactory. In addition, something like 10–12 per cent of these who pass out at the Master's level come through the channel of correspondence courses. The situation there is far from satisfactory. The problem of instruction at the postgraduate level is thus a real one and has to be seen from different points of view.

What has been suggested above is a move in what I consider as the right direction. But if someone can come up with an alternative formula which makes fewer commitments on the plane of restructuring as proposed, such a proposition may also be considered seriously.

The problem can be viewed from one more angle also. If we look at the existing structure of undergraduate education, one thing becomes apparent. In quite a few cases, a part of what is done at the undergraduate level should have been done at the school level. In certain cases, there is very poor coordination between school boards and the universities. Instances have come to notice where, at the undergraduate level, students are to some extent made to go over the same ground which they have already covered in school. This is a signal example of the lack of coordination.

In sum, therefore, various dimensions of the problem have to be taken into account. There are, amongst others, problems of academic standards, modes of testing, availability of the right kind of teachers, geographical distribution, training the right kind of students at the undergraduate level and the issue of their admission into the Master's course and so on. These and several others, will have to be taken into account. Above all, to seek to contract the system, at least to begin with, is not going to be easy. The fact of the matter is that none of these issues have been discussed or debated in recent years.

And yet, things have to change. Unless that is done, in another few years, the existing trend of a performing and a non-performing sector of education will become more or less irreversible. That would be a tragedy. Indeed it can also lead to other adverse consequences, both on the social and political plane.

VIII

Given this complex situation, what is it that should be done? In my judgement, the following steps need to be taken:

1. An overall view should be taken and an alternative system of postgraduate education be evolved. In the first round, what must be done during the first five years should be thrashed out. Certain suggestions have been made. With a little give and take, quite a few of those suggestions can be implemented. For instance, networking of colleges in some of those towns which have more than one college doing postgraduate work should not be difficult to arrange.
2. It is the second step which will be more difficult to take. To adopt the approach that in future only autonomous colleges will undertake postgraduate work would be strongly resisted. There are two ways of overcoming this resistance. One is to identify colleges which can be given the autonomous status. If all that they need is a little push, there should be no problem.
3. The second thing to recognise is that this push cannot be given by the UGC, except marginally. The UGC will have to convert

the state governments to this point of view. Almost all colleges are controlled by state governments and the concerned universities. Converting the universities to this point of view would be relatively easy. But getting the state governments to agree to this line of approach would be much more difficult. One reason for that is that it would be difficult to identify those people at the state level who have to be brought round to this point of view. The education minister might agree but then he might be replaced before the decision has been fully implemented. The same can apply to the secretaries of education in the states. They too are subject to frequent transfers.

4. This means that, without brining about a wider change of thinking, it would be difficult to bring about any change. To deal with only a few easily identifiable officials or political bosses would not be enough; there would have to be much wider involvement of all those concerned. The principal opposition will come from two sources. One would be teacher leadership and the second would the colleges which would be affected. Beyond suggesting this line of action, it is not possible to go into further details here. The plain fact is that in a situation where one group of people agree, and when they are replaced by another group, the process is reversed and would lead to confusion and worse. Therefore some kind of an academic battle would have to be fought.

5. Before such a battle is fought, there must be some kind of a unified approach as far as the UGC and the academic community are concerned. In my opinion, a working paper should be prepared and should be circulated to the universities and discussed by the vice chancellors, both at the university level and the academic community level. The Association of Indian Universities (AIU) too should be involved and so should be some of the other professional councils in case they wish to be involved. Difficulties will not arise in regard to professional courses. In the case of law, the problem has more or less been solved. The real difficulties will arise in the case of arts, science and the social sciences. Even commerce faculty will not present too much of a problem. It is already somewhat professionalised. In any case, business administration is a category by itself and needs to be handled by the AICTE. The real problem will arise in the other three faculties and this fact will have to be faced.

6. This much should be clear that without an initial contraction of the system and the two other related reforms, the situation would not change. One would be a more rigorous mode of selection and the retraining of teachers and the involvement of a larger number of people who have done their doctoral work among others. The second step that would need to be taken will be in respect of the manner in which students are examined. About 10 per cent of the universities are already on the semester model. The rest of them can be pushed in that direction over a period of time. It is equally important to recognise that the style of setting question papers will have to be radically changed. This in turn will also oblige the teachers to change their style of teaching and their own mode of setting the question papers.

7. In this connection, it may not be out of place to refer to an experiment which the NCERT undertook successfully over three decades ago. Under the advice of Prof. Bloom of Chicago University, the NCERT started training teachers in the art of setting different types of question papers. In about a year's time, around 500 persons were trained. It was felt that this number was insufficient to make a lasting impact. These very people who had been trained in the first round then spread out to the various states and trained another 3,000 teachers. The whole job was done so thoroughly and scientifically that, as of today, question paper setting at the school level is distinctly superior to and much more scientific than what happens at the university level.

8. Here a distinction needs to be drawn between undergraduate and postgraduate teaching. The job of doing something innovative at the undergraduate level can be made to wait. For 50 years, the UGC has not attended to it except casually and that too in fits and starts. But if the job is undertaken in respect of only the postgraduate students, it can be pushed through within two or three years, partly through the mechanism of the existing Academic Staff Colleges and partly through a new supplementary mechanism which can be devised for this purpose.

   In other words, were the UGC to take the decision that, for the next three to four years, it would not do much about undergraduate education and concentrate on postgraduate education, the results may be positive. The numbers at this level are small and might become even smaller if what has been proposed is acted upon. Meanwhile, the new methodology would have to be spread fairly widely. If that happens, things would start changing. This proposition is feasible.

9. Another related point might also be referred to. At the undergraduate level, the Honours system resembling what Calcutta and Delhi are doing, can be encouraged and promoted on a much larger scale. While at one time, Master's teaching was done in Presidency College, Calcutta, it had to be discontinued. Instead, what was done at the college level was to concentrate upon intensive teaching at the Honours level. Persons like Amartya Sen are products of that system. If the Honours programme can be disseminated more widely and strengthened further, students who come to the Master's level would have already, to some extent, done what they do now at the Master's level. Therefore, standards of performance even at the Master's level would *ipso facto* improve.

10. A certain amount of coordination with school boards will have to be ensured. What exists today—so far it is purely informal— is plainly unsatisfactory. This is important from another angle also. If more students have to be inducted into the Honours stream, it would be advisable to prepare them better at the school level. The Ministry of HRD has at no stage paid any serious or systematic attention to this problem. It is time that something of this kind were done.

11. Once the normal qualification for admission to the Master's course becomes a good pass at the Honours level, this would lead to a qualitative change in the situation. To elaborate it any further should not be necessary.

12. More than anything else, if the UGC is to mastermind this innovation, it must work out a coherent and well organised approach to the problem. Carrying the state governments along with it is almost a pre-condition. So is the commitment as also the involvement of the Ministry of HRD. If the state governments find that the ministry too is backing the proposal strongly, they too will come aboard readily with a certain assurance of consistency. It goes without saying that once postgraduate education is by implication detached from undergraduate education, other innovations like review of the free structure at the postgraduate level, a scheme of financial support to bright but poor students and several other things would follow.

NOTES

1. It is time somebody who knows Bengali wrote a detailed study of this man who changed the academic landscape so markedly. A good deal of the controversy between the university and the colleges was carried on in Bengali periodicals and hence the reference to Bengali sources.
2. Extract taken from UGC minutes.

VIII

The University Grants Commission and the Ph.D. Degree

The Ph.D. degree awarded by Indian universities is the only degree which is accepted at face value by universities in other countries. But if things keep deteriorating as they are doing, within the next few years, the situation may start changing. Such a scenario cannot be ruled out. Equally important, preventive steps have to be taken right away so that this scenario does not turn into an actual fact.

Two things need to be said in regard to the issue raised above. One is about the other university degrees. Whether a student gets a Bachelor's degree or a Master's degree, anyone going to another country has to face the problem that, in more cases than should happen, the foreign universities raise all kinds of questions about the academic attainment of students who have passed out from Indian universities. This fact was recognised as long ago as 1966 when the Kothari Commission reported. Since then, the situation has been declining rather than improving.

It has been declining for two reasons. In the first place, even till the mid-sixties, we in India had not taken all those crucial steps which had to be taken in order to safeguard the 'chastity' of Indian degrees. To take one example, the language policy as followed till 1947 obliged every Indian student to first learn his own language and then English. In doing so, he had to repeat certain things in English even though he had learnt them in his own language earlier. This was noted by Gandhi in his criticism of the educational policy of which he too had been a victim.

Only a small percentage of students opted to join college. To be able to do that, they invariably had to acquire the requisite knowledge of English. During those early years, soon after 1947, a change could have been engineered had the academics in position switched to their respective Indian languages, written books in those languages and indigenised the system followed at that time. In countries like Iran, the entire Middle East, Korea, Japan and several others, this was precisely what was done. In these countries, English is taught but as a second language.

In India the changeover did not take place even after 1947. This happened partly owing to lack of assertion by the political decision makers as also the somewhat ambiguous and undefined situation in the country. Instead of switching over to our own languages, more and more students started learning English in a more systematic way. Not only that, more and more schools which used English as the medium of instruction were established. By the time the Kothari Commission was appointed, this trend had caught on to some extent. But the situation even a quarter of a century after 1947 was so ambivalent that when the Kothari Commission decidedly opted for our own languages, this was not regarded as an act of imposition.

That the recommendations of the Kothari Commission were not implemented during the next few years is widely acknowledged and it should not be necessary to dilate on the issue. Meanwhile, what had earlier started happening—the increasing popularity of English medium schools—picked up further momentum. By the time the policy on education was reviewed in 1985–86, this issue was sidestepped and hardly anyone discussed it any further. It was virtually accepted without question that the medium of education at the college and university level would be English.

This long digression has looked indirectly at one academic consequence of the language policy. Every Indian student who has been educated through the medium of the English language has to spend an additional two to three years to acquire some reasonable knowledge of English. An important difference between an 18-year old student in an English-speaking country and India is that the former spends that time learning more and more about other subjects whereas in our country a student does not have that option. He has to learn how to operate in English and that sets him back by a couple of years.

This was one reason why standards of performance at the college level lagged behind those which were to be encountered in countries where the medium of education has always been English. In our country, those who come through the English medium schools have a distinct advantage over the rest as far as performance at this level is concerned. That they lose something in the bargain in the understanding of their own country is also a fact of life but it need not be discussed here.

It should not be necessary to say more about this issue. The comparative disadvantage in the knowledge of English from which our students suffer at the college level and this is the second relevant factor, the lack of awareness about the need for high academic standards combines to create a situation where an average Indian student was not as competent as another student who had been educated through the medium of English. Both these factors work in conjunction with each other and put the average Indian student behind his counterpart in other countries.

Of the non-English speaking territories which have opted for English as the medium of instruction, there are two islands, Hong Kong and Singapore, which have gone the whole hog. In every other country including those referred to above, the medium of instruction is the mother tongue of the child. The child learns English in addition to his knowledge of his mother tongue. Since he learns it somewhat later in life, he is instructed in such a way that he virtually makes up for the deficiency.

The experience of Hong Kong and Singapore goes to reinforce this point. But to apply that precedent to India was not possible. The number of people who are involved is so large here that what could be done in two small islands cannot be repeated in India. To put it plainly therefore, an Indian student is likely to remain at a disadvantage because of the language handicap.

Without going further into this problem, attention needs to be drawn to something which has been discussed in the chapter entitled 'Postgraduate Education' (see Chapter VII). A favourable reference has been made in it to the experience of universities like Calcutta and Delhi which at the college level adopted what is called the 'streaming' system. One stream of students opts for the Honours course and another for the Pass course which was less demanding. Those students who could take greater pressure opted for the former while the others opted for the latter.

This system of streaming more or less brought the Honours student to the same level of performance as a student of his age in an English-speaking country. When these students therefore went on to the Master's course, they were virtually abreast of what was happening in other countries except for one odd fact which held back the performance of our students at the Master's level. Had the UGC taken better care of the standards of performance at the Master's level, the handicap which a large number of students still have to live with would have been compensated for by now.

It should not be necessary to go on with this line of argument except to come back to the starting point which was that while those who have done the Bachelors or the Master's degree are generally marked down when compared with their counterparts in other English-speaking countries to which Indian students generally go this need not have happened. All that we had to do was to pay special attention to the Master's level courses. Since this issue has been discussed in detail in the article referred to above, it is time to pass on to a more detailed discussion of how the Ph.D. degree is awarded.

II

Odd it might sound, during the 50 years of its existence, the UGC has not at any stage applied its mind to the issue of how and in what manner the Ph.D. degree is to be handled. On a couple of occasions, there have been some limited moves and that is about all. The award of a Ph.D. degree was never considered an important enough academic issue where the different stages of work had to examined, in some detail.

Without going into the matter further, there are several issues which need to be precisely defined. For instance, how is a research student to be registered? Some kind of procedure has to be followed. Every university follows its own procedure though, to be sure, there is a broad degree of agreement among the practices evolved and followed by most of them. Similarly, there are issues regarding the range and quality of supervision by the research supervisor, the successive drafts which may be submitted to the supervisor and the comments made and so on.

The more crucial question is: when the thesis is ready for submission, how are the examiners to be appointed? How long should they take to report on the thesis? How is duplication of work to be avoided? How does one ensure that the topic covered has not already been covered and that something new is being investigated or analysed. There are scores of issues which have to be both enumerated and defined.

As already stated, almost each established university has by now evolved a format which is by and large followed. That the format need not be exactly identical is readily accepted. At the same time there should be a certain broad correspondence between what is done in one university and in another. There are also variations of approach as between the sciences and the humanities. To say no more about it, the UGC would do well to appoint a committee of dependable and experienced researchers and work out a system whereby, in regard to basics, there is no disagreement and yet there is room for variations.

When the 1973 scales were introduced in 1975, one of the recommendations made was that every new entrant should have a Ph.D. degree. This was such a break with the existing system that there was a good deal of criticism of what had been proposed. While the rest of the decade was taken up by each state almost forcing a confrontation between its wage policy and the demands of the teachers, in quite some cases the appointments made with effect from 1975 onwards were, as far possible, in conformity with the new requirements laid down. In point of fact, more or less till the mid-eighties when the Mehrotra Committee proposed a new formula of promotion from one grade of lectureship to another, the situation remained somewhat confused.

It was confused for the reason that not enough Ph.Ds were available and yet people were to be appointed. Fortunately by the beginning of the seventies, the earlier high rate of expansion—13 to 14 per cent—had come down to around 5–6 per cent per year. The number of new appointments, therefore, came down. In this connection, it might be helpful to present the growth of doctoral degrees awarded during the period 1961–62 to 2000–01 (see Table 8.1). The data is taken from the UGC Annual Reports.

Table 8.1
Doctoral Degrees Awarded from 1961–62 to 2000–01

Year	Arts	Sc	Comm	Edu	Engg & Tech	Med	Agri	Vet Sc	Law	Others	Total
1961–62	314	401	15	9	20	14	41	–	1	–	815
1970–71	876	1,103	58	42	99	33	216	26	5	3	2,461
1981–82	2,347	2,846	173	178	190	66	471	93	14	26	6,404
1991–92	3,489	3,226	409	254	299	107	653	129	60	117	8,743
2000–01	4,398	3,727	621	399	778	221	889	110	105	296	11,534

It may be helpful to comment upon some of the figures. In 1970–71, the total number of Ph.D. degrees awarded was 2,461. By 1981–82, it had risen to 6,404. Ten years later, it had gone up to 8,743 and, another 10 years later, it had gone up to 11,534.

Another figure which has not been quoted above however may be quoted now. In 1970–71, the number of those who were awarded doctoral degrees in the faculty of arts was 876. By 1976–77, the number had gone up to 1,364 and by 1980 it had risen to 2,246. The same pattern can be observed in the sciences. To go on with further details about other faculties should not be necessary.

Another thing that needs to be noted is that the number of the Ph.D. degree holders in the faculty of commerce did not rise particularly high during the first 20 years. After that, commerce as a field of study became more popular and there was an increased demand for teachers. Therefore the number of those completing their Ph.D. degree began to rise. As a matter of fact, the number began to rise in every faculty except that, seen in the overall perspective, the figures both in engineering and technology and agriculture plus veterinary science continues to be on the low side.

In engineering and technology, from 20 doctorates in 1961–62, the number rose to 778 which is quite an increase. This steep increase and, considering the low base in the 1960–61, the progress made, both are impressive. But when it is measured against the booming number of engineering colleges (240 alone in Tamil Nadu), the rise should have been much higher. A large number of those persons who complete their Ph.D. either belong to the teaching faculty or opt for teaching later on. That is how it should be. There is one additional point to be noted in respect of one country i.e., Germany, where, even unlike USA, the practice followed is some kind of a model which, if taken over, can work wonders.

Hardly any engineer who passes out from an engineering college or university joins teaching. His first job is in industry. If he has a questioning mind, within a couple of years, he writes one or two papers on the basis of the actual problems that he had to solve and the way he solved them and gets them published in professional journals. In other words, most of what is published in German professional journals by these contributors is based on actual, live experience. In a few years, those who are academically inclined generally move to an engineering university where the experience of working in a factory stands them in good stead. Traffic between the German universities and industry is somewhat more widespread than is to be encountered in other countries. After these incidental details, which at best are inadequate, it should not come as a surprise to anyone that the quality of workmanship in German industry is uncommonly high compared to a large number of other countries.

It is some such model that we in India should aspire to evolve. But nothing of that kind is happening. Most engineering colleges (around 1,200 by now) engage teachers who have only completed their Bachelor's in engineering. Most engineers in India join either industry or teaching, mostly the former. Those who join industry more or less stay there and seldom switch over to teaching as they do in Germany. Later on those who opt for teaching, to repeat once more, seldom go to industry. In consequence, the bulk of those persons who do their Master's in engineering are, generally speaking, those who joined as lecturers in the beginning. In order to get the next higher scale of pay and other benefits they like to earn their M.Tech and so on. Several universities have provisions for part-time M.Tech courses also.

Who goes on for a Ph.D. in engineering or technology then? It is either teachers teaching in engineering colleges or some teachers in the IITs and the Regional Engineering Colleges, now raised to the level of to be deemed universities. In view of the extraordinary expansion that has taken place in the case of engineering, the number of Ph.Ds passing out every year is highly inadequate. It is time for the AICTE to pay special attention to this particular problem. While the neglect of the Master's degree is receiving some attention, the situation at the Ph.D. level is not.

A good deal has been said about Ph.D. in engineering for reasons already stated. No more need be said about it. When it comes to agriculture however, the situation is even more unsatisfactory. From 41 persons who obtained their Ph.D. in 1961-62, the number rose to 889 in 50 years. This was gratifying considering the fact that two-thirds of the Indian population is engaged in agriculture and agricultural research is, without question, one of the sorely neglected areas of research. Properly speaking, something like 10 times as many Ph.Ds in Agriculture should be produced every year. A good deal has been said about the Indian Council of Agricultural Research in the chapter on 'Other Professional Bodies' (Chapter II) and no more need be said except for two things.

The first is that agricultural research does not have the kind of glamour as a career which so many other professions have. Agriculture has remained neglected for a long time and continues to remain neglected. If one-third of Indian population lives below the poverty line, the main explanation for that situation is that our agriculture is not productive enough or to be more precise, as productive as it could have been and this is the second point that needs to be underlined.

In other words, an answer has to be found to two problems. One is to give a higher profile to agricultural research than obtains today. It is not possible to go into the details of what needs to be done. The need for doing so is overwhelming and the earlier we can move in this direction, and move decisively, the better it would be. The existing state of research in agricultural universities is also not at all flattering. What happens in research institutes in agriculture is equally unflattering. The fact of the matter is that unless there are radical advances in agricultural production which can generate a new atmosphere, agricultural research will not become an attractive option for those who have talent.

Coming to the issue of greater productivity, the problems here do not entirely relate to research as much as to what is called the dissemination of the results of that research, in other words, extension work. This a complex problem and does not fall within the purview of our discussion here. Poverty will be overcome only when the results of researches are disseminated more widely than is happening at present. This aspect of the problem is therefore a matter of considerable urgency.

A related issue might however be considered here. An increase in the number of Ph.D. holders in engineering and technology can also lead to a larger out flow of talent than what is happening today. As it is, brain drain from India is fairly high. If it is not higher, that is because the state of economy in the USA and some other countries cannot accommodate a higher inflow of highly trained people at that level. The only exception is the IT area. India has made a considerable impact in this newly emerging area and India-trained engineers are in great demand.

When it comes to agriculture, unlike engineering, its most direct impact will be on agricultural universities and the various other avenues of dissemination which exist or can be promoted in the years to come. A larger growth in the number of Ph.Ds in agriculture should therefore be doubly welcome.

A minor footnote to be added here is that if the number and quality of research in agriculture increases, it will also have an indirect impact on the teaching of agriculture at the school level. This is a totally neglected field. The complete absence of agricultural polytechnics is a pointer in that direction. Since it falls outside the purview of the discussion in hand, nothing more is being said as far as its impact on school education is concerned.

III

It was stated in the beginning that there is genuine risk of the Indian Ph.D. degree ceasing to be internationally acceptable at some future date. Is this a genuine apprehension or is it an alarmist position? It is difficult to give a decisive answer. The fact of the matter is that all kinds of abuses are creeping into the system. Unless these abuses are arrested in good time, the situation can become adverse.

The most important thing, apart from the formulation of a code of professional ethics which should govern the enrolment and award of the Ph.D. degree, the one obvious thing that needs to be done is that the award of the Ph.D. degree should not take as much time as it does now. There are instances where, after the submission of the thesis, the results have been delayed for as long as three years or even more than that! In one particular university with which I was connected at one time, I pointed out that in as prestigious a university—this one was out of those five which have been identified as having the potential for excellence—the Ph.D. degree should be generally awarded within three months. Under no circumstances should it take more than six months.

Not much notice was taken of my protest. Since I kept on repeating that point at successive meetings, the vice chancellor eventually asked the office to carry out a survey. It was found out that, in the preceding academic year, 180 theses had been submitted and the results of more than 100 of them had been delayed beyond one year. In the wake of this finding, the rules were partly revised. The situation has improved but not to the extent which it could have.

The explanation is simple. Those who undertake to guide research do not take this part of the job with the kind of seriousness which the issue deserves. Unless there is a change in the thinking of several thousand people who act as research guides and examines, the situation will not improve. The greater part of the delay takes place either in the university office or when the thesis is sent to the external examiner. Once, however, they know that the university expects the results to be expedited, they would respond accordingly. Today one or two universities insist upon it and the rest do not, though perhaps, not as determinedly as they should. In the code of rules and regulations which the UGC should work out, this matter should receive serious attention.

The second issue relates to a certain degree of avoidable manipulation. This takes place both at the time of the enrolment, the choice of the supervisor and all that follows later on. There is no full proof system which can be devised against abuses creeping in except that there should be sleepless anxiety on the part of the research committee about the progress reports which are received from time to time and occasionally reviewed. There should be a system whereby such reviews are undertaken systematically and any suggestion of manipulation should not only be frowned upon but severely punished.

As a matter of fact the proposed UGC committee should go into a detailed analysis of what is happening and what can happen, identify most of the pitfalls in advance and lay down automatic punishment in each case.

In case of any misconduct by an academic, punishment should not be anything less than removal from his job. Such things may not be happening in the government. But let us remember that universities are not the government. Universities are institutions where moral values have to be upheld and enforced without exception. If there is some degree of correspondence between what happens in civic life and in the government, one can understand. But there should be no correspondence whatsoever between what happens in the government and what happens in a university. A university is an institution where anything unethical is to be rejected, frowned upon and penalised. This distinction must be drawn clearly and categorically.

One vice chancellor told me the details of this little incident and it is worth retelling. It happened in one particular department in one of the Indian languages. Whenever the head was asked to suggest the names of suitable examiners, all that he did was to forward a few names, and that too from the nearby universities. The vice chancellor had become somewhat suspicious about what was happening. On one particular occasion, he asked for a different set of names. When one of those potential examiners was sent a letter, it was stated in response that the person concerned had yet to complete his Ph.D.! This is a clear case of academic misconduct and must be dealt with accordingly. Only such a response would take care of situations like the one referred to above.

There are many more such examples that can be quoted but it is not necessary to do so. Issues like how many candidates can a research supervisor handle at a time would be taken care of in the code itself and issues like those which call into question the ethical values of the supervisor have to be treated as indicated earlier.

All kinds of unexpected issues can arise. Not so long ago, there was a case of plagiarism in a university in which a head of department was involved. The vice chancellor too belonged to the same department and his name had also appeared as one of the co-authors. When the matter became public and was enquired into, every one including the vice chancellor had to go. The point which is being made is that there should not be the slightest impropriety in the award of a Ph.D. degree. This is the highest degree conferred by a university and its 'chastity' must be zealously and consistently protected.

IV

The UGC is in the process of working out a system in respect of the specification of degrees. It would be well advised to include the Ph.D. degree also in this exercise. A case for doing so has already been argued out as above. What is now required is to frame the rules and guidelines in the form of official regulations so that they become legally binding on the universities.

In this connection there is one particular suggestion which may be discussed, and if it is found acceptable, included in the code which is to be worked out.

The UGC should empower itself with the right to ask to see the text of any thesis in any faculty approved by a particular university. There is a whole procedure for the award of the Ph.D. degree, including its final approval by the Academic Council and the Executive Council. While the earlier stages for the award of the degree are covered by the rules that have been made and the right of the examiner to award the degree or to reject it or ask for resubmission remains unamended, the UGC should empower itself with a new provision. All these rights belong to the university which enrols a student but there is one right which the UGC can take for itself. The UGC must be able to ask to see any thesis which it may pick at random. While doing so complete office record giving details about the steps taken should also be summoned.

A system should be evolved whereby any thesis approved by a university is picked out for a second reading by an independent set of examiners. Two new experts may be consulted each time and they may be asked to re-assess the thesis. This re-assessment would have no legal validity. If the degree has already been awarded to a particular candidate, no one is going to even remotely suggest that the degree be withdrawn. In other words, everything at the university level should stay intact as it is.

But what the UGC should do is to send the opinion of those two examiners to the university for circulation amongst the members of the Research Committee which finally approved the award. In addition, intimation is given both to the Academic Council and the Executive Council by the university with an indication to the effect that the new opinion received from the UGC might also be seen. A copy of the fresh opinion may also be supplied to the candidate who got the degree.

In plain language, the degree has already been awarded and no one is reopening the issue. But a second opinion has been sought and that information is not made public. However it is circulated to those who had anything to do with the award of the degree i.e., the supervisor, the candidate, the Research Committee, the committee which considered the opinion of the examiners and so on. No one who had anything to do with the award of the degree should be left out, for the intention is to convey to them that in case the second opinion differs significantly from the earlier one, there should be some rethinking on their part in the matter.

Were such thing to be done, even in 10 cases per year selected on a random basis with the help of a computer or otherwise, within a couple of years everyone connected with the award of the Ph.D. degree would become alert and careful. Everyone would know that even when a degree has been awarded, the matter is not closed. If the second report is negative or something close to it, word would go around and that would be enough. After all the purpose is to put everyone on the guard. Indeed everyone should be made aware of the fact that the award of the Ph.D. degree is a matter which cannot be treated lightly. On the contrary, it must be treated with the utmost seriousness.

Looking around the country, and this is a case where one can be right as also wrong, there are 30–40 universities in the country which take extraordinary care in regard to each one of the theses submitted and examined. I base my assessment on the basis of conversations that I have had with several examiners. They are well known scholars in their respective fields and examine, an average, something like half a dozen theses per year. In the course of the conversations, they have told me about certain universities which maintain their earlier standards of vigilance, some which are beginning to compromise and others which have already done so.

Since my survey is confined more to the humanities than the sciences, it would be misleading to generalise beyond the figure already given. Both IITs and IIMs (they do not call it Ph.D.) are included in these 30–40 universities which are known for the care that they bestow on the award of the Ph.D degree. This implies that, outside the ranks of these two high profile institutions, there are not more than a score of universities which exercise the kind of care which they ought to exercise, as they had been doing till a few years ago.

It would be in order to say another thing. A good deal depends upon the kind of vice chancellor who heads the university. Almost every degree has to pass through his hands at some stage or the other. If he is demanding and careful, the message goes around and others become careful. If he is not demanding and tends to be casual, and the number of such people has been growing of late, the alarm bells should ring. He is the one person who handles the award of Ph.D. degree at some stage or the other and therefore it is he, more than anyone else, who should be held responsible for what happens.

Having mentioned one little incident which a vice chancellor told me, it may be in order to mention another one also. In this particular case, while the examiners had sent in their reports, the viva voce had yet to take place. The person who had been selected to do so was in Shimla and he could not find time to travel down to Delhi even for one day.

In this somewhat awkward situation, a compromise was worked out. The examiner had to go somewhere beyond Delhi. What he did was to travel by the night train and disembark at Subzi Mandi, a suburban railway station near Delhi, at a little past 5 AM. He was received by the supervisor and the candidate and taken to the university where a formal viva voce was conducted. This happened before 6 AM in the morning. A little later the examiner had to take the same train again from New Delhi. It would be difficult to recall another incident of similar time management anywhere in the world! To say anything more on this issue need not be necessary.

The point of recalling these two instances is that incidents like these are occurring every now and then. Either the UGC is unaware of them or so far it has not shown any inclination to take corrective action. In either case, it is deplorable. What needs to be done is to survey the whole field and work out a detailed code as suggested above. Perhaps this will be more effective if some of the recommendations made above are incorporated in the code. Possibly, this will be more true of the humanities than of the sciences. When it comes to the sciences, there is something additional that needs to be done.

V

Scientific research is different from research in the humanities in a variety of ways. Almost invariably, scientific research has to be done primarily in the laboratory, a record of the experiments made and the results obtained has to be kept. No one can say that faking cannot take place even in this situation. It does take place off and on and generally with the collusion of the supervisor. To say no more about it, safeguards have to be built into the system of supervision. While drawing up the code, these issues can be taken care of. Quite often the results of the various experiments done can be verified by anyone.

But there is an equally reliable system of verification which takes the form of publication in science journals. Here there is a problem. As far as the humanities are concerned, an entreprising publisher brings out something like 15–16 research journals and each one of them is internationally comparable. In the case of science journals, the situation was better a few decades ago. During the last few decades, it has undergone a marked deterioration. Very few science journals published in India are internationally comparable.

There is a good explanation for it. Publication of a science journal requires careful planning and equally careful execution of those plans. Foreign universities sometimes on their own and sometimes with the assistance of professional publishers bring out hundreds of journals and each one of them conforms to the requirements of what a good professional journal should be. In subjects like chemistry, to take up one example, there are hundreds of journals and several of them deal with those sub-branches of chemistry where also the number of journals published is large and there is acute competition for attention among them.

To put it another way, to bring out a journal requires alertness, commitment, resources and professionalism of international standards. Our universities are unable to match these demands. Therefore our science and engineering students cannot publish in professional journals as foreign students do. In their case what is being done in the laboratory and what is being submitted for purpose of the Ph.D. award is already public knowledge or will become public shortly. The scope for manipulation is therefore significantly minimised.

This does not happen in our country. In the case of the sciences, therefore, it is a matter of vital importance that there is close consultation among the various science funding ministries of the union government and the UGC and a plan is drawn up whereby a certain number of science journals are brought out. To say that the UGC has completely neglected this dimension of its work would not be an exaggeration.

Not being a science man myself, I find it difficult to be more specific than that. I am however told by some knowledgeable people that, were a detailed survey to be carried out, it would be possible to bring out something like 50 science journals right away. Each one of them can be up to international standards. Another year and another 50 can be added. After that, the progress would be slow, even halting. The international competition is so intense that it would be difficult to bring out a large number of internationally comparable professional journals. Apart from everything else the output of suitable articles for publication may not be adequate enough.

It should not be necessary to pursue this matter any further. This is a scheme which can be discussed in fuller detail. As a compromise, one can even suggest that, if internationally comparable journals cannot be brought out in larger numbers, the minimum that can be done is to bring out some journals which follow the practice of getting the articles refereed and not do a shabby job. In other words, these journals should be respected at least within the country. If they can win acceptance even outside, that would be welcome. But the minimum that they should do is to win acceptance within the country.

While most Korean science researchers are opting to publish in the international research journals, the same cannot be said about the Chinese. It is difficult to find out precisely what they are doing but it is not difficult to anticipate that something of the kind suggested above is either being done or would get done in the near future. The one point that needs to be underlined is that anything which is regarded as fit enough for the award of a Ph.D. degree should also be good enough for publication, at least nationally, if not internationally.

IX

REVITALISING THE UNIVERSITY GRANTS COMMISSION*

The founding fathers of the Indian Constitution assigned the responsibility of maintaining standards in higher education to the central government. To work for the fulfilment of this task, the University Grants Commission (UGC) was established in December 1953, initially by executive action, which was reinforced by an Act of the Parliament a couple of years later. After 40 years of its being in operation, a rigorous and full-scale evaluation of the UGC's performance needs to be undertaken. This should cover its role, structure, style of functioning, reputation and its strengths and weaknesses in the context of its constitutional responsibilities, the functions assigned by the Act, and the policies laid down by the government from time to time.

The UGC Act of 1956 laid down, *inter alia*, that the Commission would 'take, in consultation with universities and other bodies concerned, all steps as it may think fit for the promotion and coordination of university education and for the determination and maintenance of standards of teaching, examination and research in universities ...'. To enable the UGC

---

*Originally published in the *Journal of Higher Education*, 16(2), Spring 1993.

to play this role, the Act authorised it to look into the financial needs of universities and allocate and disburse funds on the basis of careful consideration of the needs of each of the universities. It was also authorised to establish and maintain institutions for providing common facilities, services and programmes for all or some of the universities, and to offer advice to concerned central or state authorities regarding institutional development. In addition, the UGC was also expected to collect and disseminate relevant information relating to university education in India and other countries, and obtain data from individual universities concerning their financial position, the credibility and quality of teaching and examinations, as well as the academic viability of various faculties.

The UGC was also enjoined, by an amendment to the Act in 1984, to ensure that no candidate would secure admission to a course of study by reason of economic power, thereby preventing a more meritorious candidate from securing admission to such a course. It was also required to see whether particular programmes of study would equip students for the responsibilities of their profession and also take steps to prevent direct or indirect levy or acceptance of additional fees or donations and, for this purpose, authorised it to disaffiliate any college or to prevent the continuance of any course of study characterised by such malpractices.

MANAGERIAL SET-UP

In this analysis, it is proposed to look at the UGC as a managerial set-up. In this context, it is necessary to state that, over the years, in fact almost since its inception, the image of the UGC has been going down from year to year. This has happened partly because of external factors and shortage of funds, but to a considerable extent also because of the increasing routinisation of its functioning. This is largely due to concentrating attention mainly on the sanction of grants in respect of proposals received from various institutions. It is now regarded, by and large, as an ineffectual body which has failed not only to generate viable ideas pertaining to policies but which has, by sheer inertia, also gone on expanding in a convoluted manner largely by inbreeding. Later, in this analysis, we shall go into details about the UGC administration.

More specifically, it is proposed to look into the performance status of four aspects of its functioning mentioned below:

1. The failure of the centre and the states, to coordinate with each other.
2. The strategy of development followed over the years because of which a large number of students, irrespective of their aptitudes or the prospects in the employment market, tend to look at college education as a necessary continuation of school education.
3. The policies followed in respect of structure and composition of the UGC and the manner in which its secretariat has managed to survive with such gross inefficiency compounded maybe with a modicum of corruption.
4. The level of financial support from the government and the distortions which characterise the mode and terms of allocations.

STANDARDS

As is well-known, the Constitution has conferred upon the centre overriding powers to coordinate and determine standards in higher and professional education. However, what constitutes standards has not been defined anywhere. In the Supreme Court judgement in the early sixties, in regard to the exclusive use of Gujarati in Gujarat University, it was laid down specifically that standards had to be interpreted in a broad and flexible manner. In its opinion, the medium of education at the higher level was a crucial component of what constitutes standards. This is the law of the land as of today. Even though education was made a concurrent subject in 1976, no follow-up legislation has been undertaken so as to clarify many areas of uncertainty and overlap of roles and responsibilities. The situation, therefore, has continued to be what it was before.

In pursuance of Entry 66 of the Schedule VII, in 1951, the centre proposed the setting up of a Central Council for Universities with far reaching powers, including the power to regulate the establishment of new universities and to derecognise degrees (for which also provisions were laid down).

When the Bill was circulated, the universities protested against powers being vested in a central body to decide the fate of those universities which had also been established as statutory bodies. Because of the vehemence of the protest both from universities and states, when the Bill was eventually enacted in 1956, it was a highly diluted version of what had been proposed originally. Gone was the power to regulate the establishment of universities along with the power to derecognise any degree. In addition to the continuation of an ineffective UGC, this course of events also sharpened the controversy about whether or not universities were autonomous in the absolute sense of the word. Or could it be argued that they were inherently subject to regulation by a coordinating body such as the Central Council?

The universities affirmed that they had been set up as autonomous bodies and, therefore, had the authority to function as they deemed best. It was argued that if they were not performing better, it was only because of inadequate funding. The centre's point of view, which got lost in the course of the controversy, was that if it had to carry out the mandate of the Constitution (to coordinate and determine standards), there would have to be some agency to coordinate the functioning of universities.

Even though the issues did not get resolved in 1956, the situation then could still be managed somehow; there were only three central universities at that time and the magnitude of funding was also rather limited. However, since then, the number of universities has increased and so has the funding, though not to the same extent. In 1991, after nearly four decades, the issue erupted again. A number of central universities, though each one of them is funded by the UGC, appeared to be acting arbitrarily in different ways. What was done in one university was either ignored or distorted in another. Even leave rules in respect of teaching and non-teaching staff were not identical. When these discrepancies and contradictions created problems, the UGC discovered that it had no regulatory powers to straighten out administrative anomalies. When it tried to acquire those powers, there was resistance on the grounds of the autonomy of university.

Autonomy means the power to regulate things within the institution. Is there any doubt that Indian universities enjoy it in ample measure? It is difficult to recall an instance when a university administration was impeded by lack of powers. It is equally difficult to quote instances when universities were prevented from taking the requisite steps for lack of authority. The truth of the matter is that even though they had the requisite powers, in most cases, they did not opt to use them. Factional concerns and political considerations combined with narrowness of academic vision have combined to create a situation in which most universities are a mockery of what they should be. Actually, by itself, autonomy is neither a virtue nor a vice. It is a means towards the end of pursuing excellence.

In this context, it must be recalled that the controversy between the centre and the universities was resolved in 1953 by the innovative stratagem of re-christening the Central Council as the UGC. It was contended that the real problem facing the universities was lack of funding. This could be solved by merging the two bodies—a committee known as the UGC was already in existence, though not as a statutory body. By adding to it the functions of the Central Council, which was proposed to be set up as per the 1951 Bill, a way out was found. The primary function of the new body, notwithstanding its name, was to regulate standards and not to give funds. By combining the work of the two bodies into one, it was sought to allay the fears of the universities about the curtailment of their autonomy.

Some people, both within the government and outside, did express misgivings with regard to giving the new body (renamed as the UGC to match the acronym of the British UGC which was only a committee and not a statutory commission) the power to distribute funds. They thought that, as usual, this power to distribute largesse would militate against its basic task of regulating standards.

It is noteworthy that in Britain the UGC was responsible only for funding. The job of maintaining high academic standards was and is done by the universities themselves. That the British universities could do it successfully has been demonstrated over the years quite convincingly. Even in the sixties, when, following the Robbins report, the number of universities went up steeply, standards did not decline. Can we say the same about our universities? The answer is embarrassingly against the universities.

Apart from their poor performance on the academic plane, even the standard of ethical behaviour in the universities is no better than that operating in the marketplace. The great pity, however, is that even the UGC has succumbed to these pressures and fallen into the pattern set by universities. That is why it is difficult to return a categorical answer. Before this issue is pursued further, the problem formulated at under (2) above needs to be examined. What has caused failure on that front has contributed in a substantial measure to difficulties classified under (1) as enumerated in the last section.

Strategy of Development

Two things that stand out in respect of educational planning need to be specified here. One is the direction and thrust of Indian planning and the kind of economic system which has been established in India. The second is the impact it has had on priorities and policies pertaining to education. In terms of social and economic policies, the main thrust of development has been, more or less, the continuance of what had been happening right from the nineteenth century onwards. Instead of colonialism, we now have neo-colonialism.

Enclaves of urban progress (with all the injustice it signifies) have been growing while the countryside has been left more or less as it was. This is not to suggest that no changes have taken place in the countryside: the agrarian situation has undergone many notable changes. However, the net outcome has been the emergence and consolidation of the middle peasantry, and little more, in certain parts of the country. In Bihar, for instance, even this did not happen.

Even today, around 40 per cent of the Indian population is unable to get two square meals a day. Notwithstanding this, there has been a remarkable spurt in the educational sector. There is no need to quote figures to prove this point.

Whether we describe what happened as the impact of social forces or attribute it to the educational component of the strategy of development is a matter of detail. The pertinent fact is that in the sphere of education it led to several interrelated developments such as the consistent neglect of elementary education and the extraordinary growth of higher and professional education. Available data shows that the two phenomena have fed upon each other. That the fees at the higher and professional level remained stagnant all these years is further evidence of a mutually reinforcing process at work.

These two phenomena operating side by side were accentuated by certain shifts and changes within the educational structure. For instance, except in Assam and one or two other states, the duration of schooling was ten years. In the mid-fifties it was raised by one year. In the seventies it was raised by another year. Both these changes were somewhat unsettling. In fact, the school system had not adjusted fully to the first change-over when the second one was imposed. Today, throughout the country (except for UP) schooling covers a span of 12 years while college education (for graduation) takes three years. (The situation has changed since then.)

At one level, extending the duration of schooling by two years has led to a different mode of calculation. When around 1950, it was calculated that the number of students in colleges and universities was half a million, that calculation was based in respect of those who had completed their matriculation. Had the old system of calculation continued to be followed, the number of those enrolled at present in the tertiary sector would have come to 7 million or so instead of being reckoned at 4.5 million.

Whatever else may have been gained by juggling with the basis of calculations, extending the duration of secondary education by two years has not improved matters. Logically this should have reduced the rush for admission to colleges. This has not happened, however, because despite the two-year extension, school education has not won recognition as an adequate and appropriate stage for all but the few with special aptitudes for higher studies, to enter the world of work. Consequently, even after 12 years of education, as before, students continue to flock into colleges.

One can safely surmise that around half of those who are enrolled in the colleges are interested only in carrying on with 'studies' because they have nothing better to do. In plain words, colleges are teeming with students because the country has failed to generate enough jobs for those passing out from schools. Seeking admission into a college is thus a way of disguising unemployment. Availability of this relatively respectable outlet is regarded as preferable to open unemployment.

Instead of being a threat to the social order, students are kept perfunctorily engaged in a baby sitting kind of operation during their sojourn in colleges. In most other countries, including developing countries like Thailand and Indonesia, middle level jobs such as those of office clerks, bank accountants, receptionists, and telephone operators are given to school leavers. Nobody looks for a college graduate for routine work. Those studying in college are, on the other hand, trained seriously for jobs requiring a relatively higher level of competence and skills. In our country the general belief is that school level education over a span of 12 years does not prepare the pupils for middle level jobs. Moreover, why should anyone take them when graduates are available for the same scale of pay? All this confusion exists only because the system of education is not attuned to the job market.

Undergraduate Education

How does the UGC come into it? Had the UGC decided, as has been mooted off and on, that it would concern itself only with postgraduate education and research, and that it would have nothing to do with undergraduate education, it would not have been answerable for the various acts of omission and commission leading to the present situation. Except for Delhi, almost everywhere else, undergraduate education is handled by the states. They respond to the pressures exerted on them and if expansion is continuing unabated, the UGC is only indirectly responsible.

Unfortunately it cannot escape its share of responsibility today because it has, at no stage, clearly demarcated its role and functioning as distinct from those of the states. The fact that lack of coordination between the centre and the states is responsible for a good deal of the confusion that exists today makes it difficult for it to rebut the charge that it has been unable to perform its statutory function: to coordinate and determine standards.

Since 87 per cent of students are enrolled at the undergraduate level, it is their problems and their performance which looms large on the horizon. While there are good arguments against the centre divesting itself of the responsibility for undergraduate education, on balance, it would be easier to fix responsibility and enforce appropriate solutions were it to be decided that undergraduate education, like school education, would be dealt with primarily by the states.

We have already noted how undergraduate education is more a palliative than a seriously pursued stage of education. The UGC is really not in a position either to regulate the entry of students nor to exercise decisive influence on the content and processes of teaching. One could even describe the UGC as a victim of the decisions of others which impinge upon its working and performance. One thing is clear at any rate. The social and economic pressures being generated in the Indian society are of such an overwhelming character that the UGC would, in any case, be unable to cope with them.

The inability of the UGC to control or influence these developments is evident from various other related factors also. Even in fields like medicine and engineering, these pressures have been exerting an unsettling influence. While the situation there is not as unfavourable, it is not as favourable as it could have been. This is only a way of saying that it is not possible for any professional body, and the UGC is one (or at least ought to be one), to operate against the dominant social and economic trends moulding the country. Granting that the two cannot be delinked from each other, it must be recognised that the country's interests cannot be served by allowing populist considerations to overrule professional considerations in every instance. But this is precisely what has happened. The UGC's basic failure lies in not having been professional enough.

AFFILIATED COLLEGES

In order to be professional, the UGC has to fulfil at least two preconditions. First, it has to function more efficiently and take decisions on the basis of feedback obtained from an effective system of monitoring. This will be gone into a little later. Meanwhile, it may be noted that the other precondition relates to the UGC's interaction with the states.

Except for central universities—and till now, there are not even a dozen of these—others are state universities. While the agricultural universities are looked after by ICAR and the IITs and IIMs by the All-India Council of Technical Education, the rest of the system is looked after by the UGC. A little over two dozen institutions are deemed to be universities but, in the total scheme, their characteristics and requirements need not be discussed in an overview of the system.

What needs to be noted, however, is that the bulk of enrolment is in those 100 plus affiliating universities which undoubtedly are under the jurisdiction of the UGC. Roughly 90 per cent of the students are enrolled in these universities. The UGC especially under the present dispensation in which it has been as much responsible for undergraduate education as the states, has to answer for what is going on in the affiliated colleges. Putting it mildly, the UGC seems to have failed to exert any real influence on them.

Could the situation have been saved? There were only two ways. One was that, as suggested already, the UGC should have taken the position that undergraduate education was not a part of its obligation and it is the states which should look after it. The consequences of such a situation are difficult to visualise. Maybe, things would have been as they are today. The only advantage would have been that the UGC would not have had to answer awkward questions about the state of undergraduate education. Nonetheless the fallout of a rudderless undergraduate programme would still have confronted UGC at the postgraduate level where almost half the enrolment is in colleges.

Without dwelling upon what might have happened had the UGC succeeded in washing its hands of undergraduate education, it is obvious that the number at the postgraduate level could have been restricted to bring about qualitative improvements only with the backing of a strong political will. Realising that in the populist environment prevailing in the country, finding support for a proposal to free the UGC from the burden of undergraduate education would have been impossible, this line of action was not even put on the agenda.

It is debatable whether the UGC was justified in playing safe and not projecting a viewpoint merely because it might not find favour with the ultimate arbiters of policies. There is a general impression that the UGC has become ineffectual mainly because it always gives in to external pressures and has seldom taken a courageous stand on principles. At times it has worked against itself by giving in without a murmur to policies and proposals which would eventually weaken its position.

A Devalued Institution

The biggest weakness of the UGC over all these decades has been that it has been operating in a social and academic vacuum. While it has contributed positively in respect of many academic problems, it has often failed to grasp the realities on the ground. For instance, it failed to appreciate and take into account the fact that universities are subject to such pressures that they can seldom resist them.

After all, universities are not free agents. They are controlled by the state governments who appoint the vice chancellor and determine how long he stays in office, and who also constitute the principal university bodies, provide funds and take all the other decisions which are within their purview and some times, even those which are not within their purview.

The functioning of the state governments is determined not by the guidelines or advice of the UGC, but in response to the populist pressures exerted upon them. Every state government has to bow before these if they continue to be exerted unremittingly with the active support of influential sections of the public. This is inextricably connected with the kind of polity we have evolved in the country and with other factors such as the electoral system, the reluctance to decentralise, the regional, communal and caste pressures which play a decisive role in almost every matter.

These pressures could have been moderated (not eliminated, it ought to be added) if the UGC were functioning as a credible and decisive professional body and not as a devalued institution, drifting without resistance to the currents and cross-currents of contemporary forces. It is difficult to understand why the UGC did not lay down certain norms and unwaveringly insist upon adherence thereto.

Which agency, however, was to do the job of implementation? The UGC never set up a system of monitoring. Therefore, it has never been in a position to follow up cases of disregard of its directives. The fact that the UGC has been ineffective vis-à-vis even the central universities goes to show the extent of its decline and provides an idea of how, except in statutory matters, the state universities function without feeling accountable to the UGC.

One of the alternative courses of action would have been to keep interacting with the secretaries of the departments of education in the states. However, this would not have worked well either since secretaries are transferred so frequently that they seldom get the time even to understand, much less to improve, the working of universities. In any case, this avenue has never been explored.

Education secretaries of states and members of the UGC seldom take the trouble to get acquainted with one another. Even with the state ministers for education, the UGC has no real rapport, and it is difficult to decide who is to blame for this estrangement. Obviously the UGC will have to deliberate on how it could interact with the university authorities of the states to obtain the support necessary for the smooth and purposeful functioning of the system.

STATE COUNCILS OF HIGHER EDUCATION

It was in recognition of some of these problems that the 1986 Policy recommended the establishment of State Councils of Higher Education. These Councils were expected to function more or less as the counterparts of the UGC in the states. If nothing else, they would have been continuing bodies. Even if the chairman and members changed every few years, the body would have remained in existence and continued to function. Moreover, it was assumed quite reasonably that at least some of those nominated to these Councils would be professionals of some competence and credibility.

A third dimension too may be mentioned here. The Councils, as envisaged, were not to be limbs of the state governments. The secretary of the department of education would no doubt have been a member; but the decision making would have been guided by the chairman or the members of the Council. In other words the expectation was that replicating the central pattern of the management of higher education would have brought into existence at the state level an agency with which the UGC could have done business. Furthermore, it could also have identified and projected a certain group of people who, though not entirely free from all infirmities, would have been relatively free of them.

In this way, both the UGC and the State Councils would have worked, more or less, on the same wavelength. But even after more than half a decade, in most states, the Councils have not as yet been established.

The prevailing state of affairs inevitably raises the question as to why, in most states, the State Councils have not been established. There are two important reasons. One relates to the reluctance of the bureaucrats to part with power so that they can continue to control the universities the way they control other sectors of education. Once a State Council gets organised under different auspices, in the manner suggested, the department of education would no longer be in the driver's seat. Naturally, therefore, they have been less than enthusiastic about the setting up of these Councils.

Actually, even the state governments have been far from enthusiastic about them. Whatever might be said about the chief ministers, in a large number of cases, the quality of education ministers leaves a lot to be desired. More often than not, education is looked upon as an unimportant portfolio to be assigned to politicians on the fringes of the circle of power. That is why a legislator rarely takes the portfolio of education by choice.

It is natural that one should ponder over what, if anything, the UGC could be doing to rectify the situation. Of course, the UGC can do something but only if it gets the support of the government. One way of reinforcing the position of the chairman, UGC, would have been to project him as a person of consequence in the Central Advisory Board of Education (CABE). Otherwise, he could have been given the ex-officio status of at least a minister of state of the Government of India. After all, one chairman of the UGC was given the rank of a cabinet minister. If this were adopted as a general practice, he would be in a much better position to deal with the secretariats of the central and state ministries as well as the state ministers of education.

Even today, it is far from certain that State Councils would get established even in the course of the Eighth Five Year Plan without the active interest of the centre. CABE, at its 1992 meeting, did decide to make 1 crore of rupees available to a state setting up a State Council, in order to give this idea some impetus. But more than any financial inducement, what is called for is a powerful political push from the centre. Would that be forthcoming? One guess is as good as another.

This detailed discussion of the State Councils of Higher Education is meant to underline one simple point. The centre can be effective in respect of higher education only when and to the extent to which it has counterparts to work with, in each of the states. Without some such twinning, the UGC would remain seriously handicapped. The irony of it, however, is that till the 1986 Policy recommended the establishment of the State Councils, the UGC had not been able to identify its own basic weakness even in conceptual terms. In fact, it was so snowed under by conflicting pulls and pressures that it hardly had the inclination or the capability to think for itself.

By 1985, the UGC had been in existence for over three decades. How is it that except for stray remarks here and there, it never formulated an alternative plan? And it was left to the makers of the 1986 Policy to come up with this alternative. This has something to do with the kind and quality of persons who are put on the UGC.

RECORD OF PERFORMANCE

To talk of those who have held office in the UGC is to venture into uncertain territory. It is neither possible nor fair to discuss individuals. Not only can opinions differ; one can be genuinely wrong in one's assessment. However, it is possible to refer to a few objective facts and then link up the performance of those vested with the authority to determine and shape policies. Another reliable source of supporting evidence is the various Parliamentary bodies which have expressed informed and, on the whole, adverse opinion about the performance of the UGC.

Without going into the specifics or referring to individuals, the working of the UGC may be divided into a few identifiable phases connected more or less with the tenure of the various chairmen. In the first phase of two and a half years, the UGC had not been made a statutory body. It was not until the next phase that, for half a decade, it cut its teeth as a statutory body. Then there was spell of 12 years under one chairman, to be followed by one whose tenure was cut short on the ground of his having attained the age of 65. This was followed by three successive chairmen, each one of whom had a tenure of almost five years.

It is not intended to offer a chronological account of how the UGC has been functioning under the various chairmen. It is possible, however, to identify certain developments which may yield certain conclusions. Three of the more obvious trends that emerged over the years may be stated as follows:

1. Once the UGC was made a statutory body, it got off to a flying start. The universities were few, the funding was reasonably liberal, the pressures were not overwhelming and the leadership was strong and creative.

2. However, there was something unreal about the nature of the success achieved. Pressures had started building up, but had not yet assumed the form or dimension that they did in subsequent years. It was the misfortune of those who came later that they had to encounter a situation of unremitting pressures. Notwithstanding this, one cannot get away from the feeling that the UGC's response to the pressures was passive rather than active. As already stated, the pressures could have been moderated, though these could not have been ignored or disregarded. These were real and something had to be done to contain them; the failure lay in not even making an attempt to contain them.

3. By the time a partial attempt was made to contain those pressures, in the early seventies, the rush for undergraduate enrolment was on the decline. During the fifties and the sixties, the annual rate of growth had been 13–14 per cent. By the early seventies, it had come down to 5–6 per cent. In a sense, the situation was more favourable for organising a systematic and purposeful development of higher education. However, two things happened to thwart the attempts made during this period.

One of these has been referred to already. It had become clear by the mid-sixties that the situation had reached an impasse because the UGC had been functioning more or less without reference to what was happening in the states. Whatever it advocated or wanted to be done was listened to politely but rarely complied with. As to the mechanism of following up the compliance, none existed. What is more, the UGC secretariat by then was no longer faceless or passive, It had managed to appropriate substantial authority to take decisions. Things got more and more centralised and decision making, therefore, got progressively bureaucratised.

Second and more specifically, had the UGC devised and developed certain mechanisms for monitoring in the sixties it would have developed a means of identifying how and when and where things were going wrong. This was not done mainly because of the Commission's inability to conceptualise various contingencies. Moreover, despite the fact that the mandate of the UGC was to coordinate and determine standards, all that was done was to provide some funding, suggest certain things to the universities and leave it at that.

An objective mechanism for monitoring would, besides ensuring effective action in the universities, have taken away some of the powers appropriated by the secretariat. It was, therefore, doubly important to have moved in this direction. Whether the failure to move in this direction was because of conceptual and administrative incompetence or due to sabotage from within the secretariat are issues on which it is difficult to go beyond the realm of conjecture. In most such cases, there is an interplay of social forces as well as individuals. The upshot in brief was that nothing except the release of grants got done and the original mandate given to the UGC was both forgotten and subverted.

Once the universities got accustomed to the idea that the UGC would release funds in any case, and it would not take any action against anyone for ignoring its directives, the universities ceased to take the standard setting role of the UGC seriously.

Even the 1971 amendment of the UGC Act, which empowered it to withhold grants in case a university was set up without its prior concurrence, did not improve matters. The state governments were all the time yielding to the pressures being exerted upon them. There was no one to exercise professional influence on them to make them adhere to certain norms and principles. This happened largely because the UGC, which had been visualised as a professional body had, through sheer inertia, degenerated into a funding agency. In terms of its day-to-day functioning, all that it did was to swim with the current: it neither conceived nor put forward an alternative strategy by way of intervention.

The Personnel Factors

The second factor in the situation was the choice of members for the Commission. In the first decade or so, persons with outstanding track records were available and were put on the Commission. In course of time they became more and more scarce. What is worse, the process of selection got both personalised and politicised. A related development that must be noted is that around this period, the rules of promotion of the secretariat staff also came to be recast in the interests of expediency.

Originally there were two cadres of officers. One came from the educational pool and the other from the pool of administrative personnel. This distinction of backgrounds was based both on sound administrative principles and experience. During the sixties, however, this distinction got blurred, or it was so arranged that due importance was not attached to it. Rules were recast so as to concede parity of treatment beyond a certain level of seniority to officers in both categories. This was a signal mistake. Gradually the quality of intake from the open market began to decline. In course of time, promotions became almost automatic. Much worse than that as pointed out by the High Court was the conscious decision to keep certain jobs unfilled and allow ad hoc promotions. Whether a person was suitable for a particular assignment or not ceased to matter, and everything tended to be decided on the basis of seniority.

The matter was, to some extent, sorted out when some aggrieved persons went to the High Court, which noted the oddity of the situation in which some people with limited educational qualifications were controlling the work of those who were far superior to them in understanding as well as educational qualifications. The process which had been at work for almost a quarter of a century had, however, done great damage. With the kind of immobility which characterises our administrative system, it would be years before the right kind of balance gets restored.

The situation in regard to the supporting staff is equally disquieting. Where five people would do, 10 are in position. To have a large number of substandard people than required creates two sets of problems. First, they are unable to perform and, second, they fail to perform. Following the report of the Administrative Staff College, Hyderabad, the UGC has carried out some kind of reorganisation of work but it will be quite some time before it creates an impact. What is to happen meanwhile? A committee headed by V.C. Kulandai Swamy has made some recommendations. How and when those are implemented remains to be seen.

There is no choice except to do two things. One is to induct a small number of competent people who can give direction to what is happening and what requires to be done. Second, it is equally important to retrain those who are already in position. While some of them cannot perhaps improve, this cannot be said about everyone. Quite a few of them can be helped to improve. Something like what is being done for teachers through Academic Staff Colleges may also be done in respect of the UGC staff.

The effect of the double jeopardy arising from the decline in the quality of members nominated to the Commission as well as the extraordinary decline in the quality of personnel of the secretariat becomes apparent even to a casual visitor to the UGC. The Commission now is like any other office of the government where the work of a few people gives the establishment a modicum of respectability while the majority of people while away their time.

The most regrettable aspect of this situation is that nothing is being done to ginger up the laggards, largely because the small minority of academicians who understand the need for a good management culture to further the cause of education are unwilling to take hard decisions to stem the rot permeating the system.

In this connection another allied problem must be raised. Many people are asking what the structure of the UGC should be, since the existing structure has failed to deliver the goods. In this context, it is necessary to recall that when the UGC was set up, the size of the university sector was not even one-tenth of what it is today. Having one chief executive (about whose role and authority also there is confusion) may have been adequate when things were more leisurely and relaxed. However, within a decade of the UGC's establishment, it became clear that this institution, as it was, would be unable to take the strain. Another development which manifested itself in the mid-sixties was the gradual ascendancy of the secretariat of the UGC over the Commission. Some of the factors which contributed to this development have been mentioned already. Nevertheless some of these need to be referred to again.

One was the personality factor. If those in the secretariat worked hard, mastered the details of each case and were assertive into the bargain, it should be no surprise that they got the better of the Commission or something close to that. This need not have happened but for the passivity or the lack of administrative acumen of the heads of the Commission. Once this happened, the rest was easy. This, however, leads one to mention the second factor in the situation.

The functioning of the UGC was so organised that the members of the Commission attended a meeting lasting three to four hours, once a month, usually 10 times in a year. The agenda was so overloaded with items, both important and trivial, that there was no time for occasional unstructured dialogues to explore ways and means of grappling with problems and the policy issues relating to the basic problems plaguing the system.

The chief executives neither had the foresight nor were they assertive enough to see what was happening: a situation had developed where members of the Commission merely reacted to what was placed before it by its bureaucracy rather than acting on their own initiative in response to their perception of problems or ground realities. How it happened, and whether it was the result of manipulation, or the result of the general passivity amongst the members need not be gone into. But this is what happened, so that by the beginning of the seventies, the pendulum had swung unmistakably against the Commission.

Reacting to these developments, the UGC Act was amended in 1971 to provide for a number of full-time members to look after different portfolios. Had this amendment been put into effect, it would have ensured that the secretariat would work under the guidance of the whole-time members of the Commission. For reasons which were never made public, the 1971 Act was again amended with the result that the chairman had only a full-time vice chairman to assist him. This was hardly of any consequence so far as the ultimate outcome was concerned, decision making in the real sense remained vested in the secretariat.

The new chairman who came after these developments had only a short tenure. Therefore, he could not bring about significant changes, despite having a mind of his own and the strength to assert his authority over the secretariat.

Most people who know the UGC are agreed that in its life of five decades, it has had only two effective chairman, and both of them were made to retire under unfortunate circumstances. In contrast, another chairman who was also being retired on the same grounds as these chairmen managed to stay on because of some loophole in the rules. This lacuna was never pointed out earlier. In this case, however, it was used to good effect.

RESTRUCTURING THE UGC

Without going into further details, the basic issue requiring consideration is what the structure of the UGC should be. Should it be restructured on the lines of the Railway Board, in which portfolios assigned to members are handled by them with the secretariat providing such assistance and processing of facts and alternatives as may be laid down or, required in a particular case? In such an organisation, it is the members who take decisions and accept responsibility for the same. In the existing structure, the authority formally vests in the chairman, the vice chairman and the secretary with the other members of the Commission sitting together once a month to discuss the issues placed before them and occasionally make a few suggestions.

What happens to these suggestions is uncertain, but it is widely accepted that these are attended to at a leisurely pace. No one has to deliberately kill an unpopular proposal; the sheer immobility of the office machine takes care of that.

It has been repeatedly argued that having two types of members—full-time and part-time—would militate against the kind of parity that should prevail among the members of the Commission. This, however, is a specious argument, particularly since a similar set-up does exist in some organisations. In any case, there is nothing inherently wrong or improper in four or five out of a dozen members being appointed as full-time members. They would study problems, give directions and assume responsibility for performance in respect of the segments of work assigned to them.

That the UGC strengthened with four or five full-time members would perform better is based on the assumption that those appointed to the Commission would be persons of proven competence and integrity. Going by past experience, one cannot be sure of what will happen in this respect. Nonetheless, one has to forge ahead with the reorganisation of the Commission hoping that good sense would prevail and people with questionable bonafides would not be given berths in a body responsible for directing higher education in the country.

Another question intimately related to the constitution of the UGC is whom do the persons nominated to the Commission represent? Do they represent only themselves or do they represent a constituency? If they represent only themselves, their choice could be impeccable. If, on the other hand, they represent a constituency, certain other things (for instance, how representative are they?) would have to be taken into account.

With more than a quarter million teachers in the system, it stands to reason that at least one person should have had some connection with or some understanding of what other teachers think and feel about the problems confronting the profession. On the other had, if an activist functioning as a teacher has to be inducted, the UGC will get moulded into the shape of some of the bodies established in the universities. Plainly, we have to consider whether the UGC should be a body of well-known academicians and education administrators or an elevated Academic Council for the system of higher education.

What mechanism does or can the UGC have to ascertain academic opinion or find out whether a particular step being taken would promote the interest of the university system? The fact that a particular individual was known to a particular minister and as a consequence got nominated to the UGC does not entitle him to speak for the totality of the academic system. At best, he can speak for himself. And if his thinking and conduct are not in tune with academic opinion, all that one can say is that the UGC's decisions are likely to create as many problems as they might solve. To some extent this is precisely what has been happening.

Such situations do not arise in a country like UK from where the original model was taken for fashioning the UGC in India. Britain is a small country. Decision making, though not free from personal preferences, is not as unprofessional or subjective as it has become in our country. The committee in Britain had more members than in the Indian UGC. What is more, most of the members were chosen from the top three-four experts in a particular field. No less important, there was seldom a duplication in their area of expertise.

All these safeguards buttressed by strong conventions ensured that the UGC in Britain would function in a predictable fashion and would be able to innovate measures to tackle various problems. However, in that country also things started getting out of hand in the seventies due to economic problems which forced the government of the day to put the universities on the back burner. No wonder the UGC has been replaced by the University Funding Council (UFC) in Britain.

It is not proposed to press the comparison further. One thing, however is, definite. The work of the Indian UGC is sharply defined. Therefore, the tools to be used to fulfil the given tasks cannot be selected at random. These have to be fashioned to suit the objectives. This has not always

been done and the resultant situation has been complicated further by
social and economic forces which served to undermine any attempt to
introduce better manpower planning or financial discipline. Clearly, to
enable the UGC to work effectively, it would be necessary to ginger it up
from within and unshackle it from without.

THE FUNDING FUNCTION

Even when it is conceded that as regards maintenance expenditure in
respect of state universities, where the bulk of enrolment is, has to come
from the states, the situation between now and the early fifties, when the
UGC was established is no longer the same. During its early years, the
UGC was not so hard pressed for resources. During those relaxed days,
most universities did not know how to deal with a funding agency. It
took them some time to learn the ropes. Moreover, the number of universities was quite small so that, even with relatively meagre funding, the
UGC could make an impact on the situation.

Another factor which has affected the UGC has been the considerable
increase in the number of central universities and institutions deemed to
be universities. In the case of central universities, it is clearly specified
that funds for both maintenance and development have to come from
the UGC. For institutions deemed to be universities, the formula is different for different institutions. Some of them like the Indian Institute of
Science, Bangalore, receive 100 per cent grant. Others like BITS, Pilani,
receive only development grants. Some are funded by the states while
others have to depend upon a diversity of sources. It is not necessary to
go into these details, except to call attention to the fact that within the
limited funds allocated to the UGC, what is left for the state institutions
is hardly of any significance.

A state university getting roughly Rs 10 million during the entire VIIth
Plan does not look up to the UGC the way it did even in the seventies
when there was some balance between what the UGC gave and what the
state government sanctioned for development purposes. As long as the
UGC's share was even of the order of 40 per cent of what the states
allocated, it could not be ignored. Of late, the UGC's share has come
down so steeply that most state universities are not bothered about what

the UGC has to give. In 1981 for instance, the central sector received 33 per cent of the total allocation. A decade later the central sector's share had risen to approximately 75 per cent.

This disparity between the support given to the central and state sector institutions has had a very negative effect. If the state sector with more than 90 per cent of the enrolment is neglected, the UGC cannot play a decisive role in influencing the development and functioning of the system of higher education in the country. This situation, coupled with the fact that the UGC has no mechanism to monitor whatever is going on in the universities, rules out the hope that the UGC can mend matters as far as the state sector is concerned. Unless the overall grant to the UGC is stepped up considerably and the imbalance between the central and state sectors is somewhat redressed the situation will continue as it is.

Earlier, mention was made of the role of the UGC as a professional body. There are other all-India professional bodies which do not provide any funding to the state level institutions. Nonetheless, they do manage to have a certain amount of say with them. For one thing, they deal with a smaller number of institutions. For another, the political pressures on them are not so overwhelming. When it comes to the mainstream system of arts, commerce and science courses, the bulk of the populist pressure is extended there.

These can be countered only in two ways. Primarily the UGC's role as a professional body has to be made much more stringent than it is today. This would require an active and vigilant system of monitoring, which, most unfortunately, the UGC has failed to develop till now, in spite of the fact that the 1977 review of the UGC had made a strong case for it. This recommendation was effectively sabotaged from within by the strata-gem of masterly inaction. Nobody opposed it in principle, but nobody did anything about it.

The Ministry of Education, which should have ensured compliance, also did nothing about it in spite of the Parliamentary committees taking umbrage on account of lack of progress in this respect. The fact of the matter is that monitoring was ignored because this exceedingly difficult and complex function does not yield instant results. Even those who know that a system as large as the Indian system of higher education cannot be managed without performing the watchdog role of monitoring put it off and preferred to create a favourable impression by giving largesse to newly established institutions.

Currently, the UGC is engaged in setting up a Council of Accreditation and Assessment. This was precisely the task entrusted to it. Not having performed it for over three decades, it is now in the process of setting up another body to do what it ought to have done in the first instance. What will eventually be the outcome of this initiative remains to be seen. This move too may die a slow death if it continues to linger without a powerful thrust to give it adequate momentum.

It is indeed a pity that the UGC has applied itself almost exclusively to the sanctioning of grants, It needs to be remembered that the job of providing funds was entrusted to the UGC as an act of compromise, indeed as an afterthought. The starting point for the UGC was the need to devise a mechanism which would ensure that somebody at the centre would do the job of coordinating and determining standards.

Given this context and keeping in view the ground already lost, it has been mooted several times that the UGC should wash its hands of under-graduate education and concentrate on postgraduate education. This is not such a wild thought as might appear to those who are unaware of the limitation under which the UGC is functioning. If this proposal comes through and the UGC starts funding only the autonomous colleges (at least for some time) and postgraduate institutions, things would start changing. Having divested itself of this routine and shed the responsibility of disbursing small amounts all over the country, the UGC could then insist upon the system of higher education complying with certain other qualitatively important requirements. Had this idea got beyond a mere talking point, it might have been worthwhile speculating upon the outcome.

Since nothing of the kind has happened, it is idle to spend any more time on this line of thinking. In any case, this is something which the UGC cannot decide on its own. The central government would have to come into it with the state governments agreeing to such a division of responsibilities.

Immediately, and on its own, the UGC can do only two things. One, to repeat, is to establish a strong and sensitive system of monitoring which would then keep everybody, and itself also, on its toes and, second, mobilise adequate resources so that by ensuring a much greater outflow of funds to state universities, the UGC would regain the strength to call the shots.

Conclusion

In conclusion, it needs to be made clear that while the central government is responsible for: (a) constituting the Commission; (b) providing the required funding; (c) facilitating its interaction with states; and (d) laying down the parameters of overall and parliamentary control, the rest of the job is to be done by the Commission itself. To be specific, the Commission has to: (a) improve its procedures and performance; and (b) develop a system of monitoring so that it knows precisely what is or is not happening on the ground. It has been proposed that a part of the Commission's job be farmed out to an Accreditation and Assessment Council. It goes without saying that the two would have to work in close coordination with each other.

For one thing, all the data would be with the UGC and, for another, it would be more or less a limb of the UGC. Collaboration between the two is, therefore, unavoidable. Perhaps one of the members of the Commission, may be the vice chairman, can be made the chief executive of this Council; this would be in line with what the Review Committee had recommended in 1977. One thing that would have to be avoided at all costs would be that the two, i.e., the Commission and the Accreditation Council do not work at cross purposes.

When it comes to procedures and performance, the issue has been discussed already in considerable detail. However, one more point requires to be made. The system of grant-in-aid devised by the British in the nineteenth century for schools, and later extended to colleges, came to be applied to the universities mainly after 1947. In this regard, the UGC played a pivotal role. It refined and perfected that system to such an extent that decision making became centralised in the UGC as far as the central universities were concerned. A committee is looking into the system of grants to central universities, but unless one important issue is gone into in some detail, the whole exercise will remain sterile.

This refers to the system of unit costs. For every course in a college or a university, unit cost can and should be worked out systematically. It would also have to be revised every year. When, in 1985, the UGC was vested with the power to determine the fee structure of each course, something of this kind was intended. It is ironical, though not untypical of its working, that the UGC has hardly done anything in this regard. It is high time for this part of the job to be undertaken. Once it is done, the functioning of the UGC would get revamped by itself.

Apart from various other advantages that would accrue, four can be specifically stated at the outset. First, decision making would be done basically by academics and not by pen pushers. When the unit cost is being worked out, the job would have to be entrusted to some academics and some administrators; the academic input, therefore, would be considerable. Second, it would lead to economy of manpower both in the UGC and the universities. This can create problems of surplus manpower, but the way to deal with this issue would be to retrain and redeploy those already in position. Third, once the UGC adopts this system, various states would have no alternative except to adopt the same line of action. Either they would take over the formula developed by the UGC, or adapt it to their use. In either case it would make for neatness of operations and clarity in regard to who is responsible for what and, on what conditions and stipulations.

Possibly a fourth advantage can also accrue. Today a course like business management costs X in one central university and Y in another. The difference between X and Y is as wide as several thousand rupees. Clearly this is indefensible. But no one goes into this issue with any degree of thoroughness. Once a formula of unit costs is worked out, each university would have to ensure that it works within the parameters laid down. There would then be no headaches or arguments about approved items of expenditure, seeking of prior or *ex-post facto* approvals and such other bureaucratic hassles.

The UGC has to change its image to that of a body which, if it is there, matters and, if it were to be wound up, would be missed. In Britain, the UGC has been wound up. To entertain any such notion in respect of India would imply that the formula of state support devised by India was not the right formula. No other country had vested both the powers (to coordinate and determine standards and also to provide funds) in the same agency. If the experiment has not succeeded so far, it is not because, conceptually speaking, it was wrong. The failure lies in our inability to implement the concept.

X

THE INDIAN UNIVERSITY GRANTS COMMISSION*

I

When the UGC was established in Britain in 1919, it was primarily conceived as a buffer between the state and the universities. British universities had begun to experience certain strains even before World War I. After the end of the war, in recognition of the changing situation, the UGC was established, quite appropriately, as an advisory body to the Treasury

The situation in India was entirely different. Till 1919, education was controlled by the central government with the viceroy as its executive head. In that year education was 'transferred' to the provinces and for

---

*This essay was originally published in *Higher Education*, the internation journal of higher education and planning (Elsevier Publishers, the Netherlands) in October 1974. This particular issue dealt with only one theme: University Grant Committees in International Perspective. Apart from Britain where the UGC was first established in 1919, it spread to other commonwealth countries like Australia, New Zealand, Hong Kong, Sri Lanka etc. The experience of all these countries was projected. In respect of India, I was asked to write about the Indian UGC. The text is reproduced exactly as it was published.

the next quarter of a century or so the central government had very little to do with the way the universities were managed. A mechanism for co-ordination was, however, developed. It was called the Central Advisory Board of Education and the provinces were represented by their respective education ministers. For the rest everything was controlled by the provinces; almost the only role which the central government played was to look after the universities at Aligarh and Banaras which had been established as representative centres of learning for the Muslim and the Hindu populations, respectively.

By the time the British withdrew in 1947, the Constituent Assembly had already been set up. It look India another couple of years to hammer out a constitution for herself. One of the important issues that came up during the making of the Constitution related to the control of education. Broadly speaking, there were two conflicting points of view. One favoured education to be under the charge of the central government. The other held that for a country of the size and diversity of India this would be utterly unfeasible and the control of education should be vested in the states. Ultimately a kind of reconciliation was effected between the two points of view. Education, including university education, was accepted as a state subject. In respect of higher and professional education, the centre was given a supervisory and pace-setting role so as to coordinate and determine standards.

A proposal to make education a concurrent subject has also been mooted. This was not agreed to despite the fact that the University Education Commission presided over by Dr S. Radhakrishnan had made a recommendation to this effect only a little earlier. It was only in 1976 that education was made a concurrent subject.[1]

There were three important factors which persuaded the constitution makers to vest the centre with these far reaching powers. One was the conviction expressed most characteristically by the then union minister of education, Maulana Azad, that 'in the present state of development of education in India it is imperative [that] there should be central guidance, if not central control, on Provincial progress'.[2] This was in line with the thinking of Jawaharlal Nehru who was in favour of checking 'the growing tendency towards a lowering of the standard of university education which was already discernible in certain parts of the country'.[3] Dr Ambedkar, the main architect of the Constitution, more or less held the same opinion and in the course of an important intervention made the point that different universities ought not be allowed to prescribe or follow different standards.

Second, though some people differed with this point of view, the weight of political opinion was in favour of treating education as an agent of change. This point of view was fortified by Entry 20 of the Concurrent List under the heading 'Economic and Social Planning'. It is by virtue of this entry in the Constitution that the Planning Commission has been set up and the entire process of planning undertaken. Without some measure of control over higher and professional education, it was argued, planning could be rendered meaningless.

The third important factor derived from the nature of Indian federalism. While in theory India is a federation of states, in actual practice and to some extent, even in statutory terms, the dice is loaded in favour of the centre. Apart from the other statutory powers that the central government has, the centre is much, much stronger in respect of its financial resources. The power to raise taxes has been distributed in such a way that the bulk of the revenue comes to the centre. Not only that, the sources of revenue at the disposal of the centre are much more flexible than those at the disposal of the states so that central revenues have been growing at a much faster pace than the state revenues. Anticipating the availability of disposable funds to the centre, the Constitution created a statutory mechanism for the transfer of resources from the centre to the states: it is called the Finance Commission and is appointed every five years. In this respect the more appropriate comparison would be with federal countries like Australia and Canada and not with a unitary country like Britain.

Consequently, when the Constitution was finally adopted, in respect of higher and professional education at least, the central government had powers to coordinate and determine standards of instruction as well as achievement. These powers were so overriding in character that in the next couple of decades whenever the courts were asked to interpret the law in any respect (one of the unique features of the Indian Constitution), the judgements were invariably in favour of the dominating role of the central government.

In 1976, when education was made a concurrent subject (an amendment of the earlier provision), it was almost an unnecessary exercise as far as higher education was concerned. Without formally being so armed, the centre had all kinds of powers in that limited area of operation. Whether it used them or not is another matter. Ironically enough, there has been no further follow-up legislation after the 42nd Amendment of the Constitution in 1976. In consequence, the role of the centre as far as higher education is concerned is precisely what it was when the Constitution was inaugurated in 1951.

II

Sometime in the second half of 1951, after the Constitution had been put into force, the Ministry of Education circulated a draft Bill, entitled 'The Universities' (Regulation of Standards) Bill, to universities and the states. The statement of Objects and Reasons reads as follows:

> The Constitution of India vests Parliament with exclusive authority in regard to "co-ordination and determination of standards in institutions for higher education." It is obvious that neither co-ordination of institutions nor determination of their standards is possible unless the central government has some control over the establishment of new universities, the definition of territorial jurisdiction and the determination of standards of teaching and examination in universities, both old and new.

Of the various important provisions in this proposed Bill, the following may be referred to in a summary form:

(i) No university established after the commencement of this Act by or under a State Act shall be deemed to be a university unless the central government by notification makes a declaration to that effect.

(ii) It is open to the central government to declare any institution for higher education other than a university to be a university.

(iii) No institution other than a university will have the right to confer degrees.

(iv) In order to carry out the work of coordination and determination of standards, a Central Council of University Education is to be established. At least one-third of the members of the Council will be vice chancellors.

(v) The Central Council can ask for information about any aspect of university work from a university and will have the powers to direct the executive authority of any university to take such action as may be specified.

(vi) In case any university fails to comply with the direction issued within a reasonable time, the Central Council will be authorised to advise the central government to derecognise any degree conferred by such a university for the purpose of employment under the central government or for any other purpose.

As should be evident, these provisions were an attempt to give a concrete statutory form to the role of the centre which was to coordinate and determine standards. When circulated for opinion, only one state government opposed it. The universities, however, opposed the Bill vehemently as well as persistently. They looked upon it as an attack on their autonomy. Their main line of argument may be summed up in these words:

1. It is for the universities themselves to regulate, maintain and coordinate their own academic standards.
2. For any outside agency to undertake this job would amount to violating university autonomy.
3. If the standards were low it was mainly for lack of funds. Once adequate funds were made available, there would be hardly any problems.

The political leadership, however, was for the Bill. The Planning Commission had been established in 1950 and planning both as an agent of change and as a lever of change had been accepted by the whole country. Education too was looked upon as an instrument of change. The same political party (the Indian National Congress) was in power both at the centre and in the states. The prime minister enjoyed a high degree of prestige and was looked upon as the leader of the nation rather than as a leader of the ruling party. Above all, it was clear to the political leadership that if India was to make any progress it was important to ensure that higher education was used as an instrument of change. This is the principal reason why, despite whatever misgivings some people might have had, only one state government chose to demur. The others did not choose to say anything.

In September 1952 a special session of the Inter-University Board, which represented the Indian vice chancellors, was held at Madras.[4] Member after member got up to oppose the proposed Bill. The dominant feeling was that universities were autonomous and it was for them to maintain standards. No agency other than the universities themselves had the right to enforce anything. One of them, V.K.R.V. Rao, who later became the minister for education in the central government said:

> Even supporting that the central government agrees that the Central Council should consist only of vice-chancellors, I would very strongly put it to this body that we cannot allow any other body to issue directives. I can understand they can argue and try to persuade us

but I am of the opinion it is a complete breach of the very principle even if the constitution is changed and it consists only of vice-chancellors.[5]

Several of the members asserted that 'the question of standards is a question of finance. If the standards are low it is not because of the universities but in spite of them.' This came from the representative of Aligarh Muslim University. The vice chancellor of Baroda put it equally strongly. 'It is no use asking us to do this and that and not helping us at all with money. There was a Grants Committee appointed in the past, of which I was a member, but we met once or twice and became defunct and there was no grant to distribute. If the Government of India think of standards, they must give financial assistance.'[6]

An eloquent case against any central direction or control was made by the vice chancellor of Annamalai who only a few years earlier had been the union minister for finance. He said:

If the central government had begun to realise their constitutional responsibility in the matter of higher education, this Bill, instead of taking this shape, must really have taken the shape of a Bill to create a University Grants Committee and then to define what the powers of the University Grants Committee would be and what the functions of the central government would be in regard to their responsibility. Because once you recognise that the central government must be the source of finance to the universities, then even the most ardent advocates of university autonomy cannot deny the implications of such a statement, viz., that if the central government which is responsible for finding the major part of the finances must have some voice, in some manner or other, for the way in which all this money is spent so that the whole basis of this proposed legislation must start from the kind of financial help that the central government is expected to give and what consequences regarding control of the central government would follow the grant of financial resources to meet the needs of the universities. Instead of doing that, the Bill has been shaped in such a manner that one is tempted to think that the central government is following in respect of the education the example of non-democratic countries.[7]

At this stage a reference ought to be made to what was already in existence, though nominally so. In 1943, a Post-War Development Plan in respect of education was prepared by a committee under the chairmanship of Sir John Sargent, then educational commissioner to the Government of India. This committee recommended the establishment of a University Grants Committee and one was established in 1945 with four members. In 1946 and again in 1947 its membership was increased and its powers enlarged. None of the members was full-time and no definite funds were placed at its disposal. The committee, however, was to make recommendations to the Ministry of Education which, in turn, forwarded it with its own recommendations to the Ministry of Finance. The system had not worked satisfactorily and worked, at best, by fits and starts. Considering the insignificant role that this committee played at that time and the nominal funds that were available to the universities it was inappropriate to describe it as the UGC. But the British example was there in the background and that is why it was so described. Two things, however, must be noted here. First, that it was purely advisory in character unlike the UGC after 1956 which is a statutory body and is entitled to take its own decisions. Second, this UGC was more or less constructed on the British model which was to act in an advisory capacity and deal only with the subject of grants.

When the Radhakrishnan Commission reported in 1949, one of its important recommendations was to set up a committee or commission to allocate both recurrent and capital grants to the universities from the centre. This report visualised the UGC as an expert body with considerably enhanced powers over the existing University Grants Committee. No definite decision, however, was taken and the matter remained pending for quite some time.

When the vice chancellors of Indian universities opposed the University (Regulation of Standards) Bill so vehemently, there was some re-thinking within the ministry of education. There were two options available to the ministry. One was to go ahead with the Bill in disregard of what the vice chancellors had said. The other was to drop the matter altogether and give it a different direction. It was the second option which was exercised and in a manner which seems to have no precedent elsewhere.

A good deal of the criticism made by the vice chancellors stemmed from the fact that the universities had very limited funds at their disposal. They argued, and not without reason, that they knew what needed to be done in order to maintain high standards of performance but they did not have the means to implement their ideas. That is why they repeatedly referred to the mechanism for disbursement of grants already existing. They also referred to what the Radhakrishnan Report had recommended. In any case it was clear to the Ministry of Education that, in terms of the financial arrangements between the centre and the states, the centre had a good deal of money to transfer to the states and a statutory mechanism called the Finance Commission had been created for the purpose. It was recognised that at least some part of the funds would come to the university sector. The Ministry of Education, therefore, decided to overcome its earlier hesitation in establishing a grant-giving body.

More or less through a process of natural evolution, the conclusion was reached that the power to regulate standards should also be vested in the body which was to be created to disburse grants to universities. This was an innovation the like of which had not been thought of anywhere else. In almost all federal countries, the centre gives funds to its units. But nowhere are these funds linked with the performance of the universities.

The uniqueness of the concept of the Indian UGC lay in this fact. Accordingly, the UGC was established through administrative action in December 1953. Meanwhile the earlier Bill which the universities had opposed was abandoned altogether and a new Bill was drawn up and circulated. A Joint Select Committee of both Houses of Parliament went into the question in some detail and the Act was finally adopted in 1956. Certain features of the UGC Act as finally enacted deserve to be referred to here:

(i) Two important provisions of the 1951 Bill which gave teeth to the proposed UGC were deleted. The 1951 Bill vested the central government with the power of approving or not approving a university established by a state legislature. In the 1956 Act this provision was altogether deleted and it was open to the state legislatures to establish any university without reference to the UGC. The state legislatures made abundant use of this power.

(ii) Another important change made in the new Act as compared to the 1951 Bill was that in the earlier Bill it was open to the central government to derecongnise any degree conferred by a university provided the said university failed to carry out any directions given to it. This derecognition could be for the purpose of employment under the central government or for any other purpose. This provision now was deleted.

(iii) While the British UGC was primarily concerned with the question of the financial needs of universities and the disbursement of grants, the Indian UGC was given certain additional powers.

This was because the Indian UGC assumed the obligation of performing certain functions following authority vested in central government to ensure the coordination and determination of standards. In other words the Indian UGC was looked upon as a professional body.

To this end it was given certain specified powers. For instance, it could recommended to any university the measures necessary for the improvement of university education. It could advise the central government or any state government on the allocation of grants to any universities, for any general or specified purpose, out of central or state funds. It could also require a university to furnish it with such information as might be needed relating to its financial position or the studies in the various branches of learning undertaken in that university together with all the regulations relating to the standards of teaching and examination.

In order to be able to carry out these functions, the UGC was empowered to inspect any department or university and communicate its views to the said university and advise it in terms of its findings.

(iv) While the chairman was to be appointed by the government as also all the members, three important provisions were introduced in regard to their appointment. One, the chairman would be chosen from among persons who were not officers of the central government or any of the state governments. Two, only two persons were to represent the central government on the Commission and these by convention have been secretaries to the Government of India in the Ministries of Education and Finance. If any one or both of them were absent on a particular day, no deputies were authorised to attend on their behalf. C.D. Deshmukh who was the first chairman of the UGC after it became a statutory body regarded this particular issue to be a matter of principle. Vice chancellors of universities and the remaining three could be persons who had a background in industry, commerce or any of the learned professions, including university education.[8]

(v) When the UGC Bill was under discussion, there was a division of opinion within the cabinet as to the extent of the autonomy to be given to the UGC. It is best to state the official point of view in the words of the then prime minister, Jawaharlal Nehru:

The purpose of having a high-powered University Grants Commission is to make them responsible for the division of the money available for the purpose among the universities concerned, which means all universities in India, including the central universities. For this purpose the UGC should be practically autonomous . . . . So far as the division of grants to universities, this is the special work of the Commission and they are the best qualified to judge. Even the Cabinet is not in a better position to judge this because they cannot keep in intimate touch with the universities and their work . . . . It is for the government to determine the total amount to be placed at the disposal of the Commission for grants-in-aid to the universities. In this matter the Commission's advice might be sought, but the decision must be that of the Government. After the total sum is decided upon and the Commission is informed accordingly, the Commission will then give grants within that sum.[9]

It would be misleading however, to assume that this point of view was accepted by everyone in the cabinet. C.D. Deshmukh was then union finance minister. He was of the view that the Ministry of Finance should have the right to review and sit in judgement on the decisions of the UGC in so far as they committed the government to a certain magnitude of expenditure. Jawaharlal Nehru did not agree.

The details of that disagreement are still confidential as the cabinet papers relating to that period have not yet been made public. Interestingly enough, however, C.D. Deshmukh himself became the first chairman of the UGC when it was formally established in 1956. After a couple of years in office, he himself referred to this controversy between him and the prime minister and confessed that he had been wrong and the prime minister right.[10]

In terms of statutory powers, while the UGC became legally autonomous, in actual practice it has continued to be more or less a handmaiden of the Ministry of Education. In a recent Report (1982–84) dealing with the central universities which are presided over by the chairman of the UGC, a number of instances were referred to where the UGC could have functioned on its own in terms of its statutory power but failed to do so. The tone is one of missed chances and regret. It is difficult to understand to whom this lament is addressed. The UGC has only itself to blame if it could not function on its own and preserve its autonomy. The explanation is to be found more in the outlook and calibre of the people who were appointed to be its members rather than any other reasons, statutory or otherwise.

As the foregoing opinion of Jawaharlal Nehru clearly indicates, while the overall allocation was to be made by the Ministry of Education, the allocation to universities was to be made by the UGC. In actual practice this did not always happen. In addition, the UGC was unable to resist pressures, political and not so political. The UGC failed to withstand these pressures and submitted tamely to whatever tilted in favour of expansion and dilution of quality not only because of arm twisting by the ministry of education but also because of the lacksadaisical attitude of the members. Technically speaking, norms were laid down, committees met and there was a good deal of talk about maintaining and coordination of standards. In actual fact almost every institution, whether a university or a college, did what it pleased. The UGC in consequence came to be only a grant-giving body and its academic and professional function was pushed into the background.

One interesting feature of this entire debate about the regulation of standards and the consequent establishment of the UGC was that it was assumed that everything depended upon the flow and availability of funds. That this was a gross over-simplification of the total situation has been proved by experience. If universities have not done better it is not only for lack of funds. Equally responsible was the mistaken belief best described in the picturesque phrase 'the fallacy of more funds'.

III

The UGC got off to a flying start under C.D. Deshmukh. Universities were starved of funds. Their number was rather small at that time and at least in the beginning there were more funds available than the universities could use.

Pay scales were very unsatisfactory. One of the first things that the UGC did was to revise the pay scales upwards for all university teachers. A question arose as to what was to be done with regard to colleges. The UGC decided, and correctly too, that the colleges could not be left out of any schemes of reform and renovation. Historically, the colleges had been established before the universities. When the first three universities were established in India in 1857, the University of London model was used under which the colleges were to be affiliated to the university. The university set the syllabus for them and also conducted the examination. The universities did hardly any postgraduate teaching. That too was done in colleges. It was only with the beginning of the twentieth century that the University of Calcutta took the initiative of concentrating all postgraduate teaching in the university. Rather reluctantly, the colleges divested themselves of postgraduate teaching.

When the surge of expansion got underway in the fifties and the sixties, it was the colleges rather than the universities which began to proliferate. While the UGC could not have ignored the colleges in any significant way, it engaged itself in an unreal controversy when it sought to limit the number of universities that were to be set up but did little to regulate the proliferation of colleges. The real expansion took place in respect of colleges and yet even after three decades, the UGC has not been able to evolve a set of guidelines as to what norms are to govern their establishment. Through this single act of omission, the UGC has under-performed more grossly than anywhere else.

Reporting in 1977, the UGC Review Committee commended the work done in the first phase of activity (1956–61). The only caveat one can enter is that the UGC failed to evolve a mechanism for coordination with the state governments. Except for four universities which were controlled by the centre at that time, all others were state universities. How to deal with the state governments was therefore a matter of considerable significance.

It is in the second phase of UGC development (1961–72) that the UGC gradually lost its elan and its sense of direction. This was the decade of relentless expansion. The annual rate of expansion was sometimes as high as 13 or 14 per cent. No country in the world has experienced such a high rate of growth. The bulk of this expansion was at the undergraduate level, i.e., in colleges. While colleges had been brought within the purview of the UGC no steps were taken at any stage to either lay down any norms for regulating their growth or the academic programme that they followed. It is best for the UGC Review Committee to describe this phase of its functioning:

> The period from 1961–62 to 1972–73 saw a steep rise in enrolment as well as in the number of new universities and colleges. The number of universities rose from 48 (including two deemed ones) to 99 (including nine deemed ones) and of colleges from 1,783 to

4,158. Enrolment shot up from 1 million to about 3.5 million during the same period. The effect on standards is not hard to visualise. However, the effectiveness of various programmes launched by the UGC for standards cannot be assessed as there has been no evaluation through inspection or otherwise. Expansion so overwhelmed the Commission that doling out grants became its sole function. It did set up some good committees but nothing was done to ensure the implementation of their recommendations or assess and evaluate the impact of such implementation anywhere.[11]

The UGC was concerned about the increasing number of universities but nobody enquired in any meaningful manner how the expansion of colleges was to be controlled or regulated. When the UGC Act came to be amended in 1970 and then again in 1972, an attempt was made to curb the growth in the number of universities. It was laid down in the amended Act for instance that a university which was established without the prior concurrence of the UGC would not be eligible for receipt of grants either from the UGC or from the central government. Nothing, however, was done in respect of the number of colleges.

Apart from giving grants, the Indian UGC had also been conceived as a professional body and this latter role was neglected. On the contrary, it was argued in the Report of the Education Commission that 'the UGC can become an effective instrument for upgrading the standards only if it follows the method of persuasion rather than coercion.[12] This was virtually a plea for non-intervention by an agency statutorily empowered to determine and coordinate standards of performance. In normal circumstances such a plea could have been accepted as valid. In the situation in which social and political pressures were being exerted on the universities without any let or pause, it amounted to complete, indeed planned, inaction. The alternatives of persuasion and coercion need to be understood in the Indian context. The bulk of the population has suffered from poverty and ignorance. To such people the way to overcome these disabilities is to enter the modern sector of the Indian economy for which the western kind of education is a necessary prelude. This explains the pressure on schools and colleges. To a great extent this pressure has been met and met successfully. The requisite facilities however could not be provided. In this process, therefore, standards of performance tended to be depressed and this led to an acute dilution of standards.

The UGC could not have withstood the onslaught of the democratic pressure. The pressures were much too intense and even the government lacked the appetite as well as the will to withstand them. All that the UGC could have done was to regulate the pressure in such a way that some of its more serious side-effects could have been moderated. In the situation in which the UGC was operating, a head-on collision with these democratic pressures was out of the question. But it does not follow that the UGC should have retreated at every step and made no stand for quality in education. The UGC Review Committee has commented upon this phase of the UGC working in the following words:

> The retreat of [the] central government under pressure from states and universities from the stand it had taken in the Draft Universities (Regulation of Standards) Bill 1951 and acceptance of the radically diluted UGC Act, 1956 was a crucial event in the history of higher education in India. The result was a laissez-faire in the growth of universities and colleges whose proliferation left the UGC in the position of a hopeless spectator . . . . In an atmosphere in which any advice or caution could be construed as an infringement of the autonomy of the states, the UGC appeared to have been over-whelmed and it rarely tested the little initiative which it might have exercised. It did not even perform any clearing house function it was supposed to under the Act, on matters concerning higher education.[13]

It would be fair to add that if the UGC has not recovered from the setback that it received during the sixties, it is largely owing to its having made no attempt whatsoever to project itself as a professional as well as a grant giving body.

Regarding the third phase of UGC activity (1973–77), somewhat more complimentary things have been said by the UGC Review Committee. Not all of them are undeserved except that the damage done to the functioning of the UGC during the decade of the sixties could not be repaired in a significant manner. Apart from inaction on the academic front, the UGC had allowed itself to be bureaucratised to such an extent that it has not recovered even today. Despite that limitation, there certainly was an attempt during this phase to have some kind of perspective planning and to ginger things up but the saga of inaction had been so prolonged that it was not possible to turn over a new leaf.

Meanwhile another important development gave a new turn to events. Arising out of a report made by a committee appointed by the UGC, the scales of pay of university and college teachers were revised upwards with effect from January 1973. Two things are to be noted in this regard. One, the scales of pay were equated with those of the senior civil servants in the Government of India. This was an attempt to give a higher level of recognition to university and college teachers than had been accorded hitherto and was welcomed by almost all concerned. Two, the scales of pay of university and college teachers were equated with each other. This too was gratifying because the scales of pay in force till then were on the low side and teachers did not receive a living wage. Now at least a living wage was guaranteed.

But the academic implications of this decision were overlooked. A good deal of what is done in the colleges in India is done at schools in other countries. To equate both levels of teaching went against the principle of differentiation of wages which, ordinarily speaking, is an important principle in any system of organisation. It is even more so in an academic setting. The revised scales of pay were a bonanza for college teachers but for those working in the universities it was less exciting. That apart, parity once conceded would be impossible to revoke. As of today no one is talking of doing so. But if and when such a demand ever comes to be made for entirely academic reasons, the decisions made in the early seventies will prove a serious obstruction for two important reasons. One is the simple arithmetical fact that more than 85 per cent of the total strength of teachers in the country (approximately 200,000) work in the colleges. To talk of any kind of re-consideration of this issue would at once lead to conflict and tension. Second, teachers at that level have now become much more unionised than before. The decades of the fifties and the sixties were decades of expansion in Indian higher education. The rate of expansion was so high that a very large number of substandard teachers entered the profession.

Accordingly, the situation today in respect of academic performance as a whole is more unsatisfactory than it ever was. And yet, because of the pressure of numbers, the UGC would not act as a free agent. Less than a year ago the UGC agreed to a certain formula of promotions which, shorn of all frills, amounts to promotion by seniority. In conceding this demand, the UGC completely overlooked what its own committee, which had recommended the revised scales of pay in the first instance, had said on the subject:

We have considered the question of prescribing a running scale for teachers and feel that every teacher should be assured of a minimum scale of pay which will allow him to maintain a reasonable standard of living. At the same time, those who are more qualified or show evidence of scholarly work should be granted scale which provide them with adequate incentives and recognition. The very best people should get to the highest positions. Therefore, a single running grade to cover all categories of teachers would curb initiative and be lacking in incentives. Considering the practice prevalent in this and other countries, we recommend that there should be three tiers of posts in the universities—lecturers, readers and professors. To select the best candidate the recruitment should be through open competition at all levels and not at a single point entry like the administrative services.[14]

It should not have been necessary to quote these words but for the fact that the pressure for upgrading teachers to the next scale of pay came principally from those working in colleges. The formula now accepted by the UGC does precisely what the Sen Committee had warned against. It curbs initiative: even promotion to a professional post is based on considerations which underemphasise academic achievement and overemphasise seniority. Couples with this is the fact that the number of academic working days is seldom in accordance with the norms laid down. In plain words, while quality and productivity have been declining the wages have been rising. One can qualify this statement to the extent that inflationary pressures have eaten away a good part of the increased wages. The fact, however, remains that through its policies over the decades the UGC has come to be looked upon as the instrument for the scaling up of wages rather than as an organisation whose principal responsibility is to ensure coordination and determination of standards.

One consequence of the lack of performance on the part of the UGC has been the gradual moving of research out of the universities to research institutes located outside the university system. The process began with the establishment of science laboratories. At first these were under the auspices of the Council of Scientific and Industrial Research. Gradually the department of atomic energy moved in. Then came the departments of science and electronics. And now oceanography as well as environment have begun to establish and finance research laboratories. The principal reason why an independent sector dealing with research grew up outside the university sector was that the Indian university cannot be conceived of without colleges. Of the total student strength 85 per cent is in the colleges. Each college is affiliated to a university. The tail wags the dog— what happens in the colleges influences to a large extent what happens within the universities. Research institutes outside the university sector can function entirely on their own and have no kind of intrusion from the non-research sector. Research work in the universities, however, is impeded by the need to look after the colleges.

More or less parallel to these activities in the scientific sector, the Indian Council of Social Science Research supports a considerable amount of research. Two new entrants in this area are the Indian Council of Historical Research and the Indian Council of Philosophical Research. The sum total of these various initiatives is the fact that a whole new research sector has been established outside the four walls of the universities. In terms of outlay, scientific research attracts almost twice of what is spent on the universities as a whole. The outlay on the social sciences is much smaller but not inconsiderable. Despite the reduced outlay, universities have not been performing too badly even in the field of scientific research. A good many studies in recent years have confirmed this hypothesis.

Apart from these developments, an altogether independent sector of university activity also grew up outside the purview of the UGC. This was mainly the Indian Institutes of Technology and the Indian Institutes of Management. The meaning of these developments was clear. With the declining vigour of the UGC as a professional body, other forces and agencies started carving out their own spheres of action.

IV

Two things should be clear from the foregoing analysis. One, the primary function of the UGC was to maintain and determine standards; to disburse funds was a supportive function so that nothing remained undone for want of funds. Over the years this secondary function has been allowed to assume a primary role and the primary function has been relegated to the background.

Second, the real failure of the UGC has been its inability to establish its bonafides as a professional body. This failure is all the more deplorable because it was clear to the founding fathers of the Indian Constitution that, left to themselves, the states would not give as much attention to higher education and research as was required. It was in recognition of this misgiving that the centre assumed the responsibility to coordinate and determine standards.

While to some extent this misgiving proved to be misplaced, in another sense it proved to be completely right. It was misplaced in the sense that the states did not neglect higher education. If anything, they neglected elementary education and gave more attention to higher and professional education than was warranted by the needs of the economy of the country. This came about largely because of pressures exerted by the rising middle classes. In consequence the interests of the masses were ignored and those of the middle classes fulfilled.

But there was another sense in which the centre had a role to play and failed to do so. This was in respect of the coordination and determination of standards. Middle-class pressure was so intense that colleges and universities proliferated. The question of standards of performance, however, was almost totally neglected. One of the important formulations of the Education Commission (1964–66) was that, in order to be meaningful, higher education had to be conducted at a high level of performance. This was being consistently and systematically ignored. Situated as it was, it was the statutory duty of the UGC to seek to ensure high standards. The UGC signally failed to do so. In plain words, it failed to perform its role as a professional body.

In the conflict between populism and professionalism which has characterised India's development so far, professionalism was doomed to lose. Populism could be resisted, if at all, by moderating its inexorable march. In other words, the UGC could not have prevented what the populist pressures were seeking to accomplish. But it certainly could have moderated those pressures.

The issue erupted into a live academic and political issue when the Report of the Education Commission (1964–66) came to be considered by a Parliamentary Committee appointed in 1967 to prepare a National Policy on Education. The Education Commission had called for selective admissions. The Parliamentary Committee rejected it and their view ultimately prevailed. Even when this recommendation had been turned down, it did not follow that a decision had been taken for all time. Moreover, this decision was more applicable at the undergraduate than at the postgraduate level. But the UGC's role in resisting these populist pressures at both levels was one of total passivity. In such matters, what is required is a will to fight at the level of policy and persist at the level of administrative action. The UGC was deficient at both. The UGC issued all kinds of circulars to universities. There is very little to fault these circulars on the grounds of poorly formulated policies or wrongly placed emphasis. In regard to both these aspects, the UGC by and large said the right things. But, having said them, it never stopped to find out for itself to what extent the universities agreed to disagree with them and to what extent they put them into practice.

An obvious step would have been to establish a monitoring unit. The UGC never did so. It appeared as if it was afraid of finding out for itself that the universities were interested mainly in their funding but not in the range of ideas and policies being worked out by and under the auspices of the UGC. Even in the third phase (1973–77), when an attempt was made to break with the supine attitudes of the earlier decade, no attempt was made to establish a monitoring unit. Even the UGC Review Committee reporting in 1977 commented adversely on this omission. Though more than half a decade has gone by since that Review Committee reported, the UGC still does not have anything like a monitoring unit.

In countries where the university systems are strong and where high standards of performance have been built into the system, it would be totally unnecessary even to think of such a mechanism. In India it was not only necessary but the very condition of survival. The UGC has failed to accomplish its professed objectives largely because it has failed to ensure that what it recommended to universities was put into practice. Universities were constantly subjected to pressures both from within and without. Had the universities been committed to excellence in the best sense of the word for any length of time, there would have been no problem. As it was, the universities were operating in a situation where the notion of excellence was regarded as more or less inimical in local and regional terms to what they were established for. It was in this context that an all-India, statutorily empowered body like the UGC had a role to play.

Not only that, the UGC did not choose to develop any capacity of its own to evolve and project new ideas. Whatever ideas were forthcoming emerged almost incidentally and as a part of the day-to-day administration. No unit was established to do any thinking on behalf of the UGC nor was any attempt, formal or informal, made to undertake any systematic research studies.

The task before the UGC, therefor, is now to establish its bonafides as a professional body. Everything so far has worked against it. To assume that a change of direction can take place overnight is to fly in the face of experience. The process by which the UGC gradually lost its professional character was a slow one. Miracles do not happen in the realm of public policy. They have to be worked for, slowly and systematically. The choice before the UGC therefore is how and when to start this reversal of direction.

NOTES AND REFERENCES

1. According to the Indian Constitution there are two lists of subjects, one to be handled by the central government and the other to be handled by the states. There is also an intermediate list where a particular subject is regarded as concurrent. In terms of it, any law framed by the central government has precedence over any law passed by the state government.
2. Ramamurthy, K.S. (1974). 'The constitutional framework', in Philip Altbach and Amrik Singh (eds) *The Higher Learning in India*. Delhi, Bombay, Bangalore: Vikas. Report of the University Education Commission (1949, 1951). Government of India.
3. Ibid.
4. Proceedings of the Inter-University Board, 6th and 7th September (1952).
5. Ibid.
6. Ibid.
7. Ibid.
8. When one-third of the membership was reserved for vice chancellors there were some unexpressed misgivings. When the Act was amended in 1970 and then again in 1972, this provision was deleted and, instead, it was made mandatory that one-third of the membership be drawn from amongst the ranks of the teachers. There is no bar against a vice chancellor being appointed but he can be a member of the UGC only under the category of being an educationist.
9. Kothari, D.S. (1967). Address to Indian vice chancellors.
10. This is based on a personal communication written by an ex-secretary of the UGC to the writer of this paper.
11. Report of the Review committee on the University Grants Commission 1974–77 (Chairman, Dr V.S. Jha) New Delhi: Ministry of Education, Government of India.
12. Education and National Development: Report of the Education Commission 1964–66 (1966). (Chairman, Dr D.S. Kothari) Ministry of Education, Government of India.
13. Report of the Review Committee, *op. cit.*, see note 11.
14. S.N. Sen Committee Report (1971).

PART III

Two
Perspectives

XI

STUDENT ASSESSMENT OF TEACHERS

I

Any one talking about student assessment of teachers in India invites either ridicule or criticism. 'This is an American idea', some people would say. 'It cannot work in India' would assert others and so on. Why are there such strong reactions to such a simple proposal? This issue requires some elucidation.

To be fair, one must understand the American system a little more precisely than is generally understood. In that country, student assessment of teachers (through a proforma administered after every semester) is used for two purposes. One is to find out what students think about the instruction being imparted to them and the extent to which they profit from it and the other is to use this input not only for academic promotions but also to determine how much raise in salary is to be given to a particular teacher.

Unlike our country, there is no fixed scale of pay for most academics in that country nor is the rate of annual increment certain or pre-determined. Everything depends upon the performance of the teacher. One way of judging his performance is to find out what students have to say about him. It must also be added that this is not the only yardstick used. Peer judgement is also given a certain degree of weightage. So is the research work done by him and a couple of other things.

In our situation, the introduction of this system would be regarded as somewhat farfetched. Teacher absenteeism is widespread in our country. As to the kind and quality of teaching done in the classroom, several misgivings can be, and indeed are, expressed from time to time. With the kind of system that has evolved, there is no way any one can find out if a teacher even came to the institution on a particular day or not.

So far no method has been devised to deal with this problem. This is for three reasons. One of them is obvious. The American system cannot be transplanted to India. It has to be indigenised, if one may put it that way. Any suggestion of a teacher—or any one for that matter—being penalised for not doing his job will not work beyond a point. In our situation, underperformance is not an offence. On the contrary, it is lived with, day after day and year after year. If this particular dimension of the problem can be taken care of, the quality of teaching will improve immensely. And hence the case for student assessment of teachers.

Second, we cannot have a situation where we swing over from complete passivity to unremitting activity overnight. In other words, it will take time both for teachers and students to get adjusted to the new drill in the classroom. Today a large number of teachers are convinced that they have nothing to learn from their students. As for the students, they would not deny that they have a good deal to learn from their teachers. That they have also something to 'teach' their teachers is a thought that has never occurred to them. It takes some time for a teacher to learn that students not only 'learn' from their teachers, they have something to 'teach' them too. This notional reversal of roles is an exciting experience and should be a part of the teaching–learning encounter.

To move from the existing *laissez-faire* situation to one of active and productive cooperation in which both students and teachers are equally involved will take a few years before it is accepted as a part of our academic functioning.

Third, in tactical terms, it would be best to begin at the postgraduate level. Students at that level are mature enough to understand what is happening to and around them. In plain words, the switchover should begin at that level, and then work downwards. At the same time, there are something like a thousand colleges where, even at the undergraduate level, the quality of students is fairly good. It would require only a little effort to involve them in this new experiment and most of them would gladly play the game.

What about the teachers? It would require sustained effort to draw them into this exercise. They would distrust, even oppose, this system. But partly through patient explanation and partly through enforcement of the new system, things will begin to change. In the first phase which, in my judgement should be spread over two years, the following developments can take place.

(i) At the end of each term, every student is asked to fill in a proforma in regard to the regularity, overall performance and several other relevant features of the teacher/s instructing him. All details like the format of the proforma, the date and time when it is to be administered, who is entitled to participate in it (more details later), reports about the safe custody of the responses and a dozen other things would have to be worked out by the principal or dean of the faculty. But the actual exercise would be done by the teacher concerned at the time and place specified and a report to that effect submitted to the authorities.

(ii) This proforma, once filled up, would stay with the teacher concerned and not be handed over either to the dean of the faculty or the principal or anyone else connected with the management. In other words, the whole thing would be a strictly private transaction between the students and the teachers.

(iii) It follows that there would be no question of any kind of penal action being taken against any teacher. Data in regard to how teachers are performing would be with the teacher concerned and it would not be available to anyone else. There is no question therefore of anyone taking any punitive action against any teacher.

Somebody may turn around and ask, 'will all this effort serve any purpose?' The answer is two-fold. First, all those teachers who get a favourable reaction from their students would go out of their way to share this information with their colleagues, friends, and even the principal or the dean. They would feel happy at the fact that their performance in the classroom is being appreciated. It is natural for everyone to talk of things that go in one's favour and not talk of those which go against one.

Second, whether we plan it or not, it would get known within a year who is performing well and who is not. Would this have an impact on those who may be described as the confirmed sinners? The answer would depend upon how the college or the university is run. If the vice chancellor/ principal does his job sincerely and functions not because he is a manipulator but because he is looked upon as the natural leader of the team, there would be no problem. But if either of them somehow managed to get that job and all that goes with it, the situation would not improve except marginally.

It stands to reason that even the most hard boiled of evaders would sooner or later feel embarrassed about the negative verdict on them. That such a verdict would be repeated term after term, year after year, does not have to be underlined. Even if the transaction is private and not public, it would have an undoubted impact.

As of today, a substantial number of people take their job casually. A little less than one quarter of them take it seriously and the system is functioning because of them. The majority would like to copy their example, adopt their approach and ways of doing things. But the negative example of the unrepentant 10 per cent or so unsettles them. What is required is how to isolate this 10 per cent of professional non-performers. That quite a few of them are politically influential and are aligned with one political group or another is not entirely an accident. Hence this proposal to have student assessment of teachers.

II

As projected here, the process would soon get entirely Indianised and there would be nothing American about it. If some teachers feel that this system is open to certain objections, let them come forward with their misgivings and give reasons why they find this harmless novelty unacceptable.

After about two years, it would be time to move to the second phase of this initiative. Reporting in 1986, on the pay scales of university and college teachers the Mehrotra Committee made several important recommendations in order to ensure the accountability of teachers. One of them was student assessment of teachers. This proposal was reiterated by the Rastogi Committee in 1997.

The earlier Committee had recommended that, though not indigenous to the soil of India, its introduction on a gradual and selective basis would be welcome. Along with several other similar recommendations, this one too was not implemented. The earlier Committee had left things to the good sense of the teachers. However almost nothing was done. Returning to this issue, the Rastogi Committee said that there was no further time to lose and rather than introduce it selectively or gradually, it recommended that it be introduced right away.

Such a thing is easier said than done. The number of colleges is so large that it needs no argument to show that the UGC alone would not be able to handle the job. Since it is the state governments which look after 99 per cent of the colleges, they will have to own up to this responsibility, otherwise it will remain undone as is currently happening. What should be done in this situation?

Before everything else, the UGC should set an example. It should ensure that institutions funded by it directly i.e., those in the central universities, start enforcing it. What the UGC has to do is to make up its mind about enforcing this particular item of work. More than anything else, this single step would achieve much more than several other steps either suggested or contemplated. At the same time, it should be recognised that the UGC, as constituted at present, would talk about it but do little in the matter.

Second, in this unenviable situation, it can at least resolve to do one thing. The next revision of scales, still several years away, should be made contingent on the introduction of this system. Indeed such a statement should come from the minister of HRD rather than the UGC. In the ultimate analysis, it is all a question of what is generally described as political will. If everything around us is administered casually, to expect the UGC to function differently would be hoping against hope.

But surely the UGC can still do one thing. This condition can be made mandatory wherever and whenever a grant is given. Every grant, sanctioned and released, should be subject to certain conditions. Why can't student assessment of teachers be one of the conditions? This is not as difficult as some people think. Once the UGC fine tunes its conditions of grant, the rest would follow almost automatically. There would be problems about the follow-up. But that is an issue which requires to be discussed in some detail.

III

The argument put forward so far amounts to this: the system of teacher assessment needs to be introduced but it is not advisable to rush headlong into it. There are two principal reasons why this system cannot be introduced right away. The most important of them is the gap between undergraduate and postgraduate teaching. Despite the same scale of pay for both categories of teachers, they are to be distinguished from each other in respect of the background of their students, their earlier track record, level of instruction and career expectations.

At the postgraduate level, it can be introduced right away and indeed it should be made mandatory. Two-thirds of those enrolled at the postgraduate level are enrolled in colleges. A substantial number of these colleges do not perform well though there is no reason why they should not. Student assessment of teachers at that level would in any case for that reason alone improve things. Since this category of colleges are likely to receive a grant from the UGC, to insist upon this precondition, as suggested above, should neither be difficult nor unfeasible.

At the undergraduate level however, things are different. The situation is far from uniform throughout the country. In most states, students are anything but serious about what they are doing. A large number of them join college not because they are interested in pursuing higher studies or are even hopeful about securing a job eventually. They join college because this is the only alternative available to them.

The tuition fee at this level is so low that not many people think twice before joining college. More than that, colleges come to be established not always because there is a demand for them but for all kinds of other, generally political, reasons. A significant proportion of these undergraduate colleges do not even have adequate student strength. They, therefore, are inclined to admit whoever comes along. Approximately half the colleges affiliated to different universities are ineligible for the UGC grants. The latter has laid down certain minimum conditions for this purpose but almost half the colleges are unable to fulfil them.

To ask these undergraduate students to assess the teaching performance of their teachers would not exactly be the right thing to do. As one of the teachers put it graphically, it would amount to letting a monkey use the shaving blade and the monkey would not know how and where to use it. Nor can it be ruled out that such students will not sometimes be manipulated by clever individuals. In other words, a certain element of selectivity would have to be introduced.

Second, and this is logical without question, the right thing for the UGC to do would be to set up a committee with some experienced persons and a select group of teachers to thrash out these issues in detail. Hopefully, they will come up with a set of recommendations which would take into account the differing conditions of colleges, the state of development of the area in which the college is located and so on. Student assessment must be made mandatory in certain circumstances. At the same time, some colleges may be exempted from the operation of this particular provision for a stated period of time and for reasons to be made public. For how long and subject to what conditions this exemption is granted, are issues to which the UGC committee should provide an answer. But there should be no question of any university or university-level institution being exempted.

The experience of one of the leading colleges of Tamil Nadu, Loyola College, Madras, struck me as particularly noteworthy and may be referred to here. Like some other colleges in the country, it started following the same format of assessment which others were following. With the passage of time, it came to be seen that the opinion expressed by the student, even though completely anonymous, could not be taken as its face value. If a student was himself absent, how could he sit in judgement over a teacher? Eventually the college came to the conclusion that only those students may be asked for their opinion whose bonafides were impeccable. But how can their bonafides be converted into a mathematical formula? The answer was that full value should be attached only to the opinion of those students who had attended 80 per cent of the classes. That in consequence of this decision, students take their attendance in the class much more seriously than before goes without saying.

IV

What weightage is to be given to student assessment of teachers? The obvious answer is: in whatever way the weightage is eventually quantified. At the postgraduate level, the weightage should be substantial. By that time, students are fairly mature, have had exposure to college education for a number of years and, all said and done, do not generally join a postgraduate course because they have nothing else to do. This last statement may not be true in certain individual cases but is true in general.

At the undergraduate stage, wherever this system is enforced, the weightage cannot be particularly high, at least to start with. It may be one-third in the first year of the college. In the second year, it may be raised to half and, in the third year, what students have to say may carry something like a two-third weightage. Even this cannot be enforced right away. The introduction of the system will have to be preceded by a certain degree of systematic and sustained student education. As of today, our students are not accustomed to this mode of working which involves the simultaneous assessment of the teachers who instruct them. Clearly, they have first to be educated about the whole concept, then introduce it gradually and it is only after that that it can be enforced. Once introduced, it would be found that there is no more decisive mode of assessing teachers' work than to go by what the students have to say.

Sometimes students are carried away by a particular teacher's style of delivery, his ability to handle people and similar social skills. But these personal characteristics should not be allowed to influence decision making beyond a point. What should count is the ability of the teacher to communicate what he knows, the quantum and content of what he knows and imparts to his students and, no less important, his willingness to establish some kind of a rapport with students. In the ultimate analysis, students are the best judge of how they are being taught.

There is an additional point to be made here. While opinion may be divided as to the extent to which students who are still on rolls can be relied upon to return a responsible response by way of assessment, those who have passed out or are in the process of doing so or are ex-students who passed out a few years ago are in a unique position to sit in judgement on those who instructed them. A minor variation on the recommendation made by the Rastogi Committee may thus be considered as an alternative. To be called the Exit Poll, it may be described as follows.

When students are leaving, they may be asked to grade their teachers. Or they may be asked such questions as would bring into focus the strength and weakness of the various teachers under whom they have studied. Informally speaking, this is being done all the time. Older students are always telling younger students about how a teacher is to be approached, what kind of interaction they can expect and so on. In plain words, they are, even without being asked, sharing their assessment of the teachers with the newcomers.

This is how legends are born. Over the years, certain teachers come to acquire certain reputations. These are based on what, generally speaking, students are glad to say about their respective teachers willingly and even without being prompted to do so. What is proposed is a formalisation of that phenomenon.

In those undergraduate colleges, particularly in certain states, where a systematic use of a proforma may not be easily possible, the Exit Poll system may be tried out with profit.

V

That the UGC itself has been passive about the whole thing so far should be clear from one single fact. At no stage has the UGC gone into this issue with any degree of depth or thoroughness. Committees appointed by it have made recommendations in their own sleepy way, and, the UGC has simply endorsed them. At no stage did anyone in the UGC go into the question of how precisely the job is to be done. The issue of the limitations of the scheme as well as the safeguards to be provided was never gone into. But, as should be evident even from this brief discussion, the issue has many more dimensions than has been recognised until now. The distinction between undergraduate and postgraduate classes is basic to the whole issue. Once this is recognised, so many consequences would flow from it.

Not only that, a methodology of assessment is yet to evolve. Mistakes that can occur have to be identified and guarded against. Indeed a number of other salutary safeguards can be anticipated and provided for. In what manner this information is to be used is an issue by itself. The fact of the matter is that, as in so many other things, the UGC has not chosen to go into this matter thoroughly.

Going further, it should be clear by now that unless we make a beginning at the postgraduate level, this innovation will not take off. This single fact underlines the importance of choosing the right strategy. While beginning at the postgraduate level is the obvious thing to do, there is also another minor dimension to it.

Of the three things recommended both by the National Policy on Education (1986) and the Mehrotra Committee (about the same time), student assessment of teachers is one, the other two being self appraisal by the teacher and appraisal by his peers on the basis of his published work. Both these requirements are difficult to quantify and enforce whereas instituting the system of student assessment is much more feasible as argued above. More than that, once this particular requirement is complied with, the other two will more or less get taken care of almost automatically.

Therefore, comparatively speaking, to institute the system of student assessment of teachers is not so difficult an undertaking as is generally believed and, as if to reinforce the first point, relatively easy to enforce. What it requires is a change in the mode of thinking and a somewhat easy to understand procedure of work.

Two things should be clear from the foregoing analysis. It would not be possible to enforce one uniform, unvarying system across the board. Regional and other kinds of variations and a certain degree of time differential would have to be allowed for. At the state level, there would have to be some kind of a nodal agency to keep a tab on these things. Second, the UGC would have to have a Standing Committee which would review the reports received from the states. In any case, the UGC would have to reformulate the scheme as argued above and, no less important, concretise it in terms of priorities, mode of working and the eventual objective of close and fruitful interaction between students and teachers.

Its other job would be to keep an eye over how the system is evolving, what difficulties are being encountered and how those are to be resolved. It may not be out of place to add however that what students have to say about teachers would eventually come to be the single most decisive factor when it comes to how the latter are eventually evaluated.

Those who have been accustomed to a system of non-performance are not going to accept this proposal willingly or easily. A certain degree of enforcement would have to be ensured. Some kind of provision for review would also have to be provided. When it is first introduced, the system should be somewhat flexible. But, within a couple of years, as more and more experience is gained, it can be made mandatory while retaining those elements of flexibility which would make it workable as well as credible.

On a visit to Pondicherry as a member of a NAAC team some years ago, it was gratifying to discover one thing. This university had introduced the system of student assessment of teachers only a year earlier. When, towards the end of the visit, we compared our assessment of what we had observed for ourselves over three days and what the students had to say about their teachers, there was an uncanny resemblance between the two sets of perceptions.

Was it a coincidence or was there an inner logic at work? I would like to believe that it was the latter. As the saying goes, you can fool some people for all times, a large number of people for some time, but not all people for all times. If that can be done, as they say, you deserve to win in any case. The truth of the matter is that as there can be no secrets between parents and children, there can be no secrets between students and teachers.

At the postgraduate level, if one may sum up, students seldom go wrong. Indeed their perception is unerring. Whether students at the under-graduate level would be equally perceptive remains to be seen. Once the system is established, their judgement would be perhaps as weighty as that of their seniors.

VI

In conclusion, the argument may both be recapitulated and expanded in this manner.

1. The system of student assessment of teachers will have to be comprehensively and thoroughly Indianised.
2. It would be advisable to begin with postgraduate students who constitute something like 10 per cent of the total student strength. To handle them and the teachers who instruct them would be a manageable proposition, to start with. Even here, students would have to be educated about the objectives and the process in the full sense of the word. This whole idea of as-sessment by students is something so new in India that it would take everybody some time to understand its significance as also how its objectives are to be carried out. Some kind of a manual would have to be drafted and appropriate guidelines laid down. It is necessary to repeat however that to begin at any level other than the postgraduate level is likely to create more problems rather than solve them.
3. For the first two years, as suggested, teachers and students may get used to the new system. Since the whole thing is to remain confidential at that stage, a whole series of lessons would inevit-ably be learnt from the procedures that would be evolved. Almost everything will be tentative and it is more or less at the end of two years that a well established system will be evolved.
4. Without the willing and unqualified cooperation of the state governments, the system will not be able to get off the ground. In a sense, this is likely to prove the most contentious part of the scheme. More than 65 per cent of the students are enrolled

in postgraduate colleges which are entirely controlled by state governments. Except for a handful of central universities, all the other universities are controlled by different states. Procedures and mechanisms will therefore have to be evolved through discussion with the state governments. Let some of these state governments be represented on the committee which will be set up by the UGC. Should some of them choose to put forward any new proposals at any stage, those can be immediately discussed and an appropriate decision taken. Total collaboration between the UGC and state governments would have to be ensured in the way suggested here or in any other way that may be thought up.

5. This is a task which the UGC would find difficult to do entirely on its own. Substantial cooperation of the Ministry of the HRD is imperative. In regard to several other matters, there has been disagreement between the Ministry of HRD and state governments. But in regard to this matter, there is no room for disagreement or contention. What states have to do is to accept the proposal which is formulated by the UGC and the Ministry of HRD. Furthermore, the central cabinet will have to take a decision to this effect that unless the system of student assessment of teachers gets enforced within the next three to four years, there would be no question of the next revision of scales of pay. Both the Mehrotra Committee and the Rastogi Committee had made out a case for the introduction of this scheme. But there was no follow-up with the result that the job remained undone. Teachers who are not accustomed to this mode of assessment do not want to accept the system for reasons that do not have to be elaborated. If they could get the revised scales of pay without any of the other related recommendations being enforced, as has happened so far, why bother about other things? Since it is this state of mind which is sought to be changed specific political intervention by the centre is of the utmost importance. While the UGC can prepare a detailed plan of action, political intervention is imperative and that is precisely what is being suggested.

6. Introducing the scheme even at the postgraduate level would be a massive operation and would require the whole-hearted support of state governments. Indeed the latter would have to evolve a certain system of management and control which does

not exist as of today. This is where the bottlenecks are likely to arise. Let it also be added here that, if the job is undertaken seriously, the number of autonomous colleges will rise substantially within the next three to four years. Perhaps the number can go up to 3,000–4,000 by the end of the Tenth Plan. Thus if this system gets introduced both in university departments and the better-managed colleges as proposed, there would be a modest but significant advance upon the existing, virtually stagnant, situation. This should be the target in the first round. In the second round which will come after two to three years, the rest of the colleges can be covered.

7. Can this political intervention be challenged on legal grounds? The brief answer is in the negative. It is sectors other than higher education which were given the concurrent status in 1976. That there has been no follow-up legislation after 1976 is something to be deplored. As far as higher education is concerned, the centre always had powers to coordinate and determine standards. In pursuance of that power, if the centre wants student assessment of teachers to be introduced, no one can question that directive. In plain words, the states would have no legal right to disregard this direction of the union government. The painful truth is that the centre has not chosen to exercise the powers already vested in it. An initiative in this direction will be accepted by the states, perhaps after a certain amount of discussion and adjustment in terms of the local situation.

8. There is another angle to this issue. States have been responding to all kinds of questionable pressures, often setting up colleges even for no reason other than this that a local politician wants it done that way and so on. At no stage was any form of planning undertaken. Today, almost all states have reached a stage when they do not have enough funds to meet even their existing commitments. Once, the system of student assessment of teachers is introduced, they would have no choice except to undertake a review of what they have been doing and also initiate a certain amount of fresh planning. In other words, the existing chaotic system of ad hoc decision making will have to be, in the minimum, moderated. In about five years, expenditure on higher education will get rationalised and, to that extent, become more productive. This will be a gain of enormous importance. If, between them, the two key sectors of power (some crucial steps

are already in progress) and education (as proposed now) are better managed, the performance of the states will undergo a dramatic change.

9. Should the proposal under discussion get implemented within the next two to three years, it will have two types of consequences. One would relate to the impact on the student body as a whole. This issue will be taken up a little later. But the other consequences would be no less significant. To take one simple example. Today, colleges are set up without any forethought or planning. Not only that, rules regarding the establishment of colleges and their affiliation to universities are not all that precisely defined. The UGC hardly figures anywhere in the picture. Indeed it comes into the picture when, some years later, the issue of recognising a particular college under Section 2 (f) of the UGC Act is to be considered. By then, the college has been in existence for something like half a decade, if not longer. Not to recognise it would not mean that the college would cease to exist. Since it will continue to function, this is likely to lead to further dilution of standards. The minimum, therefore, that would happen is that once student assessment of teachers gets under way, hopefully, colleges would be set up according to a certain plan and the state grants would be given only on certain conditions. The policy of squeezing the universities at one time and then the colleges at another time would be given up.

The ugly truth is that there is no clear cut mechanism either for the establishment of new colleges or their regulation. Whoever happens to be in power (i.e., politicians) or in position (i.e., the bureaucratic category) takes a decision and it becomes binding on the state to honour it. The job, as a matter of fact, is so immense that through the weight of sheer default the UGC has virtually given up any intention of seeking to regulate the colleges. This is tragic from the policy point of view and indefensible from the academic point of view.

10. Another variation of this theme might be found to be equally pertinent. In most of the substandard colleges, there is not even a chair and a table for a teacher to sit. There is only the staff room to which teachers go, wait for their classes to begin and then come back after the classes are over. The staff room therefore has a social personality but performs no other function.

Nor does it have any academic context whatsoever. The situation of the college library is equally pathetic. Indeed the less said about it, the better. Students rely upon made-easy guides and other shortcuts to learning. No wonder approximately half of them fail in their examinations. In some of the rural colleges and even the urban ones, most people work for only three to four hours per day. Nobody spends any extra time in the college. There is no occasion to interact with students even when some of the teachers would like to do so. A certain proportion of teachers are thus obliged to become part-time teachers. They may draw wages of a full-time teacher but, in terms of the hours of functioning, they are virtually part-time teachers.

When students are required to sit in judgement on their teachers, there would be something phoney about the process if the teaching hours are so limited and interaction between students and teachers is so casual. In supporting the case for student assessment of teachers therefore, one is also supporting the case for better physical and academic arrangements in colleges. The minimum requirement is a chair and a table for each teacher and more fruitful visits to the college library, both for teachers and students, than is possible today.

11. One unavoidable outcome of the provision of some of these minimum facilities would be that the state governments would have to think twice before they accord permission to set up a new college. The present day response in certain situations shows nothing but ad hocism. In certain states like Maharashtra, for instance, new teaching positions are not sanctioned easily. In certain other states, Punjab for example, the rate of government grant, which is currently 95 per cent of the deficit, is sought to be lowered. A compromise might be worked out and the awkward moment tided over but, sooner or later, these problems are bound to recur.

There is also the issue of distribution between the two sectors—universities and colleges. How much to give to one and how much to the other? A related question is about postgraduate education. Can a college insist upon a certain teaching position being filled because the postgraduate course being run in a particular department is weak? There are scores of issues like that. But most of them remain unaddressed.

12. Also there would be the issue of what happens to those students who do not attend 80 per cent of the lectures? Will they be permitted to express their opinion about their teachers? If they are, what weightage would be given to their opinion? There can also be alternative solutions. In most universities, the permissible limit of attending lectures is generally between two-thirds and three-fourths. What about those students who do not measure up even to the minimum requirement? Furthermore, can some other solutions be thought of? Different states while participating in the deliberations of the UGC Committee might come up with new ideas. That is why it has been said that it will take a few years before the scheme gets properly evolved and suitably indigenised. In brief, instituting the system of student assessment of teachers is going to amount to a virtual revamp of the entire system of higher education.

13. Nothing will transform the academic atmosphere and the mode of working of colleges more decisively than this system of assessment by students which must be imposed (there should be no doubt about it) in the manner suggested above. Simultaneously, the UGC will have to amend its rules so that all grants made by it are subject to this additional condition that whatever be the nature of the grant or its quantum, assessment by students will be an inseparable part of it.

14. So far, the focus of discussion has been on what the teachers say or think. This is an important dimension of the problem without question. What about the students however? In my opinion, introducing this system would have a strong impact both on their thinking and conduct. Their first reaction might be in the direction of a certain kind of wildness, even delinquency but, within no time, the teachers themselves will bring them back to the right path. One or two incidents in different parts of the country and the wildness will get tamed! Then will follow the next phase of how to conduct themselves in a more responsible way. Both these phases of development will take a few months to crystallise. Once things get stabilised, as they will, the atmosphere will begin to change. It would be a new experience for the young people to discover that their word counts and what they say would eventually make a difference in their lives as well as the functioning of educational institutions.

15. To dwell on it any further should not be necessary. The only safe thing one can say at this stage is that this system, if successfully introduced, will bring about a striking change in the life of everyone concerned. The journey from delinquency to responsibility is a journey which is both necessary and self-rewarding. No one grows up without becoming responsible. As of today, the journey is erratic and uncertain. Once adolescents are treated like adults, they will grow up fast. There are problems which are peculiar both to adolescence and adulthood. What happens today is that adolescence gets much too prolonged and adulthood is delayed more than it should be.

XII

A Note on Teacher Leadership

I

While teacher leadership at the state level came to be noticed some time in the mid-fifties, it took another decade or more for the all-India leadership to emerge. The establishment of the UGC to some extent lent an all-India character to the profession of teaching at the college and university level. In its own way, this helped the all-India body crystallise into an all-India entity before long.

Even though a body which came eventually to be called the All-India Federation of University and College Teachers Organisations (AIFUCTO) representing all teachers at the level of higher education had emerged, there was no occasion for it to play a role on the all-India stage. It was in this background that, in the early seventies, the then minister of education, Nurul Hassan, mobilised some of the office bearers of AIFUCTO when the scales were being revised in the early seventies. Till then, hardly anyone had taken notice of them. Now they were brought into the picture. Initially reluctant, the prime minister had to be persuaded to see things from a different point of view. Teachers had not been given their due for a whole quarter of a century even after the transfer of power in 1947.

While the notional leadership was with some persons hailing from Madhya Pradesh, Delhi and one or two other places, the real control was with the teacher activists based in West Bengal. Most of them were connected with CPM. More than any other sector of teachers, it was the college teachers who were closely linked to the CPM. In fact, a couple of them were members of the key cell which guided and controlled teacher leadership in the country. Once the all-India connection was established and projected, their control over the state unit became absolute and unchallenged. That is what happened in the middle of the seventies and it continued to remain so all these years except that, of late, some of the other left organisations too came to have a voice in the all-India leadership.

What was being attempted in the early seventies was something radical. College teachers, some of whom were seriously underpaid were proposed to be brought into the network of the all-India fraternity of teachers. It was proposed to have an unconditional parity between university and college teachers. Even in the early seventies when prices had risen somewhat, in certain places there were college teachers (as noted by the S.N. Sen Committee which reported in 1971) who were in the pay scale of Rs 300–600, and no more. There seemed to be no other way to improve their salaries except to bracket them with university teachers.

In addition to ensuring parity between university and college teachers, the 1973 decision taken by the union government did another thing. It equated university and college teachers with Class I officers of the Government of India. In a sense, this was like breaking the sound barrier. This was talking in the language that the bureaucrats understood. This new notion of parity soon began to circulate widely and without any significant resistance from them.

Both these decisions were radical without question. Since the seventies, though the formality of a committee set up by the UGC is observed as a ritual, the ultimate outcome is no more and no less than what the relevant Pay Commission says. Whatever is sanctioned for Class I officers in the Government of India is sanctioned to university and college teachers. Two contributions which the Ministry of Human Resource Development, the nodal ministry made may now be referred to.

One was to virtually ignore the recommendations made by the various UGC Committees which reported from time to time. The second was to leave their implementation to other agencies. The recommendations made were well meaning and fairly progressive in character. But the implementation had to be done partially by the UGC and largely by the state governments. In regard to both, the proprieties were observed but the objective was never really fulfilled. The basic objective was to ensure teacher accountability. Everything right and meaningful was said in the reports submitted to the UGC but teacher accountability is as non-existent today as it was a quarter century ago. In the eyes of the Ministry of HRD, this is a job which has to be done by the UGC. If the job does not get done, as has happened all this time, no one in the Ministry of HRD is bothered about it.

Quite some teachers will find fault with this line of approach. In their view, absence of accountability is so widespread in other walks of life, particularly in the government, that to seek to ensure it in respect of teachers alone is to over-stretch the point. There is some merit in this contention. In order to discover the fallacy in this line of argument, it is necessary to stretch the argument further. Lack of accountability in the teaching profession, it needs to be recognised, virtually destroys the profession of teaching. Something along these lines has been happening in the last few decades. If things have not collapsed, it is basically owing to the sense of commitment of those 15–20 per cent of teachers in the profession who, despite so many things happening to the contrary, have continued to do what was expected of them.

The issue that arises here is what is the role of the state which provides the bulk of the funding. If the state fails to do its duty, and this is precisely what has been happening, it makes it difficult even for the upright teacher to do his duty. Underperformance in the government can be lived with. But, underperformance in the field of education ends up destroying, or almost so, the future of coming generations. Other kinds of damages can be rectified within a year or two. In the case of education, the damage is virtually permanent and, what is more, slow-acting and insidious in character. If someone does not subscribe to this point of view, the only thing one might say in response is that the person concerned is in the wrong profession.

As far as the UGC is concerned, its principal area of operations is the sector of central universities. Implementation could have been ensured if the UGC had been energetic as well as pragmatic. It has displayed neither of these two qualities. As far as the state governments were concerned, none of them had any agency other than the customary bureaucratic apparatus at their command. The states never got attuned to academic or, more precisely, university administration at any stage. In other words, even if the state governments wanted to implement the UGC recommendations, they did not possess the means of doing so. It would not be far wrong to say, therefore, that the mode of working of the state governments was tailor-made to ensure that none of the recommendations made by the UGC committees got implemented.

A ray of hope could be discerned in the State Councils of Higher Education. By now, around a dozen states have set up these Councils. Had each state set up such a Council and had a system of coordination between them and the UGC been developed and enforced, things might have been somewhat better. But the secretaries incharge of education are hostile to the notion of ceding any part of their power to the State Councils. As far as the ministers for education are concerned, except for a few of them, they do not stay in office long enough to implement what they say they would like to do. The secretaries of education are in any case birds of passage. Between the two of them, virtually nothing gets done except that the day-to-day business is attended to and some initiatives (largely under public pressure) get taken. And the ground situation remains what it is.

Second, it might be added that in the case of the Mehrotra Committee the UGC had at least endorsed the recommendations of the committee. In the case of the Rastogi Committee which reported in the late nineties, the UGC went to the extent of virtually rewriting the Report and putting forward an alternative plan of action.

The Ministry of HRD, however, had its own style of working. An important component of it was the close contact which it maintains with the teacher leadership who on their part are equally keen to do so with those in office at a particular point of time. It is difficult to say that when different universities got entangled in various court cases in the eighties after the recommendations of the Mehrotra Committee had been put into effect, why the Ministry of HRD did not choose to intervene and help out the UGC and the universities. In all likelihood, it was sheer apathy. But some kind of collusion between the HRD officials and teacher leadership cannot be ruled out.

The biggest contribution of the Ministry of HRD to the various schemes of promotion floated by it has been two-fold. Even if the rules laid down could not be invoked to cut short the damage that was being done, one course of action was always open to the Ministry of HRD. It could have taken the position, particularly when any new scheme was being introduced, that if the promotions went beyond a certain limit, the whole scheme of promotions would have to be reviewed. To put it in plain language, if everyone who goes up for selection virtually gets promoted, there is surely something wrong with the procedures laid down or those who operate the scheme. The rate of rejections is as significant an indicator as the rate of selections. But this was a yardstick to which no one paid any attention. The outcome is what we see.

In technical terms, while one running scale of pay had been demanded by the teachers repeatedly before 1973, it was not accepted as being consistent with the health and vitality of the academic system. In actual practice, this is precisely what has been happening.

The second lapse of which it was guilty was to leave everything to the UGC. But the UGC, unassisted by the Ministry of HRD, could not do many things. For instance, the institution of the State Councils of Higher Education could not be strengthened or given teeth. The Ministry of HRD did try to help but it did not work. In consequence, the era of higher productivity which could have been ushered in remained untapped.

II

The greater part of the blame for this state of affairs should, therefore, attach to the Ministry of HRD and the various turns and twists that it took every few years. It is not possible to go into details because those would be much too specific and cannot be brought up in a general discussion of this kind. The plain truth is that whatever the rules framed and the reservations introduced, each one of them was systematically and invariably sidelined or defeated. Today a situation has arisen where those who feel committed to high academic standards have no choice except to lament over what has happened. The application of bureaucratic rules on the scale that has happened has been an unmitigated disaster for the university system in India.

At this stage, it would be in order to say one thing. The entire operation from the stage of conceptualisation to implementation was masterminded by Nurul Hassan. He persuaded the then prime minister to undertake this act of social engineering. In order to achieve this objective, he made use of his contacts in the ranks of teacher leadership to ensure that they talked to the prime minister and influenced her thinking. Teachers at the university and college level were co-opted into the middle class in a manner which had a wider social significance and those at the school level, even at the higher secondary level, were excluded. It took almost a decade before the imbalance created could be partially set right.

Both steps, parity between university and college teachers and the bracketing of these teachers with Class I officers had the potential of being self-destructive. This is precisely what came to pass. It must be added however that it was his successors who were overwhelmed by the forces released and the pressures constantly exerted on them. They could see that they were going in the wrong direction but there was little that they could do to reverse the gears. As far as Nurul Hassan was concerned, he had played a historic role. It is what happened after him that now needs to be discussed.

After the revision of pay scales in the mid-seventies, teachers in almost every single state had to go on strike in order to get the state governments to introduce them. The state governments had yet to accept the idea projected by the centre that the university and college teachers were not to be equated with second grade employees as had been happening during the quarter of a century after 1947, indeed even earlier. Hardly any state therefore acted on what the centre had recommended. This was despite the fact that the central support had been raised from 50 to 80 per cent of the additional expenditure for a period of five years. Eventually the financial burden got more or less taken over by the centre through the mediation of the next Finance Commission. Despite these seductive features of the scheme, the states were simply not prepared to accept the position that teachers at this level could be considered and treated differently from the way they had been treated all these years.

That is why, in state after state, teachers went on strike and rightly so. After a certain amount of hesitation and downright reluctance, ultimately one by one the states agreed to the revised scales of pay. Details do not have to be gone into here. Only Kerala and Jammu and Kashmir did not totally conform for reasons peculiar to them. But they accepted the scales of pay and differed in regard to one or two minor details. This phase of confrontation lasted for almost half a decade. Gujarat was the last state to accept the revised scales of pay. Even that came to pass in 1980. In that year, the Congress returned to power both at the centre and the state of Gujarat. It was the Congress party under the leadership of Indira Gandhi which had sponsored these scales. After her return to power again, there was no reason now for the Congress to remain out of step. Therefore that state also followed the lead given by the centre.

In the decade from 1975 to 1986, the AIFUCTO became a powerful body at the all-India level. It had never been so powerful earlier and a few years later it lost this standing to a great extent, as we shall presently see. This came about partly because of a feeling of arrogance on its part. The Mehrotra Committee recommendations were sensible and promotion from one grade to another at the lecturer level was linked with certain academic steps that were to be taken. Still the matter got mishandled in two ways.

One was the fact that the entire mode of functioning was bureaucratic. Within a few years, matters started going to the courts. The UGC was the agency acting on behalf of the Ministry of HRD. When things began to go out of control, the ministry should have intervened and sorted things out. Between the lack of leadership at the UGC level and lack of assertion by the ministry, things got distinctly complicated.

The second explanation for implementation having been bungled was the overnight establishment of something like 50 Academic Staff Colleges (ASCs) for the orientation and inservice training of the general run of teachers. While the inservice part did succeed in certain places, the orientation part did not succeed all that well. For one thing, there was hardly any literature available, nor any academics who were competent in related areas like the constitutional status of education, techniques of teaching and testing, the history of higher education in India, the social and economic context of the profession of teaching and several related areas. There was just no expertise available in these areas and the UGC paid no attention to what ASCs were asked to do. Whatever limited initiatives were taken were not given due recognition with the result that these staff colleges developed into centres of patronage and a subsidised holiday for those who attended.

There is a good deal to be said on this subject but this is not the occasion to do so. A comparison with teachers in other countries is a humbling experience. Most of them are knowledgeable about educational policies. Compared to them, our teachers are virtually ignorant of the complex dimensions of higher education.

There is hardly any organ of opinion or information about education which circulates throughout the country. For a university system which has a strength of over 400,000 teachers, this level of ignorance on matters educational is indefensible. But more about it later. For the present, it is enough to say that while the first step towards making teaching into a respected profession was taken when the scales of pay were radically revised upwards, the second step in equipping the teachers with appropriate professional expertise has yet to be taken.

III

Currently we are victims of a double misfortune. While other sectors of education were put on the Concurrent List in 1976, as far as higher education is concerned, there was never any doubt that the centre always had the power to coordinate and determine standards. The establishment of the UGC as also the various other professional councils is a testimony to this statement.

Right from the day that it was established, the UGC has been crippled both by the designation given to it and the mode of working that it evolved for itself. The UGC in India might have been an appropriate abbreviation of the University Grants Committee which was functioning in UK but it was an egregious mistake to have set up a body with the same initials. The controversy surrounding its establishment has been described elsewhere. What requires to be said here is that to have given it the same designation as its counterpart body in UK became a foretaste of things to come.

But is that the purpose for which the UGC was set up in India? The answer to this question constitutes the second misfortune. According to the Indian Constitution, the centre has been empowered to coordinate and determine standards of higher education. The mention of the word 'Regulation of Standards' in the 1951 Bill met with considerable suspicion and resistance. It was in order to overcome that resistance that the centre agreed to vest the power to distribute funds to the same body which was to coordinate and determine standards. The giving of grants was a secondary function. The basic function was to coordinate and determine standards. By giving it a misleading name, the focus got shifted which resulted in the bedevilling of the functioning of the UGC all these years.

No more need be said about this particular issue because it has been dealt with elsewhere. The basic issue however is who is to raise questions like these. There is a small segment of dedicated public opinion which understands these issues and is prepared to talk about them. But their area of influence is limited. In any case, over the years, the universities have got so highly politicised and their functioning has deteriorated to such an extent that even though some people are interested in university and college education, they feel disenchanted and marginalised.

There are indeed three other sections of opinion which have the potential to take interest in the matter. The first one is of those who control policy making i.e., the political bosses. If the last five decades have any message to convey, it is this that our political class lacks both a sense of commitment and a sense of direction. Even in a key sector like power which is the cornerstone for any kind of economic progress, they have made a mess. If they have also made a mess of education which is the second key sector of activity, there should be nothing to be surprised about. In plain words, the political leaders have acted in character, so to speak. They have mucked up the entire educational system and also the economy. To expect anything else from them, therefore, would be a somewhat extravagant expectation.

What about the civil servants? Strange as it might sound, despite all the criticism of the bureaucracy, it is the odd individual who belongs to this category who has, here and there, refused to be swept off his feet and managed to adhere to the mandate given to him and done a few good things. This refers to a few secretaries of education in different states and their counterparts at the centre. Something like 10–15 per cent of them have stood their ground and, despite all the knocks that they received, responded to the call of duty. A handful of ministers too have been farsighted and understood the problems. Between them and the few civil servants with a conscience, they have initiated and executed some good policies. But then the overall achievement has not been all that substantial.

What about the teachers? Properly speaking, it is they who understand the issues they deal with more than anybody else. Indeed they know where the shoe pinches, as they say. Were they to participate more actively and more creatively than they do at present in how educational institutions are run, what is sought to be achieved and to what extent it is achieved and so on, things would become vastly better. The painful truth is that it is this abdication of their role as standard setters and policy makers which is largely responsible for the existing sorry state of affairs. Not only that, quite often they project their own personal interests, though, to be fair, not in all cases. In the approximately 300 odd university-level institutions which we have in the country, all kinds of decisions are being taken. Some of them are positive and forward looking without question and these too are taken by some of these teachers. On the whole, it is a mixed situation.

In other words, decision making, such as it is, has got into a rut largely because of the apathy of teachers and teacher administrators who are vested with the responsibility of running universities and colleges. In certain cases, they do manage to impart a touch of excellence. But it needs to be acknowledged that their number is very small. It would be invidious to pick out individuals and institutions and talk about them.

The fact however remains that something like 5 to 10 per cent of the institutions are performing reasonably well. For the rest, either there is the wrong kind of decision making or, worse, motivated decision making.

This questionable kind of motivation largely comes from the naked pursuit of power, a game in which quite some teachers are engaged. That some of them are appointed as vice chancellors or principals is a fact of life. Having got appointed with the help of their supporters, they feel that their primary obligation is to their supporters. They promote this kind of thing all the time; in season and out of season. Most motivated decisions get taken largely for this reason.

To rationalise this fact is not going to be the end of what is happening. Sometime, while talking in private, quite a few people are prepared to admit to the fact that what they do leads to dilution of standards. But they know that they cannot survive unless they support their supporters. That is how the rot keeps growing all the time.

Could the media have played a helpful role? In theory, yes. In practice, we all know that they are more interested in sensation mongering than in serious or sustained analysis of issues. It is but rarely that issues which have long range implications and affect the shape of things to come are taken up for discussion. The ugly truth is that there is no substitute for those committed teachers who understand things and know what is possible and what is not and act accordingly.

IV

The question to ask is: are the teachers a party to this racket? A certain number of them are, it has to be admitted. Those who are included in this category are the more lazy or the more influential ones. In any case, it is difficult for most people to detach themselves from what is happening around them and strike out an independent path of action. A few individuals have done so but then they have remained individuals and their efforts have not become anything like a movement. In the absence of a movement, decision making remains with those who control things. Those who do not play the game or refuse to be co-opted are generally ignored. This is something which happens day after day, and year after year in universities and colleges.

Can things change? They can, provided a much larger number of teachers start taking interest in what is happening to them and around them. For that to happen, they have to be alert as well as well informed and understand the issues which arise from day to day, why certain decisions are being taken and how some of those harmful moves can be checkmated. What is happening is almost the exact opposite of what ought to happen. If teacher leadership had chosen to play the role that it should have, and indeed could have, the situation would have been different. To imply that the teacher leadership is not doing what it could have done would be to assume that they are free to choose. The truth of the matter is that they are not.

They have become prisoners of the events of 1973. What was not visualised at that time was that such a decision, even though well inten-tioned, would be difficult to reverse. For such a thing to happen, the consent of the majority must be forthcoming. But if the majority stand to benefit from what is happening, the situation is not so straight forward as one would like to assume. The majority in this case consists of college-appointed teachers and not of the university-appointed teachers. The former are afraid that if there is a change in the system or even a minor shift, it would mean reduction in their scale of pay or something equally damaging. The latter who work in university departments would like things to be different but they are too few in numbers and too ineffectual in their impact to be able to influence decision making.

After the 1986 one-month long strike, a new body called the Federation of Central University Teachers Organisation (FCUTO) came into exist-ence. But it has not been able to achieve anything so far. Not only that, quite a few of the leaders in this Federation have even colluded with the bigger organisation called AIFUCTO which has almost three decades of solid achievement behind it. AIFUCTO has consistently received un-conditional support from CPM as well as CPI. This organisation, to repeat, has its roots mainly in Calcutta but it has an all-India presence without question. Every issue that comes up is discussed or debated by the political bosses in terms of whether it would suit AIFUCTO or not. If it would help AIFUCTO, they are for it. If not, they would let things go by default.

What has been the role of the Ministry of HRD in this whole business? Something has been hinted at here and there but one thing needs to be more specifically identified now. Till the end of the nineties, power at the centre was not with BJP. Earlier, it was with the Congress party and then it was wielded by several miscellaneous people in succession. Deci-sions in regard to scales of pay had to be made during these uncertain days. As a result of the momentum which AIFUCTO had acquired over the years and because all state government had been decisively defeated in their stand in the seventies, they felt intimidated by it. Therefore they were not prepared to take on the college teachers once again.

Those who wielded political power at the centre were broadly in sympathy with AIFUCTO and chose to go by the recommendations of the Fifth Pay Commission. One uncertain factor was the new government. Everyone was wary of how the BJP government would respond. People connected with CPM and CPI chose to play second fiddle and projected those sections of the teacher leadership who had a say with the new government. It should not be necessary to go over the ground covered elsewhere. The fact of the matter is that the NDA government's performance was neither better nor worse than that of the earlier rulers. Does it mean it is a hopeless situation? It is difficult to return a clear answer.

What is the way out? There can be no other way out except to delink undergraduate and postgraduate teaching. The two are qualitatively different. To treat them at par with each other as was done in 1973 was to have ignored the ground reality. In any case, this step was academically wrong. The kind of competence that one requires at the undergraduate level is utterly inadequate at the postgraduate level. This issue has been discussed in my piece Ravages of Affiliation[1] in greater detail and need not be discussed here except to say that even those who took this decision in the first instance and then reiterated it in the eighties and the nineties recognise the untenability of the existing arrangement.

Sooner or later, therefore, the policy makers are bound to come to this conclusion that the existing system would have to be changed. How precisely that is to be done and in what manner are details that one cannot go into here. But it should be clear to the present teacher leadership that a contingency like this can arise within the next decade, indeed before the next revision of the scales of pay becomes due. It is difficult to be more precise than this. As and when it happens, the solution which the policy makers are likely to opt for is to remodel the existing system. If those connected with teacher leadership imagine that this will not happen, they are assuming that the politicians are not capable of an about turn. They are very capable of that kind of a thing, particularly when they are confronted with a difficult situation. Indeed it does not take very long for a politician to reverse the gears.

The situation as it is unfolding is therefore, to use a hackneyed phrase, full of perils as well as possibilities. The perils need not be referred to any further here. Perhaps it would be helpful to turn to the possibilities inherent in the situation.

V

In every country of the world where higher education is a strong and viable system, the teachers have consistently, indeed invariably, played an important role. The general pattern of development is somewhat like this. Teacher organisations are formed to take care of the interest of their members and ensure appropriate conditions of work for them. This does not happen overnight. Quite often it takes decades and decades before teachers get their due and sometimes even that cannot be ensured. In this process, the teacher organisations begin to move from the stage of agitation to the stage of participation in decision making.

They participate in how the educational institutions are run. They have as much of a stake in the proper running of their institutions, as those who shape and determine policy making. A kind of partnership develops between the two and, as things evolve, this partnership gets stronger and stronger. Our misfortune is that this last thing is not happening. Teachers do not generally participate in decision making except in a limited sense of the term. On the contrary, decision making is in the hands of people who are already in power and also those sections of the teachers who have got co-opted into the power structure. These teachers participate in decision making fully and enthusiastically. But in respect of the larger issues, most of them remain indifferent and we are witness to what is happening all around us.

To put it bluntly, the profession of teaching at the university and college level has yet to properly evolve. Had we been professional in our outlook and functioning, things would have been different. But we have driven from one extreme to another and meanwhile a wrong turning on the road has been taken. Teachers at the college level are interested in only one thing and that is to retain their parity with postgraduate teachers. Teachers at the postgraduate level are too few and too involved in other things to be able to even defend their own limited interests. Therefore, the universities and colleges are full of people who have learnt how to operate the system, come to terms with whatever is happening or participate mainly with those individuals and factions which control things. And this is how things go on and on.

Thus we are caught in a situation from which no one other than the politicians can rescue us. But is it really advisable to wait until D Day when such a decision will have to unavoidably be taken? In the chapter on 'Student Assessment of Teachers' (Chapter XI), a proposal has been mooted. That proposal, if implemented, can prove to be a shortcut to some of the problems. It has been suggested there that the centre should take this view that unless the system of student assessment of teachers is implemented as recommended by all the committees that have gone into this issue, there would be no fresh revision of scales of pay in the next round. In other words, what should have been done after 1987 can be done even now—many, many years later.

Once the system of student assessment of teachers gets implemented in the manner suggested there, a large number of the ills of the existing system, both at the university and college level, will get taken care of. There is a direct link between these two developments. Whether the present government does it or the succeeding government does it is a matter of detail. It is bound to happen. Unless something of this kind is done, the situation would remain what it is. But once student assessment of teachers is honestly and systematically enforced, the kind of stubborn resistance which is encountered today will begin to decline. Once that starts happening, the situation would be ripe for any kind of change that might be made under the new dispensation.

VI

Every university brings out an annual report as per the requirement of the law. Furthermore, all professional councils have to do the same and submit a report to Parliament. Till the early eighties, when the UGC was the principal professional body in existence, its annual report used to be discussed in Parliament. What was said on that occasion was seldom very enlightening. The MPs who participated in that discussion talked of things relating to their constituencies or their state and seldom gave evidence of having an all-India perspective on things. Even that limited exercise has now been discontinued.

It may be of interest to mention why this exercise was discontinued. The minister who took charge of education after Indira Gandhi returned to power in 1980 raised the question—why is it necessary to discuss the UGC report in Parliament? The only legal requirement is that the report is placed on the table of the House. Evidently, the minister did not feel comfortable even with that indifferent kind of discussion which took place in the House. Since that change of routine, it is laid on the table of the House and that is that. In other words, the document is there and it contains a good deal of information which admits of debate and discussion, especially by the teachers. But nobody insists upon discussing it. This suits those in power. A situation in which no one questions what the decision makers do is tailor made for those who habitually underperform or want to play politics, if it may be added.

One can live even with that. But it is relevant to raise a related question; is it discussed in any meeting of the Teachers' Association in any university? Indeed one can go further and raise the question: is the university report discussed in the general house of the Teachers' Association? If not, as seems to be case, why not? Is it a matter of concern to only those who already wield power and sit in the various councils and take decisions which affect the wider body of teachers?

If the answer is in the negative, as it should be, clearly there is a basic misperception on the part of the teachers in so far as they think that they have nothing to do with the decision making process and this is something which is best left to them who deal with such matters. Decision making is criticised by certain individuals some times from their own point of view and some times from a group point of view provided the matter affects a large number of people. But it is never discussed from the point of view of the teachers as a whole. Could anything be more shortsighted, even self-destructive?

Here is a situation where decisions are being made, grants are being released or withheld and yet no one seems to be bothered by the fact that the process of decision making needs to be questioned, scrutinised and turned upside down, if necessary. It is this total lack of commitment to the profession of teaching which is responsible for what is happening in the universities and colleges.

In the colleges it is much worse than in the universities. In the universities the annual report is at least prepared and submitted to the Court or the Senate and then to the State Assembly. In colleges, nothing of that kind generally happens. Things are so organised that decisions get taken more or less as the decision makers want them to be taken. In certain cases, principals get the decisions made as they prefer them. In certain other cases, decisions are taken even against their wishes and by people to whom the principal is answerable. Obviously, the right kind of understanding between them is lacking. But the principals generally put up with that situation.

As to the teachers, except for a few difficult ones and some who are ambitious, there is seldom a problem. Here, it is pertinent to say that democracy does not lie only in voting at a poll once every few years. The essence of democracy is participation in things that concern those involved, a certain measure of give and take, mutual adjustment and understanding and, as far as possible, agreed decisions. This is as much applicable to colleges and universities as to the political bodies which establish these institutions in the first instance.

The real tragedy is that there is no sense of participation. The sense of participation is lacking in most other walks of life too. One can at least explain it away by saying that most people are illiterate or half literate and so on. In the case of universities and colleges, most teachers are highly educated. Not only that, they are charged with the responsibility of training the next generation and to a certain extent they do that job with some degree of competence. But the kind of training that they impart to students is partial, even lop-sided. More than anything else, teachers have to be models of the right kind of decision making. It is only when they are seen as the right kind of models that their students will learn to distinguish between what is right and what is wrong. Unfortunately the teachers themselves are lacking in this particular quality of participation in decision making.

The UGC has been in existence for five decades. Every year it puts out an annual report. So do the various other professional councils. Of them, the All India Council of Technical Education and the Medical Council of India deal with a substantial number of teachers. There are around a thousand technical colleges and about half that number of medical colleges. Is the situation different there? The question has only to be asked and one knows the answer.

More than the teachers in professional colleges, the largest numbers of teachers are to be found in the arts, science and commerce faculties. They constitute something like three-fourths of the total number. A good many teacher leaders also come from the ranks of these teachers. None of them can in any way affirm that they have even read the annual reports, let alone discussed them.

And let no one assume that the annual reports are a faithful record of what happens. Most of them are doctored, if it may be said. The point of discussing the reports is no more and no less than this that, after an intensive discussion, the truth should be uncovered. This requires a strong, uncrring commitment to truth and a desire to uncover it when it is sought to be manipulated. Clearly, there is much more to insist upon participation, especially when others attempt to keep the prying eyes away

On one occasion, I happened to ask a middle level officer of the UGC who used to deal with the publication of the annual report. My question was if the UGC had ever received a request from any teacher organisation for a copy of the annual report. His answer was, 'none to my knowledge'. Let us assume that it was an inadequate answer. After all, he had been incharge of that assignment only for a few years and it is not fair to generalise that from limited experience. On the whole, however, what he said in reply to my question seemed to be right.

Leaving aside the role of these teacher organisations, do the bulk of the teachers give evidence of interest in educational matters? Above all, do the teacher organisations function as if they are interested in problems of policy making? On the whole, it seems safe to say that this is one area of interest which they have yet to develop.

The fact of the matter is that an average teacher is, for the most part, ignorant of what is happening in his institution. He may be well informed about his own discipline and here the situation would differ from person to person. But of matters educational or what, broadly speaking, may be described as policy making, he is supremely ignorant. Perhaps he is unconcerned with what is happening at the policy-making level. In this situation, who takes over? Mostly those who have either an axe to grind or an ideology to promote. In either case, the right decisions are not taken.

By contrast, in decision making at every level in universities in advanced countries, teachers regard it as a part of their duty to take part in whatever is under discussion and bring to bear their judgement and independence of thought upon whatever decisions are being taken. This does not happen in government nor in business. University administration is unique from this point of view that decision making at the administrative level is shared with some people in public life who are interested in education. At the academic level, most decision making is done by the academics themselves though, in certain cases, academics from other institutions too are invited to participate.

A precondition for the right kind of decision making is that the teachers should be well informed, indeed knowledgeable, about the issues connected with education. In our country, most teachers are by and large apathetic to what happens in education . The only ones who get involved are either those who have a motive for getting involved or the bureaucrats. In more cases than I would like to recall, I have seen decisions being made by those who are more knowledgeable than the teachers sitting around the table are and generally they are bureaucrats. After that, if some teachers feel aggrieved by the decisions made, they have no right to blame any one other than themselves.

The honest truth is that, over the years, the teacher movement has boiled down to a one-point agenda. Are the scales of pay safe or is there a danger of those being taken away? Since more than three-fourths of the teachers think along those lines, it is patently difficult for the teacher leadership to think differently. This situation has endured for a whole quarter of a century. In the phase into which higher education is now entering, this may not be all that tenable.

In plain words, things are changing. If they change further, as can happen, the teacher leadership will not know how to come to terms with the changing situation. Clearly, this is a short-sighted policy. Every leadership must anticipate what is likely to happen or can happen. There is a good deal now to be said about this issue but it should not be necessary to do so here.

To put it another way: the issue before the teacher leadership is how to adjust to things in such a way that there is not much of dislocation nor setback to the profession while at the same time, ensuring that academic standards improve rather than decline. This is a tall order. But, given the situation, any other approach to the problem would create further difficulties.

VII

Two things have happened during recent years to bring about a qualitative change in the situation. One is the fact that as a consequence of the growing rate of expansion in education at all levels, more and more colleges are coming up. Therefore, the states are finding it difficult to meet their financial commitments. In the state of Punjab, for example, the state government told the teachers that instead of continuing to meet 95 per cent of the deficit as it has thus far done, the state was planning to reduce it by 10 per cent per year. The teachers were unhappy about it and worked out a deal with the state government. It was decided between the two of them that the tuition fees would be raised and the level of government support to aided colleges would remain the same. This arrangement has not worked however. It has led to a public outcry and it is difficult to anticipate how things will shape up eventually.

In the state of Maharashtra and several other states, additional teaching posts are not being given. The number of students is increasing but the number of teachers is not increasing. The situation in West Bengal is equally difficult. What would be the eventual outcome of these developments? Some kind of adjustment would have to be made. The only thing one can be certain about is that the existing level of financial support to college education might become difficult to sustain.

The second factor in the situation is that the public perception of what the teachers do has tended to become increasingly unfavourable, even hostile in certain cases. Most comments are along these lines: It does not matter even if you pay more to the teachers because, whether you pay more or less, they are not going to do their job. This situation is not only peculiar to college teaching. One is referring to it for the simple reason that 88 per cent of the enrolment (and the student strength today is 9 million or so) in colleges.

This means that almost 8 million students are everyday witness to whatever is happening. Whether the teachers are being sincere in their work or not is no longer an academic question; it is being debated in a large number of homes. In other words, teaching is not a private activity. It is, without question, a public activity. These things travel and, if there are as many as 8 million witnesses to something, it cannot remain concealed for very long. That is how the public sentiment has become somewhat hostile to teachers. Unless the teachers are prepared to change their ways of functioning and were the state governments to adopt a somewhat aggressive attitude, as compared to what obtains today, the teachers would not be able to fight back.

Every sensible teacher leadership must take this changing situation into account. To say anything more than that should not be necessary.

There is also a positive reason why the teacher leadership should encourage participation of teachers on a much larger scale than what is happening now. Today all kinds of decisions are being taken and quite a few of them are not right. A large number of teachers are dissatisfied about these decisions. But, over the years, because of their unabashed apathy, they have allowed decision making to slip out of their hands and go into hands which are not always sympathetic or well informed. In any case it is highly desirable to promote better standards of performance. Therefore, a change of gears is urgent, both for negative and positive reasons. In plain words, the teacher leadership will have to change both its mode of thinking and its style of functioning.

As dealing with the policy makers would require a good deal of skilful handling, nothing may happen within a year or two. But, by the end of the Tenth Plan, the crisis would be ready to blow up. There is one thing which is on the positive plane that the teacher leadership can do meanwhile.

It should take immediate steps to bring out a weekly or a fortnightly publication which would carry two-thirds of news and one-third of views and analysis. Further details cannot be gone into here except to underline the point that the existing system whereby underhand contacts are established with those in power and the decision makers in search of a vote bank are willing to oblige will not work any longer. Both the objective and the fiscal situation will not permit them to do so.

In plain words, the compulsions of the unfolding events will make it difficult for the policy makers to concede those demands which, so far, they could. The times are changing and so will they. The teacher leadership will have to come to terms with these developments.

And, as already argued, they will have to do two things. One is to re-think the situation and the second is to help the average teacher to educate himself about matters educational much more actively than they have done in the past. Bringing out a journal will only be the first step. Subsequent to that, they will have to sit in judgement upon how the universities, the UGC and the other professional councils are performing. This critical stance might not be easy to adopt but the devious ways being followed today neither do credit to the teaching profession nor are likely to prove productive in the long run.

REFERENCE

1. *Economic and Political Weekly*, 38(30), July 26, 2003.

INDEX

ACAR, 160
Academic Staff Colleges, 240
Accreditation and Assessment Council, 191-92
Accreditation and the UGC, 115-30
Advocates Act, 60
Affiliated Colleges, 177-78
All India Council of Technical Education (AICTE), 19, 50, 54-59, 74, 78, 86, 89, 126, 150, 160, 177, 249; objectives, 55; performance of, 55-56; UGC and, 58-59; working of, 57-59
All India Federation of University and College Teachers Organisation (AIFUCTO), 234, 240, 244-45
Ambedkar, B.R., 195
Andhra Pradesh universities, 20
Association of Indian Universities (AIU), 150
Atomic Energy Commission, 63
Azad, Maulana, 37, 43, 46, 76, 195

B.Ed, through correspondence, 17
BITS, Pilani, 189
BJP, 244-45
Banerjee, A.C., 34
Bar Council of India (1961), 50, 59-62, 75, 80-81; legal education and professionalism and, 61-62
Bloom, 151
British UGC, 173, 201

CPI, 244-45
CPM, 235, 244-45
Capitation fees,
    Supreme Court judgement on, 53, 56; system of, 52, 55

Central Advisory Board of Education (CABE), 45, 180-81, 195
Central Council for Universities, 171-73, 197-98
Central Council of Indian Medicine (1970), 50, 53
Central Council of University Education, 33, 73
Central universities, 49, 74, 203
Centrally Sponsored Schemes, 84
Centre-state relations,
    and professional councils, 76-78, 83-98; implications on education, 83-98, 106-7
Chandalvarkar, Vithal N., 34
Committee of Members of Parliament on Higher Education, report of, 99
Committee of Principals and Vice Chancellors, 108
Committee on Standards, 116
Company Secretaries Bill, 68
Congress Party, 244
Constitution of India,
    Amendment, 1976, 31, 42-43, 75, 83, 196; Schedule VII, 46, 62, 76, 81, 100, 171, 197
Correspondence course, 18
Council of Architects (1968), 50, 57, 67
Council of Higher Education, 88
Council of Scientific and Industrial Research (CSIR), 209

Das, M.N., 22
Deemed to be universities, 74
Dental Council (1948), 50, 53, 67
Deshmukh, C.D., 202-3

About the Author

Amrik Singh has held numerous positions during his long and distinguished career including serving as Director of the South Delhi Campus, Delhi University (1973–75); Vice-Chancellor, Punjabi University, Patiala (1977–79); and Professor of English, Punjabi University (1963–65). He was also Secretary of the Association of Indian Universities (1965–82), and Visiting Professor for Educational Policy at the University of Wisconsin (1969–70). Dr Singh has written extensively on issues affecting higher education in India. In addition, he has founded and edited two journals: the *Journal of University Education* (1962–67) and *Indian Book Chronicle: News and Reviews* (1976–85).

49